THE BATTLE FOR ROME

The Battle for
ROME

W. G. F. Jackson

BONANZA BOOKS · NEW YORK

This edition is published by Bonanza Books
a division of Crown Publisher, Inc.
by arrangement with Scribner's Sons.

a   b   c   d   e   f   g   h

Manufactured in the United States Of America

Contents

Illustrations

Illustrations

Acknowledgment

The Author and Publishers wish to express their thanks for permission to quote from the following sources: Clark, *Calculated Risk*, Harrap (originally published in the USA by Knopf); Juin, *Memoirs*, Arthème Fayard; Nicholson, *The Canadians in Italy 1943–45* (The Official History of the Canadian Army in the Second World War, Vol. II), Roger Duhamel, FRSC, Queen's Printer, Ottawa; Truscott, *Command Missions*, Dutton; Alexander, *The Report by the Supreme Allied Commander Mediterranean to the Combined Chiefs of Staff*, HMSO.

Grateful thanks are also due to MacDonalds for permission to reproduce Plate 4, and to the Pentagon Library for permission to reproduce Plates 9, 10 and 29–33. All other illustrations appear by courtesy of the Imperial War Museum.

Bibliographical Sources

1 *Official Reports, Despatches and Histories*

The Report of the Supreme Allied Commander Mediterranean to the Combined Chiefs of Staff: Parts I and II, HMSO, 1948.
The Despatches of Field Marshal the Earl Alexander of Tunis: The Allied Armies in Italy, *London Gazette*, 12 June 1950.
The History of the Second World War (HMSO): Grand Strategy, Vol V, by John Ehrman, 1956.
The History of Fifth Army in the published version *Salerno to the Alps*, by Colonel C. G. Starr.
The Official History of the Canadian Army in the Second World War: *The Canadians in Italy*, by G. W. L. Nicholson, 1951.
The Royal Air Force 1939–1945, Vol III, HMSO, 1954.
The US Army Air Force in World War II, Vol II, 1949.

2 *Memoirs and Biographies of Senior Commanders*

An Army in Exile, by General W. Anders, 1949.
The Second World War, Vol V, by Sir Winston Churchill, 1952.
Calculated Risk, by General Mark Clark, 1950.
The Memoirs of Field Marshal Kesselring, 1953.
Neither Fear nor Hope, by General von Senger und Etterlin, 1963.
The German Army in the West, by General Westphal, 1951.

3 *Additional Background*

Monte Cassino, by Colonel R. Bohmler, 1964.
Cassino; Portrait of a Battle, by F. Majdalany, 1957.
Anzio, by Wynford-Vaughan Thomas, 1961.
Anzio; An Epic of Bravery, by F. Sheehan, 1964.

THE BATTLE FOR ROME

Preface

This is the story of one of the military masterpieces of the Second World War which is in danger of sinking into obscurity without the recognition it so richly deserves. Much has been written about the planning and execution of the Invasion of Normandy in June 1944, but far less is known of the diversionary operation which helped to make Eisenhower's success possible. Everyone has heard of Operation 'Overlord', but few know anything about the complementary Operation 'Diadem'—the Battle for Rome.

It was the thankless task of General Sir Harold Alexander (now Field-Marshal the Earl Alexander of Tunis) and his Allied Armies in Italy to draw upon themselves as many German divisions as possible to force Hitler to weaken his forces defending the Channel coast by the time Overlord was launched.

For a major diversionary operation of this kind to succeed, it had to present a real threat which could not be ignored; and it had to be pressed with a determination which spelt reality. Hitler could not ignore the loss of Rome; nor could he safely allow Allied bombers to settle on the complex of airfields around Rome from which they could pound Germany's southern cities at far shorter range than hitherto. Moreover, if Rome fell, the Allies would soon be knocking at the back door of the Nazi Reich, forcing the German High Command to divert more and more of their dwindling resources southwards and away from the decisive battle area in Normandy and on the Russian front. The most economic military solution from Hitler's point of view was to hold the Allies as far south as possible, preferably on the shortest and strongest line across the Italian peninsula—the famous Gustav Line—based on Cassino. Any threat to this line was a threat to Rome and was bound to cause a violent German reaction, thus making it the ideal setting for an operation whose primary purpose was to attract and, if possible, decimate successive waves of German reinforcements.

This story of the final Battle for Rome is an account of how Alexander and his Chief of Staff, General John Harding (now Field-Marshal the

Lord Harding of Petherton) put life and reality into this diversionary threat without allowing their operations to become a campaign of attrition. Alexander had fought in most of Haig's offensives on the Western Front in the First World War—offensives like the Battles of the Somme and of Passchendaele which were also diversionary in character and aimed at drawing German strength away from the French sectors of the Western Front—and so he knew how costly and debilitating such operations could be. Now in command of an Army Group ordered to draw the German strength away from Normandy, he was determined not to repeat the unimaginative tactics of 1916 and 1917. So successful was he that not only did Rome fall just two days before Eisenhower's Armies crossed the Channel, but he had also drawn upon himself twenty-three German divisions and forced Hitler to send the equivalent of seven more into Italy at the most critical stage of the Normandy campaign. The magnitude of his diversionary success is shown by the fact that there were only twenty German field force divisions left within striking distance of the Channel coast when the invasion of Normandy began.

But this is not the full measure of Alexander's success. It was achieved in country which favoured the defender in every way. The hills and mountains gave excellent observation over the attacker; the rivers provided ideal obstacles on which he could be held under fire; and there was just enough cover to conceal the defenders without marring their fields of fire. Wire entanglements of great depth were not needed in front of the defenders' positions as they had been in Flanders; nature provided obstacles enough, particularly in winter. As long as the winter weather lasted in Italy, Allied superiority in the air, and in tanks and artillery on the ground, were at a discount and could not be used with effect. And yet, if Alexander did nothing while the winter weather lasted, there would not be enough time in which to draw the German divisions away from Normandy when the ground hardened in the fine spring weather and Eisenhower's Armies set out to cross the Channel. The Battle for Rome had to be fought throughout the winter and early spring of 1944 if Alexander was to carry out the task set for him by the Combined Chiefs of Staff. It says much for his generalship that he never allowed the grim Battles of Cassino and Anzio to go to extremes. What was practical without immense loss of life, and without letting the Germans feel that his efforts were a strategic feint, was done—but no more. For instance, Cassino might have been taken at the third attempt, but when pressed by General Maitland Wilson, Supreme Allied Commander Mediterranean, to carry on the battle, he used the one word 'Passchendaele' and called the battle off.

This is not all. Churchill's restless demand for action based on his acute political sense, which told him that great advantages would flow from the capture of Rome, had to be resisted if new 'Sommes' were not to occur in Italy. Churchill had fought at every Allied summit conference from Casablanca onwards for a greater share of Allied resources for the Mediterranean which he felt held the key—the soft under-belly—to the defeat of Nazi Germany. Any faltering steps on the Italian front hurt him deeply and brought forth a stream of messages urging greater effort, often in impractical military circumstances. Alexander managed by balanced and forthright arguments to resist these encroachments into his sphere of responsibility whenever it was necessary. But this was only possible because Churchill respected his military judgment and, in his turn, rewarded Alexander with his full confidence. This enabled Alexander to win great military successes for Churchill when the time was ripe.

It can be said that there were two battles for Rome—the winter battles of Cassino and Anzio which were stalemates; and the spring battle—Diadem—which is one of the outstanding examples of British and American military planning, organisation and execution. The winter battles have been written about by many authors and so in this account of the Battle for Rome they will only be sketched on a backcloth to the story of Diadem—the final and decisive Battle for Rome and the forerunner of Overlord.

The strategy of the Italian campaign as a whole and an outline of all its battles are to be found in the author's *Battle for Italy* which was written from the strategic point of view. *The Battle for Rome* places a magnifying glass over one part—the most important part—of the Battle for Italy, in which Alexander and his Armies accomplished their difficult and self-sacrificing task almost to the hour, capturing Rome and throwing Kesselring's Army Group into headlong retreat as Eisenhower's troops began to board their landing ships, assault craft and transport aircraft.

The story of the Battle for Rome is like a three-act play, each act centred upon one of the major German defensive lines across the Italian peninsula: first, the destruction of the Gustav Line based on Cassino; then the breaching of the Hitler Line, built with teutonic thoroughness as a longstop behind Cassino; and finally the disintegration of the

Caesar Line—the last defences before Rome. Before any play, or military operation, reaches the stage, many months of tedious work have to be done: the birth and development of the concept; the translation into a script; the casting of the actors; and the laborious business of training and rehearsing. The Battle for Rome was no exception and so the story will be told in two parts:

Part I   Writing the Script for Diadem
Part II Diadem—a Play in Three Acts
         Act I—the Gustav Line
         Act II—the Hitler Line
         Act III—the Caesar Line

In the appendices at the end of this book there is a list of conventions and abbreviations used on the sketches, together with an order of battle of the Allied and German divisions which took part in Diadem. There is also a brief description of the Allied and German divisional organisations used at the time which may be useful to readers not familiar with them.

Part I Writing the Script for Diadem

'He who holds Rome, holds the title deeds of Italy.'
Churchill at Teheran, December 1943

Chronology
The Preparatory Phase of Operation Diadem

17 January	Opening of the winter Battle for Rome with X (Br) Corps' crossing of the Garigliano
20 January	36 (US) Division's repulse on the Rapido
22 January	The Anzio Landings
24 January to 12 February	The First Battle of Cassino fought by II (US) Corps
16–20 February	The First German counter-offensive at Anzio
16–18 February	The Second Battle of Cassino, including the bombing of the Monastery, fought by the New Zealand Corps
22 February	Alexander submits his proposals for Diadem to the Supreme Allied Commander, Mediterranean
28 February	Alexander's First Diadem Conference with Army Commanders
29 February to 4 March	The Second German counter-offensive at Anzio
4 March	The German Fourteenth Army resumes the defensive at Anzio
15–23 March	The Third Battle of Cassino, including the bombing of Cassino town, fought by the New Zealand Corps
23 March	Alexander orders consolidation of positions gained and start Diadem relief programme
24 March	Combined Chiefs of Staff agreed to postpone Anvil, giving the green light for Diadem
2 April	Alexander's Second Diadem Conference with Army Commanders
1 May	Alexander's Final Diadem Conference with Army Commanders
11 May	Diadem D-day

22–28 February 1944

1   *The Birth of Diadem*

'To force the enemy to commit the maximum number of divisions in Italy at the time Overlord is launched.'
Object of operations as stated by General Harding in his appreciation of 22 February 1944 (Despatches 2916)

On 23 March 1944 an unusual silence fell on the battlefields of Italy. Three weeks earlier, General Eberhard von Mackensen had given up his attempts to drive the Allies back into the sea at Anzio and had ordered his Fourteenth German Army on to the defensive around General Lucian K. Truscott's VI (US) Corps beachhead. Now General Sir Bernard Freyberg VC, the commander of the New Zealand Corps attacking Cassino, which was held by General Heinrich von Vietinghoff's Tenth German Army, had to give a similar order. The 1/9 Battalion of the Gurkha Rifles, which had hung on so tenaciously to the barren rocks called Hangman's Hill just beneath the ruins of the Monastery throughout the Third Battle of Cassino, was to be withdrawn and the Allies' third attempt to break through to Rome was to be called off. The winter battles on the Italian front were over. Both sides fell back exhausted and started preparations for the decisive phase of the war which everyone sensed would come with the summer weather of 1944.

On the Allied side the winter battles had started in the middle of January under the optimistic title of the 'Battle for Rome' which had been inscribed as the heading on the top of General Alexander's operation order to his Army commanders. After three months' bitter fighting and exhausting effort, his operations had turned into the twin battles of Cassino and Anzio. Rome lay beyond his reach as long as the winter lasted, but it remained a glittering political prize which Churchill had coveted for many months.

'He who holds Rome', Churchill had said at Teheran when discussing

Allied strategy for 1944 with President Roosevelt and Marshal Stalin,
'holds the title deeds of Italy.'

On the German side a similar change had taken place. When Italy
defected from the Axis in the summer of 1943 after the fall of Sicily,
Hitler had gloomily concluded that his commander in southern Italy,
Field-Marshal Albert Kesselring, had little or no chance of saving the
German troops fighting south of Rome. The Allies would land in their
rear, adding them to the large number of German troops already lost in
Tunisia and Russia during the disastrous campaigns of 1943. When this
did not happen and when Kesselring showed that he was not only
capable of extricating his troops from the Allied trap but also of bringing
the Allied advance northwards from Salerno to a halt in front of the
Gustav Line, Hitler changed his mind. German pessimism swung to
well-founded optimism, and Kesselring was ordered to stand south of
Rome. Kesselring's subsequent success in defeating the Allies at Anzio
and Cassino invested Rome with a significance for the Führer which it
had not possessed a few months earlier. Orders of the day issued by the
German High Command whenever a crisis occurred in some sector of
the Gustav Line usually began with the familiar Hitleresque ring:

> The Führer demands that . . . must be held at all costs for the sake of
> the political consequences which will follow a completely successful
> defence. . . .

Rome had become a symbol to the political and military directors on
both sides—a target which was to enable Churchill and Alexander to
draw German strength away from Normandy, and a mirage which
caused Hitler and Kesselring to fall into the Allied trap.

Allied planning for Diadem had started many weeks before the Third
Battle of Cassino came to an end. Indeed, the strategy on which it was
based had been decided amongst the Allied leaders in July of the
previous year when Churchill, Roosevelt and their Combined Chiefs of
Staff had met in Washington for the Trident Conference. It had then
been agreed that the invasion of Normandy should be the primary
Allied effort in 1944 and that the Mediterranean Theatre's operations
should be planned in such a way as to

> force the Germans to commit the maximum number of divisions to
> operations in Italy at the time Overlord is launched.

1   The situation in Italy at the start of Diadem planning: 22 February 1944

Looking at the situation maps at the start of Diadem planning, the two sides seemed and were, in fact, evenly matched. On the German side, Kesselring's Army Group 'C' consisted of two Armies—the Tenth under von Vietinghoff and the Fourteenth under von Mackensen. Behind Kesselring's Army Group, but not under his direct command, was Army Group von Zangen garrisoning northern Italy and the major industrial cities of the Po Valley. The divisions under von Zangen's command would be rotated with Kesselring's to provide a relief programme for divisions in the front line.

Von Vietinghoff's Tenth Army was responsible for the defence of the Gustav Line on which all the Allies' winter assaults had foundered. He had two Corps: General Fridolin von Senger und Etterlin's XIV Panzer Corps held the southern sector of the line from the Gulf of Gaeta to the watershed of the Apennines; and General Valentin Feurstein's LI Mountain Corps held the rest of the front northwards to the Adriatic. These two Corps commanded on an average about ten divisions, their numbers varying with the ebb and flow of operations. Von Mackensen's Fourteenth Army was responsible for holding and, if possible, eliminating the Anzio beachhead. He had two Corps as well: General Alfred Schlemm's 1st Parachute Corps holding the northern side of the beachhead and blocking the direct road to Rome; and General Traugott Herr's LXXVI Panzer Corps holding the southern half of the beachhead and ready to resist any break-out designed to link up with the main front. Von Mackensen's force also varied, but on average he had three divisions under Schlemm and two under Herr with a variable number in reserve and earmarked by Kesselring for use in either Army's area.

On the Allied side, Alexander's Fifteenth Army Group, which was also known as the Allied Armies in Italy, had two Armies: General Mark Wayne Clark's Fifth (US) Army and General Oliver Leese's famous Eighth (British) Army. In the original invasion of Italy, Fifth Army had landed at Salerno and Eighth on the toe and at Taranto. Subsequently Fifth Army had operated up the west coast based on Naples and Eighth Army up the Adriatic coast based on Brindisi, Bari and Taranto.

Mark Clark's Army was a very mixed force consisting of two American, one British, one New Zealand and a French Corps. His headquarters was staffed by Americans and organised on American lines. Truscott's VI (US) Corps held Anzio with two British and two and a half American divisions. General Sir Richard McCreery's X (Br) Corps held the extreme southern end of the main front along the Garigliano River. Then came General Geoffrey Keyes' II (US) Corps on the upper Garigliano, followed by Freyberg's temporary* New Zealand Corps facing Cassino. Finally General Alphonse Juin's French Expeditionary Corps of North African troops held the Apennine sector of Mark Clark's front.

Oliver Leese's Eighth Army on the Adriatic coast had three Corps: General Sir Charles Allfrey's V (Br) Corps, General Sir Sidney Kirkman's XIII (Br) Corps and General Wladyslaw Anders' II (Polish) Corps. Since Montgomery had handed over command of the Eighth Army to Oliver Leese at Christmastime, operations on the Adriatic coast had been kept in a deliberately low key. Eighth Army divisions had been moved one by one over the Apennines into Fifth Army. It was clear that it would only be a matter of time before the Army headquarters and the rest of the Army followed because the Adriatic sector was now a cul-de-sac in which decisive operations were unlikely.

The main events during February had been two major counteroffensives launched by von Mackensen to drive Truscott's Corps into the sea at Anzio and an attack by Freyberg at Cassino to relieve German pressure on Anzio. In spite of the immense weight of artillery and the mass of tanks with which Hitler lavishly supported von Mackensen, both German offensives had been beaten back by the dogged determination of American and British troops in the beachhead and by the devastating fire support given to them by the Allied Navies and Air Forces. Freyberg's relieving attack had been no more successful. After the controversial bombing of the Monastery of Monte Cassino his Indian and New Zealand troops made little impression on the German defence, and so the Second Battle of Cassino† was stopped and the New Zealand Corps set about planning the Third Battle.

While these operations were in progress, General Harding had been working with the 15th Army Group staff on a careful and detailed appreciation of the situation on which Alexander could plan the Diadem offensive. The work was complete on 22 February when Alexander forwarded the results to Maitland Wilson, Supreme Allied Commander, Mediterranean. Although Diadem would not take place before the end of April or beginning of May, Alexander needed early approval in principle so that detailed planning could start with a minimum waste of effort. No

---

* Temporary because it was only formed for the Second and Third Battles of Cassino and disbanded immediately afterwards.

† The First Battle of Cassino was fought by Keyes' II (US) Corps in January.

masterpiece, and certainly no great military plan, is ever born overnight.
It develops and matures as new facts emerge, fresh brains are brought
to bear, and current events make their full impact felt. Early
ideas change until the initial concept of the work is so altered that it
becomes almost unrecognisable in the finished product. One of the
fascinations of Diadem is the way in which this development occurred
and, later, how the battle itself grew and matured. It is well worth going
through the birth and development of the Diadem plan as it occurred
over twenty-five years ago.

Most strategic appreciations have to be made months ahead of events
and it is always difficult to decide what the position will be when the
resulting plans have to be put into effect. Diadem was no exception.
Only the most senior staff officers knew that Overlord was timed for the
early summer and even they did not know the exact date. This meant
that they could not judge with any precision where the front line would
be when the moment came to launch the offensive. Their first problem
was to envisage what were the most likely starting situations. After some
discussion it was decided that there were three possibilities.

The first was a voluntary German withdrawal to the northern
Apennines or even to the Alps in anticipation of the Allied spring
offensive. They had adopted such a policy in 1918 when they withdrew
to the Hindenburg Line, throwing Haig's plans out of gear and conserv-
ing their own troops for another stand later in the year. If Hitler
allowed Kesselring to copy Hindenburg, Alexander might find himself
opposed only by rearguards, while the Tenth and Fourteenth German
Armies fell slowly back up the Italian Peninsula leaving a logistic desert
behind them. There would be little he could do to stop the German
Supreme Command—the Oberkommando der Wehrmacht (OKW)—
withdrawing a significant number of divisions from Italy to strengthen
Field-Marshal von Rundstedt's forces in Normandy. This prospect
worried the American planners in Washington, who were, in any case,
opposed to further operations in Italy, but Harding suggested in his
appreciation that this contingency was unlikely. Kesselring would
hardly throw away the very considerable success he had achieved in his
winter defence of southern Italy. Harding felt that there was every
reason to believe that Kesselring would continue to hold his immensely
strong positions in the Gustav Line even when the fine spring weather
came, thereby enabling the Allies to manoeuvre more freely. Even if
Kesselring had some personal doubts about his Army Group's ability to

go on resisting the Allies south of Rome, Hitler's reaction to the Anzio landings suggested to Harding that an emulation of the withdrawal to the Hindenburg Line was not being contemplated by OKW.

The second possibility was that the Allies might themselves make a successful break-out from the Anzio beachhead as soon as von Mackensen's counter-offensive had been worn down, and this might result in a corresponding break-through at Cassino if the Allied Air Forces managed, as they hoped, to smash a way through for Freyberg's New Zealanders. The two Allied forces might join hands south of Rome and there be held up on a new line just south of the city by German resistance and by their own logistic problems. Harding believed that with luck and good weather such an advance might occur, but he realised that with so few fresh troops left and in view of the exhausting nature of the fighting to date, the chance of events turning so soon in the Allies' favour was very slender. He believed that the third possibility—that the front would remain much as it was until the spring—was the most probable case and the one upon which future plans should be based. This did not mean that no further efforts should be made at Anzio and Cassino, but that on balance it seemed the present front would be the most likely starting point for the summer offensive.

There were certain factors which were applicable to all three possibilities. These were the state of the troops on both sides; the general operational conditions in Italy; the organisational and training problems; the amphibious possibilities; naval and air considerations; and finally logistic capability of both sides. Harding and the Army Group staff scrutinised each of these in turn before looking at the factors peculiar to the three possible starting situations.

On the Allied side, only one division—Charles Keightley's 78 (Br) Division—was fresh enough for offensive operations. All the rest needed varying periods out of the line for rest, reorganisation and re-training. The Germans had suffered just as severe losses in men and equipment, and were bound to be trying to regroup and to withdraw their mobile divisions into reserve for transfer to France and elsewhere. Reports suggested that von Mackensen's efforts at Anzio were almost spent and a further German counter-offensive could be discounted in Italy. The Allies should, therefore, risk withdrawing their own tired troops from the line in rotation for rest and refit. While this was being done the Germans should be kept on tenterhooks by minor offensives and by deception plans. The real problem to be solved, however, was how to force the Germans to retain their mobile divisions in Italy and to send more into the theatre from elsewhere. Harding pointed out that merely pushing back the German line would achieve nothing. His first important conclusion was that tactical plans must be designed to bring about situations in which enemy formations could be destroyed or so reduced in strength as to be ineffective, rather than for the primary purpose of gaining ground. Only the successful destruction of German formations would compel Hitler to replace them from elsewhere.

Studying the second factor—the operational conditions in Italy— Harding came to his second major conclusion. Experience had shown that in country like Italy a superiority of three to one in infantry was needed to ensure a breach in the German defences. Tanks could only act as supporting weapons because there was so little room for manoeuvre. Consequently, the only sound basis for assessing relative strengths was the number and state of the infantry battalions on both sides. The Allies would, however, gain considerable help from their superiority in artillery if they attacked in areas where a great mass of guns could be deployed, and this meant attacking up the widest available valley—the Liri Valley blocked by Cassino. He calculated that the ideal striking force would need about twelve divisions which should be organised under four Corps' headquarters—two for the break into the German line and two for the break-through and pursuit. Each 'break-in' Corps should have three infantry divisions, while the 'break-through' Corps would have one armoured and two infantry divisions. Each 'break-in' Corps would attack the front of not more than one German division— preferably less—providing the necessary three to one concentration to ensure a wide enough and deep enough penetration to allow the 'break- through' Corps to make a decisive breach, leading to the collapse of Kesselring's front. It would be preferable to use this striking force on one axis, but the problem of finding suitable roads and assembly areas for deployment of the mass of guns and tanks needed for the attack and the equally difficult problems of logistic support might make this impossible.

Harding's conclusion that a striking force of twelve divisions would be needed led directly to the third factor—organisational and training problems. How could a force of this size be found from the resources of the Army Group and the Mediterranean Theatre? Bearing in mind how many divisions would be needed to hold the static sectors of the front, Harding estimated that he would need a total of twenty-eight or twenty-nine divisions before he could constitute the striking force properly.

There would only be twenty-one Allied divisions in Italy by the end of March. The extra seven or eight divisions would have to reach the theatre by mid-April to allow time for training and familiarisation with the conditions of the theatre if an offensive was to be launched early in May as he suspected Overlord would require.

There was another organisational problem to be solved. The command and logistic structure of the Army Group was seriously unbalanced with divisions of different nationalities hopelessly mixed up as a result of the tactical crises during the winter battles. For really effective offensive operations on a grand scale there must be extensive regrouping to bring all American and American-equipped units, such as the French North African troops, under the American-staffed and American-supplied Fifth Army headquarters, and all the British, British Commonwealth and other British-equipped troops like General Anders' Poles under British-staffed Eighth Army headquarters. Harding could not calculate so far ahead exactly how long this regrouping would take but even if it started at once, mid-April seemed the earliest date for completion.

The next factor—amphibious operations—was the easiest to deal with. The American insistence on an attack on southern France meant that there would only be enough landing craft and ships left available to Alexander for minor amphibious operations of about divisional size around the German flanks. At the most only one US and one British division need be earmarked for such operations and the details of possible operations could be left to the tactical planning staffs. Naval considerations could likewise be dealt with equally shortly, because Allied naval strength had already been redeployed to support the Normandy invasion. The Navies' paramount tasks were firstly to accelerate the arrival of the seven to eight reinforcing divisions in Italy, and secondly to interdict coastal shipping which the Germans were using to supplement the Italian railway system which was suffering the effects of continuous Allied bombing.

Harding gave great prominence to the air factor. His appreciations belie the charges often made by senior airmen that the soldiers never really understood the capability and problems of the Air Forces. He acknowledged the importance of maintaining air supremacy and the need to frame the land battle in such a way as to capture the airfields which the Allied Air Forces needed to give themselves greater scope. He also appreciated the shape of the narrow Italian peninsula and the alignment of its roads and railways offered an ideal opportunity for air interdiction of the German logistic system. On the other hand, he also appreciated more clearly than most of the airmen at the time that, to be decisive, the interdiction of German communications would have to be prolonged and continuous and this effort would have to compete with the Army's need for air support in the land battle once the main offensive began. Nevertheless he concluded that the interdiction programme should be second only to the maintenance of air supremacy. The tactical plan on land should be framed to take full advantage of combined air and artillery bombardment, and techniques should be developed and practised by divisions during their refits so that such combined fire plans could be put into effect quickly. He asked that the Air Forces should state as early as possible the capture of which German airfields were of greatest importance to them.

The final common factor was logistic capability. Twenty-eight divisions was almost more than the administrative system could handle even on the present front. Everything must be done to prevent the Germans completing their demolition plans once they started to withdraw. The ports of Civitavecchia and later Leghorn would become vital objectives for the Allied advance if it was not to be slowed or even halted by lack of supplies.

Harding now turned to the specific problems of the three possible situations which might exist when Alexander started his major offensive in support of Overlord. If the Germans withdrew north of Rome they were unlikely to give battle, and there seemed to be no means of forcing them to do so before they reached the northern Apennines between Pisa and Rimini. They would probably leave a shattered country behind them—bridges destroyed, railways rooted up, local supplies of food and fuel removed or destroyed, and mines and booby traps sprinkled liberally along the Allies axes of advance. If the Germans did copy Hindenburg, Harding believed that the Allied Armies should be ready to send forward light, hard-hitting and highly mobile units, grounding the rest of their divisions to solve the logistic problems of the advance. Once the Germans showed signs of offering battle, the grounded divisions should be brought up as quickly as the logistic system would allow.

In the second case—if the Germans stood south of Rome—it would be easier to mount a decisive battle of the type which Alexander hoped to fight. The main problem was to decide the best axis on which to launch the striking force. To the east of the Apennines, the country was extremely difficult and had been Montgomery's undoing in the Eighth

Army's autumn offensive which had failed on the Sangro and Moro Rivers. An attack just west of the Apennine watershed through Avezzano-Rieti-Terni-Perugia would encounter similar difficult country. This left the wide Tiber Valley and the west coast. Although the latter was obstructed by the mouth of the Tiber itself, a secondary attack along the coast supported by an amphibious landing, might lead to the capture of the port of Civitavecchia. The main attack would probably be most successful if launched up the Tiber Valley east of Rome. A break-through here combined with an attack up the coast might result in the destruction of the right wing of Kesselring's Army Group.

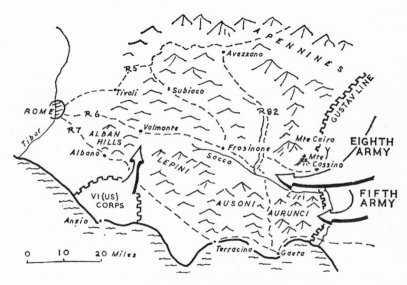

2 *The strategy of the third case*

The final situation—the front staying where it was—offered the greatest possibilities for a successful battle of annihilation. The Anzio beachhead was the key to these possibilities. As long as the beachhead existed, it was a potential threat to the German lines of communication to their troops in the Gustav Line. It was, of course, a liability to the Allies as well because it absorbed naval, air and logistic resources to keep it strong enough to resist German counter-attacks. The waste of these resources would be worthwhile if an attack could be launched from the beachhead by a force of, say, three to four divisions directed on Valmonte in the Alban Hills which lay astride von Vietinghoff's Tenth Army supply lines. Such an attack carried out at the time the main striking force was launched against the Gustav Line would have a reasonable chance of cutting off and destroying most of the German divisions holding the main front west of the Apennines. Unfortunately there were two difficulties to be overcome before this plan could be put into effect. First, the Anzio beachhead had to be made secure. (At the time of Harding's appreciation—22 February—it was far from certain that it could be held until the spring.) And secondly, the entrance to the Liri Valley—the widest and only suitable axis for the main striking force with its mass of artillery—was blocked by the defences of Cassino and the Rapido River which had defied all attacks so far. At least a limited bridgehead should be gained over the Rapido before the main offensive was launched, otherwise Diadem might break down at the very start through another failure to take Cassino.

Harding concluded his survey of all the factors by suggesting that it was to the Allies' positive advantage to allow the front to remain where it was until the spring, provided the beachhead was made secure and a bridgehead could be won in the Cassino area. He appreciated that this policy would entail a severe drain on naval and air resources to maintain the Anzio beachhead, but this was a matter for the other Services to argue and for the Supreme Commander to decide. Whatever the decision, there would have to be a pause in operations once the New Zealand Corps had shot its bolt at Cassino because there were no fresh troops available to attempt further offensive operations for some weeks.

The plan which Alexander recommended to Maitland Wilson was based on this appreciation. The current operations by Freyberg's New Zealanders should be continued until a bridgehead was secured over the Rapido; and those at Anzio should be pursued until the beachhead was secure enough to form a base for a break-out and advance on Valmonte. If these operations or some unexpected decision in the German High Command resulted in the premature collapse of the present front, then Kesselring was to be pursued with light forces until he turned to give battle. On the other hand, if, as seemed much more likely, little further progress was made by the time Freyberg's troops were exhausted then there should be a pause in operations so that divisions could be rested and refitted in rotation ready for the major offensive, synchronised with Overlord.

The outline plan for the offensive was to move Eighth Army across the Apennines as soon as possible leaving only one Corps to cover the quiet Adriatic sector. Eighth Army would become the main striking force with four Corps totalling the prescribed twelve divisions under command. Its task would be to break through the Gustav Line at Cassino and to advance as rapidly as possible up the Liri Valley towards Rome. Fifth Army, after handing over the Cassino sector, would mount a subsidiary attack from the southern sector of the front, while Truscott's VI (US) Corps attacked from the beachhead to sever von Vietinghoff's line of communications. The timing for Truscott's break-out would be decided at a later stage. It might be the first move to draw German reserves away from the Gustav Line before the main attack; or it might be launched after the main striking force when the German reserves had moved south to reinforce the Gustav defences.

The tasks of the Allied Air Forces would be to ensure the maintenance of Allied air supremacy, to continue the air interdiction plan up to the last possible moment, and then to give direct support to the land battle.

Alexander's first thoughts on the deception plan was to create the illusion of an impending attack by Fifth Army on the south coast of France. The presence of Juin's French Expeditionary Corps in Fifth Army would lend credence to such a possibility, and the preparation of the one-divisional assault landings round the German flanks could be magnified to increase the illusion. An invasion of southern France would be such a major venture that it would not take much to persuade the Germans that Alexander would be left too weak to mount a major offensive in Italy.

Alexander hoped that all preparations, including the complex move of Eighth Army across the Apennines, could be completed by 15 April but he did warn the Supreme Commander that no date could be fixed until detailed calculations had been made at the lower levels of command which had not yet been consulted.

Alexander's outline plan for a spring offensive received a cool reception at Supreme Headquarters in Algiers. In the first place it ran counter to Maitland Wilson's concept of operations for the Italian theatre; and secondly, if accepted, it would mean changing one of the major strategic decisions taken at the highest political level at Teheran.

Maitland Wilson's concept of operations in Italy had something of a

First World War ring of attrition about it. He intended to use the combined pressures of his air and land forces to compel Kesselring to withdraw north of Rome.

> My general plan for Italy is to use the air to deprive the enemy of the ability either to maintain his present positions or to withdraw his divisions out of Italy in time for Overlord. (Despatches 2916)

While the Allied forces hammered their communications, the pressure of the Allied Armies would force the Germans to consume more and more ammunition and supplies until the point came when consumption exceeded supply. Kesselring would then be forced to withdraw. The two efforts—air and land—were to be complementary. Any slacking of pressure on land would enable the Germans to rebuild their reserves. Maitland Wilson was opposed to Alexander's suggestion of a pause for regrouping and refitting for a major offensive in the spring. He would have preferred steady but unrelenting pressure until Overlord was launched. In his reply to Maitland Wilson's doubts about his plan, Alexander pointed out that pressure would not be relaxed sufficiently for the Germans to take any advantage of the lull. The operations with which he planned to secure the Anzio beachhead and to capture a bridgehead over the Rapido at Cassino would keep the Germans on their heels. Moreover, he was just as keen as Maitland Wilson to disrupt the German communications by air action. His only doubt lay in what he believed to be exaggerated claims by the Supreme Commander's air and scientific advisers as to the efficacy of the proposed interdiction plan which had been appropriately called Operation Strangle. This plan aimed to destroy the Italian railway marshalling yards and engine repair facilities as the Achilles' heel of the German logistic system. On the advice of Alexander's staff, rail and road bridges were added to the Strangle Plan, but, in the event, even this addition did not prove sufficient to reduce Kesselring's reserve stocks to a level which might have forced him to withdraw. Alexander contented himself with remarking that he hoped 'the weather will improve in time to give our air forces a chance to carry out their part of your plan' (Despatches 2917).

Although the differences between the Theatre and Army Group headquarters' concepts of operations were amicably resolved, the strategic stumbling block remained. Alexander's plan would absorb all the Army Group's existing resources plus the further seven or eight divisions which he asked should be shipped into Italy by mid-April. There would be nothing left for the attack on southern France upon which the American Chiefs of Staff had set their hearts. Maitland Wilson put Alexander's case to the Combined Chiefs of Staff and in so doing started one of the longest and most intractable strategic disagreements between the British and American Chiefs of Staff. The Americans were firmly wedded to Anvil—the code-name for the attack on southern France—whereas the British favoured Alexander's arguments that the best way to hold German divisions in Italy and to draw more in from elsewhere was to destroy those which were there already. The fact that the German divisions were defending Rome, which had become a symbol to both sides, should ensure that they stood and fought it out, giving Alexander the chance to win a decisive victory at exactly the right moment. He could only do this if all the Allied resources in the Mediterranean were concentrated upon the Battle for Rome. The ensuing argument was long and sometimes acrimonious, and it was not until 24 March that agreement was finally reached to postpone Anvil until after Rome had been taken and Overlord had been launched. This was the green light for Diadem.

While the strategic arguments went on between London, Washington and Algiers, Alexander set in train detailed tactical planning and regrouping arrangements so as to anticipate the decision if it was favourable. Unless regrouping started at once his Army Group would not be ready by the target date of 15 April which he had suggested to Maitland Wilson.

On 28 February he called his Army commanders to his headquarters at Caserta, near Naples, and gave them the outline of his plan and the reasoning behind it. This included the tasks which they were to undertake in the offensive and the Corps headquarters which would be under their command. He could only give the approximate number of divisions which would be available to each Army at this stage. The exact nominations would depend on the outcome of current operations, on the regrouping programme which had yet to be worked out in detail, and on the agreement of the Combined Chiefs of Staff to the diversion of the extra divisions which he needed in Italy.

The provisional Order of Battle was:

Eighth Army

> Kirkman's XIII (Br) Corps ⎫
> McCreery's X (Br) Corps ⎪ 12 divisions (including
> Anders' II (Polish) Corps ⎬ 3 armoured divisions)
> Burns' I (Canadian) Corps ⎭

Fifth Army

> Truscott's VI (US) Corps at Anzio ⎫   11 divisions
> Keyes' II (US) Corps ⎱ on the ⎪   (including 1
> Juin's French Expeditionary ⎰ main ⎬ armoured
>   Corps ⎰ front ⎭   division)

Under Army Group Control

> Alfrey's V (Br) Corps on the Adriatic—2 divisions

This made a total of only twenty-five divisions against Harding's assessment of twenty-eight to twenty-nine divisions, but it was no use planning on troops which might not, in the event, be allotted to the theatre by the Combined Chiefs of Staff.

After the conference Mark Clark and Oliver Leese returned to their headquarters to think out how they could best carry out their respective tasks and how much extra assistance they would need to ensure success. Regrouping instructions were sent out by the Army Group headquarters on 5 March. Mark Clark's Fifth Army headquarters issued its first planning instruction on 11 March, and on the same day Oliver Leese's Eighth Army headquarters moved across the Apennines into its new sector. The tactical planning of Diadem had begun. The first coordinating conference was to be held on 2 April at which the Army commanders would be required to give their plans and state what changes they believed would be necessary in their orders of battle to make their tasks practicable.

28 February–2 April 1944

2 The Development of Diadem

'. . . if Kesselring correctly appreciated our intentions, he could concentrate his strength opposite the threatened point as fast as we could.'

Alexander discussing the Diadem concept in his Despatches
(London Gazette 6 June 1950)

One of the hallmarks of professional military planners is the ability to achieve concurrent planning at several different levels of command without losing the flexibility needed to take advantage of the changing pattern of events and of the development of new ideas. Alexander and Harding were masters of the techniques involved. If the initial concept of an operation is given in too much detail too early, constructive suggestions are stifled which might otherwise have worked their way up the chain of command. On the other hand, if direction is not firm enough at the top, then confusion results at the lower levels. The balance is a fine one and depends essentially on the personality, style and judgment of the commander-in-chief. Some commanders achieve success using what might be called the 'Montgomery' style in which everything appears to stem from the brain of one man—the commander-in-chief; others, like Alexander, depend on a highly developed sense of team work in which every man in the machine feels he is personally contributing something to the whole. Whichever style is used, the fundamental reasons for success or failure lie in the commander's ability to see through events, to shape his concepts so that he cannot be thrown off balance by short-term considerations, and to judge the practicability of the tasks he allots to his subordinates so that they have confidence and give their best.

Concurrency in Diadem planning was achieved by three coordinating conferences held at Army Group headquarters. The first was held on 28 February at which Alexander gave out the initial concept of operations described in Chapter 1. The second was to be on 2 April, after Army commanders had developed their ideas in conjunction with their Corps commanders. The results of this conference would form the basis for detailed planning down to divisional level. And on 1 May there would be a final coordinating conference at which all the remaining issues would be resolved before the last minute preparations were made and deployment started for the offensive.

While Oliver Leese and Mark Clark were working on their initial ideas, Harding and the Army Group staff had four major problems to resolve before the next conference on 2 April. First, there was the development of a new deception plan. The Combined Chiefs of Staff had only postponed the landing in southern France, so Alexander's original idea of making Fifth Army simulate such a landing was no longer appropriate. A new means of achieving strategic and tactical surprise had to be thought out. Secondly, there were the detailed timings to be worked out: when should D-day be; which attack should come first; and what should the interval be between the attack on the main front and the break-out from Anzio, or vice versa? Thirdly, a forecast of operations was needed beyond Diadem because without such an assessment the logistic plan, which always has to be prepared many months ahead, could not be soundly based. And finally, the logistic plan itself had to be drawn up. Let us consider each in turn.

Any deception plan must be based on the commander's real intentions and on his assessment of the mental processes of his opponent. The latter had to be formed largely on the known dispositions and past reactions of the Germans in Italy. The Army Group intelligence staff managed throughout the Italian campaign to keep a very close check on the location of all German divisions and, in addition, air photography enabled them to locate the main German defensive positions under construction in the rear of the Gustav Line. From this information and the usual plethora of intelligence reports of varying reliability it was possible to build up a reasonably accurate picture of Kesselring's dispositions and likely intentions.

In March there were known to be twenty-four German divisions in Italy excluding one division, which was still forming, and a training division. Five of these were under von Zangen in northern Italy carrying out garrison duties; seven were under von Mackensen surrounding the Anzio beachhead and the remaining ten were under von Vietinghoff

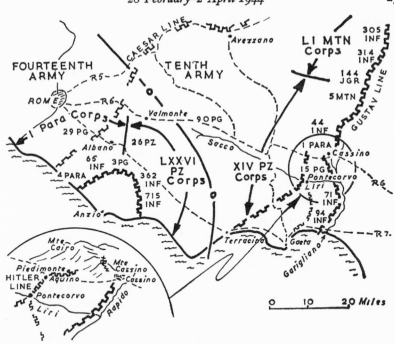

3 *German defensive plans as seen by the Allies in March 1944*

holding the main Gustav Line. The German divisions were, like the Allies, hopelessly mixed up with detachments from the mobile divisions* holding parts of infantry divisional sectors where they had been rushed to stem some crisis during the winter battles. Even the infantry divisions themselves had detachments serving in other divisions' sectors. Until the end of Freyberg's Third Battle of Cassino, the Allied pressure had been so continuous that the German staff had been unable to tidy up their patchwork of operational improvisation. There was no doubt that as soon as the Germans appreciated that the Allies' offensive was spent for the time being and that they were withdrawing divisions in rotation for rest and refitting, they would do the same. It was not possible to assess exactly how Kesselring would dispose his divisions when May came, but from his previous tactics it was fair to assume that he would hold as many of his panzer and panzer grenadier divisions as possible in reserve while leaving the infantry to hold his main defensive positions. He would

* That is to say panzer, panzer grenadier and parachute divisions as opposed to normal infantry divisions which marched and were comparatively immobile.

probably deploy his parachute divisions,which could no longer be used in their true role due to Allied air superiority and lack of German transport aircraft, to block the most dangerous approaches to Rome, i.e. Route 6 through Cassino and Route 7 from the Anzio beachhead. The aim of Alexander's deception plan must be to persuade Kesselring to dispose his mobile divisions as far away as possible from the areas which he intended to attack and on such tasks that would make Kesselring hesitate to commit them to the main battle until it was too late.

Although the German dispositions in March were only a partial guide to Kesselring's defensive plans, air photography filled in some more of the gaps. There were four German defence lines in varying stages of fortification. Furthest south was the Gustav Line itself which was now immensely strong, having withstood the winter battles and in so doing congealed into a hard and proven position whose weaknesses had been gradually eliminated in the light of experience. About eight miles behind the Gustav Line, Kesselring had begun to build a reserve position, which he called the Hitler Line.This ran across the northern half of the Liri Valley to block any successful Allied penetration of the Gustav defences along Route 6 past Cassino. Work had begun on the Hitler Line in December and was known to consist of concrete emplacements, anti-tank ditches, mines and wire, but there were a number of camouflaged objects in the line which the air-photo interpreters could not identify. The significance of these did not emerge until the Allies actually attacked the line. The fortifications ran from Piedimonte on the slopes of Monte Cairo through the village of Aquino to the ancient town of Pontecorvo on the Liri River. All the villages and farms on the line had been heavily fortified, particularly Piedimonte which was to serve as the pivot or 'Cassino' on the slopes of Monte Cairo. The country to the south of the Liri River seemed to have been considered too difficult for a major Allied offensive. Between Pontecorvo and the sea two extensions of the Hitler Line—the Senger and Dora extensions (*see figs. 3, 4*)—were sketched out, some simple earthworks had been dug and a number of deep minefields laid to block weak sectors, but the work had obviously been given a low priority and was not advancing very quickly. The steepness and tracklessness of the Aurunci Mountains seemed to be sufficient to discourage a major Allied threat south of the Liri.

The third German defensive line was Line 'C' or the Caesar Line, covering Rome. Kesselring clearly appreciated that, if the Allies did succeed in breaking out from the beachhead in strength, he might have to pull back von Vietinghoff's Tenth Army very quickly to save his divisions in the Gustav Line from being cut off. He would need a position to which he could withdraw both his Armies to stabilise his defences south of Rome. The Caesar Line was planned for this purpose and ran from the west coast just north of the beachhead to the Alban Hills, then via Valmonte to Avezzano on Route 5, and finally over the Apennines to Pescara on the Adriatic. Throughout the winter the Caesar Line was nothing more than a planning line sketched on German General Staff maps with divisional sectors worked out in case a withdrawal from the Gustav Line became necessary. In March, work was seen to be starting on this line with an emphasis on the areas blocking the main approaches to Rome, i.e. between the sea and the Alban Hills, astride Route 6 and astride the minor roads which could be used by a force thrusting round the eastern side of Rome.

The fourth and ultimate German defence line was the Green or Gothic Line (*see fig. 1*) in the northern Apennines between Pisa and Rimini which defended the Po Valley and the major industrial complexes which lay around the great cities of the north. This line had been started soon after Italy's defection from the Axis the previous summer and had been worked on spasmodically ever since. If Kesselring was defeated and his forces were so badly shaken that withdrawal became necessary then it was to this line that he would probably retreat to gain time for reinforcements to arrive from the German central reserves held inside the Reich. Whatever cover plan Alexander decided upon must avoid encouraging Kesselring to break off the battle too soon and to withdraw to the Gothic Line. Such a withdrawal would be the worst possible course of events from the Allies' point of view. They would have to advance over a devastated land in the face of German rearguards who could use to the full the ideal defensive characteristics of the Italian countryside. The destruction of a large part of Kesselring's Army Group 'C' would become unlikely once such a withdrawal began. On the other hand, the only way to persuade Kesselring to hold his reserves well back from the front was to threaten his lines of communication—the very thing which might cause him to withdraw. The Allied deception plan would have to be very carefully balanced between these two requirements.

There were two closely connected factors which could be used to help delude Kesselring. The Germans were known to overestimate the Allies' amphibious capability and would almost certainly assume that an amphibious operation would play some part in any offensive which Alexander might launch. Linked with this was the fact that Kesselring had already been caught off balance by the Allied use of sea power during the Anzio operation. On that occasion the Allied attack had opened against two sectors of the Gustav Line—on the Garigliano and at Cassino—and Kesselring, on the advice of OKW Intelligence that there was no sign of an Allied amphibious force assembling, committed all his mobile reserves to the main front. When the Allies landed at Anzio five days later there was little left in the Rome area with which to oppose them. Alexander decided to play on Kesselring's fears of another Anzio. Clear indications would be given of the preparation of another Anzio-sized amphibious force which Kesselring could not ignore, and yet which would not be so strong that he felt obliged to withdraw to the Gothic Line. The resolution which he had shown at the time of the Anzio landing suggested that it would have to be a very large force to make him consider withdrawal and that, even if he did wish to withdraw, he would not be authorised to do so by Hitler, whose 'no withdrawal' policy was by now well known to the Allies. As an experienced and prudent commander, however, he was likely to make some provision to seal off any new amphibious landings. The only way this could be done was to hold back some of his divisions to cover such amphibious targets as the ports of Civitavecchia, Leghorn and Genoa. If he held back his mobile divisions as he had done in the past, so much the better because these were the hardest hitting units in the German Army. If everything went well and he fell for Alexander's deception plan, the chances were that he would consider the attack on the Gustav Line to be another feint to draw his reserves southwards away from the potential landing area. Provided he could be prevented from knowing that there was no amphibious force at sea for several days, then he might hold his reserves back just long enough to enable Fifth and Eighth Armies to smash the Gustav Line before he realised his mistake.

Plan 'Nunton', which was the deception plan for Diadem, was designed to simulate an amphibious force assembling in the Naples–Salerno area. The I (Canadian) Corps with 1 (Canadian) Division, 5 (Canadian) Armoured Brigade and 36 (US) Division were to be placed on wireless silence on 18 April so that the German wireless interception units would report their disappearance from active operations. Canadian Corps signs and the signs of its divisions and those of 36 (US) Division would appear on the roads round Naples and Salerno, and amphibious training would be carried out by detachments from most of the units likely to be in the amphibious forces. On 22 April simulated Canadian wireless links, passing bogus traffic, would re-open purporting to show the Corps operating as an independent formation direct to Army Group headquarters from somewhere in the Salerno area. The real Canadian and US units would remain on wireless silence and would remove all tactical signs from their vehicles, bivouac areas, gun lines, supply points and so forth to conceal their true locations in assembly areas near the main front.

There was one Allied move which could not be concealed from the Germans and that was the transfer of Eighth Army from the Adriatic coast to the Cassino area. Both sides had abandoned any idea of making the Adriatic front a decisive sector; both had been withdrawing troops from it for some time; and both looked upon it as a backwater or cul-de-sac which could not be used for major operations. The undisguised presence of Eighth Army to the west of the Apennines could be used to heighten the illusion which Alexander wished to create. Preparations for a major assault on the main front, probably up the Liri Valley, were so open that Kesselring was bound to suspect that this was the feint attack and that the real attack would be delivered much later either from Anzio or from the sea.

The problems of timing involved the Army Group staff in considerable thought and discussion as to the most suitable date for D-day and the most advantageous sequence of attacks—whether the attacks from Anzio and on the main front should be made simultaneously, and, if not, which should come first. As regards D-day, detailed planning of the regrouping and arrival of new divisions from the Middle East and United States showed that the last reliefs in Eighth Army could not be finished before 23 April, and in Fifth Army by 25 April. Allowing a week to ten days for accidents and finishing touches all preparations should be complete between 3 and 5 May. It would be an advantage to have a full moon for movement of troops and supplies by night during the offensive. The moon would be new on 22 April and full on 8 May. The offensive should take place, therefore, between 1 and 15 May to obtain full advantage of the moon. A plan had been prepared to sabotage the German communications by dropping small parties by parachute just before the offensive began. The best phase of the moon for this purpose was between 4 and 7 May. Then, of course, there was the essential connection with Overlord's D-day. At this time Alexander had not been told when this was to be. He could only conclude that his own D-day would be best from his point of view if set between 3 and 7 May, but he appreciated that he might be compelled by Overlord timings either to hasten or delay his own operations.

The timing of the attacks was more difficult to resolve. The Army Group staff initially favoured attacking from Anzio first in order to unsettle the Germans in their very strong Gustav Line positions. After careful consideration Alexander reversed this proposal. In his notes written for his conference of Army commanders on 2 April he gave the reasons for deciding to attack on the main front first and spelt out how he saw the battle developing. These notes show that in his quieter way he was just as clear and far-seeing about the course of operations as the more extrovert commanders, but he kept his forecasts to his immediate staff and so did not reap the benefits of apparent omniscience. His train of thought at the time was along the following lines:

> the point at issue was when to time the two punches, i.e. on the main battle front and at Anzio.
>
> There were three possibilities:
>
> i.   Main battle front and Anzio simultaneously
> ii. Anzio first followed by the main battle front
> iii. Main battle front followed by Anzio

The main objection to (i) was that the Allied air effort would be split. The weakness of (ii) was that no German reserves would have been drawn off—the offensive once launched would have to continue until it reached Valmonte—and it might not, unassisted, be able to get as far as this.

Course (iii) appeared to be the best—it was the main battle which should be primed first, followed by the flank attack which was Anzio.

Therefore he suggested that the battle might go as follows:

The offensive on the main battle front should open with the attack of Eighth Army and II (US) Corps with the full support of the air.

This attack would continue until seriously checked or until a pause was essential to regroup.

At that stage all the enemy's resources should have been drawn in, and he hoped the enemy's troops guarding the beachhead would have been drawn on and weakened. This would be the moment to strike from Anzio—under the full protection of the air. If this flank attack was successful and got as far as Valmonte it might well be decisive and lead to the destruction of all German forces between the bridgehead and the main battle front.

At the conference on 2 April the Army commanders confirmed the practicability of the Commander-in-Chief's timing except that Eighth Army would prefer a D-day nearer to 10 May to allow more time for essential rehearsals. 10 May thus became the target date for Diadem. The attack on the main front would come first and the Anzio force should be ready to break out across the German lines of communication from D + 4 onwards. The exact moment for the Anzio attack would be decided by Alexander personally.

The forecast of operations beyond Diadem and the logistic plans based upon this forecast are complex documents which go beyond the needs of this account of the Battle for Rome but they do include two essential features whose importance will emerge as the story unfolds. Harding and his staff produced a very detailed appreciation of future operations for the 2 April conference. This envisaged two possibilities—cases X and Y. Case X assumed that Kesselring failed to stabilise the Caesar Line in front of Rome and pulled back behind rearguards, demolitions and mine-fields to the Gothic Line. Case Y envisaged a major Allied operation to break the Caesar Line. Shadow plans were made for both eventualities with an emphasis on Case Y as the most likely contingency. Eighth Army would attempt to outflank Rome to the east by breaking through the Caesar Line with a thrust directed on Tivoli (*fig. 1*) while Fifth Army would attack from the Alban Hills direct on Rome. This intention to direct Eighth Army east of Rome, which is expressed so early in planning is worthwhile noting because of the misunderstandings which arose between Mark Clark and Alexander in the final stages of the battle.

In the Army Group appreciation the attack on the Caesar Line was to be carried out with all available resources concentrated as follows:

Eighth Army with first priority astride Highway 6 directed on the area between Tivoli and Rome.
Fifth Army astride the Anzio–Albano road directed on Rome.

Thus even at this early stage, it was envisaged that Rome would fall within Mark Clark's Fifth Army's objectives.

The logistic plan was to switch Eighth Army's line of communication from Taranto and the roads east of the Apennines to Naples and the western routes. No major logistic difficulties were envisaged by the chief administrative officer, General Sir Brian Robertson, until the Caesar Line was reached. Thereafter, any further advance by Fifth Army would have to be supplied by sea making the early capture of Civitavecchia important; and Eighth Army would have to be supplied by road making it essential to reduce all transport on the roads to a minimum. He hoped that reserves and non-essential units would be held well back—a hope which was not fulfilled in the event.

At his conference on 2 April Alexander discussed his plans in their more fully developed form with his Army, Air and Naval and Logistic commanders and agreed tasks, groupings, timings and the air, naval and logistic support plans. These were confirmed in the minutes of the conference issued next day. During the rest of April the lower formations developed their plans and on 1 May Alexander held his final coordinating conference with his senior commanders and advisers as a result of which Operation Order No. 1 for Diadem was issued on 5 May. In this order the intention was to destroy the right wing of the German Tenth Army; to drive what remained of it and the German Fourteenth Army north of Rome: and to pursue the enemy to the Rimini–Pisa Line inflicting the maximum losses upon him in the process.

D-day and H-hour were now finalised at '11 May and 2300 hours' with the Anzio break-out timed at twenty-four hours' notice from D + 4 on orders from the commander-in-chief.

The scriptwriting at Army Group level was complete. In the meantime detailed casting of commanders and troops had been taking place at the lower levels. Let us now look at the men concerned on both sides of the Gustav Line and of the beachhead perimeter.

1   Field-Marshal the Earl Alexander of Tunis, talking to troops of 5 (British) Division

2   Field-Marshal Lord Harding of Petherton, Chief of Staff, 15 Army Group

3 (above) A photo taken during Alexande[r's]
final coordinating conference on 1 May 19[?]
outside his command train. (Left to rig[ht:]
Captain Everett, representing Flag Offi[cer]
Western Italy; General Harding, Chief [of]
Staff; General Leese, Commander Eigh[th]
Army; General Lemnitzer, American Liais[on]
Officer (who became Supreme Allied Co[m]-
mander Europe in 1963); Alexander; Gene[ral]
Clark, Commander Fifth Army; Air Mars[hal]
d'Albiac, Deputy Air Officer Commandi[ng]
Mediterranean Allied Tactical Air Force[.]

4 (left)   Field-Marshal   Kesselring a[nd]
General von Senger und Etterlin conferring [at]
Frascati

3 ## The Casting on Both Sides

'. . . the Gustav Line had been further consolidated in the probable battle sectors; it was so deepened by the construction of armoured and concrete switch lines and intermediate and advanced positions that even very strong enemy attacks could be intercepted. . . .'
Kesselring's 'Memoirs', describing the strengthening of his
defences before Diadem

Each Army commander—Allied and German—had to decide which of their subordinates should play the leading roles in the coming battle. Von Mackensen and von Vietinghoff had the easier task because they were commanding formations which were essentially German with only one or two divisions containing troops of East European stock and hence not wholeheartedly committed to the defence of the German Reich. On the Allied side the picture was very different. Alexander's Army Group was perhaps the most mixed national grouping which has ever been welded into a successful fighting machine. The British and American divisions were outnumbered by Commonwealth, Polish and French formations. Each national contingent commander held one ear towards his own Government and the other to the official military chain of command. Each was a prima donna in his own right or believed he should be treated as one in return for the war efforts of his own country. Moreover, each national contingent had its own special characteristics, its strong and weak points in battle, its own political sensibilities and its own special affinities or antagonisms to other contingents in this polygot Army Group. Peremptory orders which could be issued to a wholly British formation would have created friction and misunderstanding in such a force. Fortunately, Alexander had the ready knack of making each commander feel that he had thought of the idea first and that his contingent was honoured to carry it out. Alexander's orders were always couched in the form of suggestions, which by their obvious sincerity and logical reasoning were accepted by the recipients with better grace, though no less authority, than a dogmatic order would have been.

Oliver Leese had succeeded Montgomery in command of the Eighth Army at the turn of the year when the latter had returned to England to take over the 21st Army Group. It was not easy to step into such a man's shoes, but, in reality, Oliver Leese did not take over Eighth Army. Apart from the New Zealand and Indian divisions, few of Eighth Army's formations had belonged to it in its desert days. The divisions which had seen the transformation of Eighth Army from the beaten disillusioned force into the victors of El Alamein had returned to England ahead of their master. And amongst the Eighth Army staff few of the old team remained. Eighth Army was little more than a reincarnation of the First Army which had landed in Tunisia at the end of 1942. The transformation had begun in Sicily when 78 (Br) Division arrived from the disbanded First Army to join the Eighth Army in·breaking the San Stefano Line around the base of Mount Etna, with scrawled across its trucks, 'no connection with Eighth Army'. Over the next few months four El Alamein divisions left for England together with the headquarters of the experienced XXX (Br) Corps which had been Oliver Leese's Corps in the desert and throughout the Sicily campaign. Oliver Leese had often deputised for Montgomery who trusted him and recognised his sound common sense and integrity. He was thus the obvious choice as successor, but he was a very different type of commander: more orthodox, more ponderous in appearance and manner, showing less originality and lacking the flair of showmanship which was part of Montgomery's technique for raising the morale of his troops. The Eighth Army was now a more ordinary force run by its commander and staff—instead of by its commander alone as it had been in its heyday in the desert. Moreover, it suffered from the shadow of its past. Newer and less famous headquarters were always ready to denigrate its successes and magnify its failures. Its critics would claim that it never mastered the problems presented by operations in Italy. There is a grain of truth in this but it was always fated to assault in the more difficult sectors where the German defences were strongest and the topography more suited to defence than attack. Its real weakness, however, lay in the loss of many of its ablest and most experienced staff officers who followed their old master back to north-west Europe.

The task given to Oliver Leese at the 2 April Conference was to break through the enemy's front into the Liri Valley and advance astride Highway 6 on Valmonte. The same task had been allotted to various commanders four times since Christmas and on four occasions the Allies had been frustrated by the German defence: General Fred Walker's 36 (US) Division heavily defeated on the Rapido by General Eberhard Rodt's 15 Panzer Grenadier Division in January; General Charles Ryder's 34 (US) Division beaten above Cassino in February by

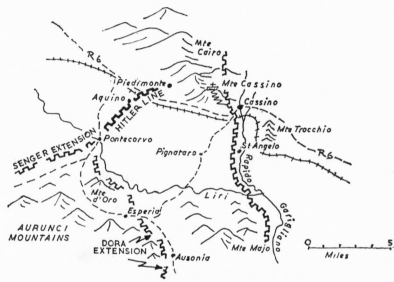

4   *The Liri Valley and Cassino Area*

a combination of the tenacity of General Ernst Baade's 90 Panzer Grenadier Division and bitter winter weather on the mountainside; General Bernard Freyberg's first attack with 2 (New Zealand) and 4 (Indian) Divisions after the bombing of the Monastery also stopped by Baade; and his final attack after the bombing of Cassino town frustrated by General Richard Heidrich's 1 Parachute Division. This time there were two great differences: the attack would be launched with ten instead of one or two divisions; and in, it was hoped, fine spring weather with the ground off the roads hard and passable to tanks, guns and vehicles, and the sky clear for the Allied Air Forces.

Eighth Army's front for the Diadem assault is easily described. It consisted of two distinct sectors: the flat Liri Valley up which ran Route 6 from Cassino to Ceprano, Frosinone, Valmonte and Rome, and the mountain mass of Monte Cairo of which Monte Cassino is only the most southerly spur, jutting out into the Liri Valley and blocking Route 6 which clings closely to its foot and which could not be used until Monte Cassino was firmly in Allied hands. On the top of Monte Cassino lay the ruins of the Monastery, sheltering German artillery observation posts which could scan all approaches into the Liri Valley; and at the foot of Monte Cassino sprawled the ruins of Cassino town, a third of which was still held by Heidrich's unbeaten paratroopers firmly blocking the exit to Route 6. The Liri Valley was rolling agricultural land, cut up by a number of streams and ditches, and although today it appears to have ample cover amongst the hedges, orchards and small woods, most of these had been stripped of foliage or destroyed by constant artillery fire during the winter months. Across the entrance of the valley ran the small fast-flowing Rapido River (or Gari, which is the more correct, but less-used name*) in a deep dredged channel with low flood bunds either side. In the middle of the valley, halfway between Cassino and the Rapido's junction with the Liri River, lay the small village of Sant' Angelo on a low bluff on the German side of the stream. German positions in and around Sant' Angelo could cover the Rapido in both directions. The River Liri formed the boundary between the Fifth and Eighth Armies and to the south of the Liri the ground was much more broken, rising steeply to the Monte Majo Massif and the difficult limestone crags of the Aurunci Mountains which filled the gap between the course of the Liri and the Mediterranean coast. After the Liri–Rapido junction the two rivers become the Garigliano River, flowing into the Gulf of Gaeta.

On the German side of the line regrouping started at much the same time as Eighth Army began to cross the Apennines. Von Senger's XIV Panzer Corps had been responsible for the whole of the southern half of Tenth Army's front from the passes north of Monte Cairo to the Gulf of Gaeta. Von Vietinghoff decided that with the increased number of Allied troops deployed south of Monte Cairo, the sector was becoming too much for one Corps' headquarters to handle efficiently. Much to von Senger's annoyance the inter-Corps boundary between Feurstein's LI Mountain Corps and von Senger's Corps was moved southwards to the Liri River. Quite fortuitously this gave Feurstein the whole of Eighth

---

* The Rapido and Gari join just south of Cassino and the resulting stream should be called the Gari, but usage which grew up during the battles named the whole stream the Rapido.

Army's sector and von Senger the Fifth Army's sector of the main front. Von Senger considered this a wrong decision because he had successfully held the whole southern front throughout the winter with conspicuous success. The front was now split and Feurstein's headquarters, which did not know the Cassino sector, was made responsible for the main road to Rome. Personal feeling obviously swayed von Senger's views, since there is little doubt, as the fighting showed later, that the frontage was far too wide for one Corps. In the event, even two Corps' headquarters were not enough to coordinate the defences properly.

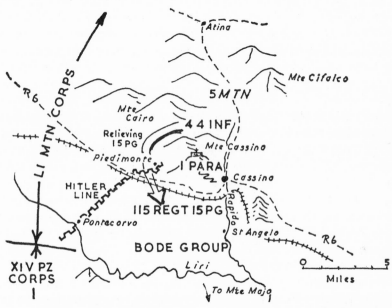

5   *The German dispositions in the Liri Valley and at Cassino*

In Feurstein's sector General Max Schrank's 5 (Mountain) Division held the passes north of Monte Cairo; General Bruno Ortner's 44 (Hoch und Deutschmeister) Division—an Austrian formation—held the eastern slopes of the mountain; and Heidrich's 1 Parachute Division held Monte Cassino, Cassino town and Route 6. Between Route 6 and the Liri Valley General Eberhard Rodt's 15 Panzer Grenadier Division had held the Gustav defences behind the Liri throughout the winter. In the general regrouping which took place in April, Rodt's mobile division was to be relieved so that it could be drawn back into reserve behind von

Senger's Corps. Early in April a regiment from 305 Division on the
Adriatic coast was brought over to relieve Rodt's most southerly regiment holding the line between Sant' Angelo and the Liri. This force was
called the Bode Blocking Group, named after its regimental commander.
The intention was to relieve the rest of Rodt's troops with Ortner's
Austrians of 44 Division but the relief programme was not due to be
completed before the middle of May. In the meantime a number of
regiments found themselves holding parts of other divisional sectors so
that all troops could spend some time out of the line. Such ad hoc
grouping is always necessary in a rest and regrouping period. Unfortunately for the Germans, they misjudged the timing of Diadem and were
still in the middle of their relief programme when Alexander struck—
but this is anticipating the story. The point to be noted at this juncture is
the unsatisfactory nature of the forces holding the Liri Valley—parts of
three divisions; 305, 44 and 15 Panzer Grenadier—not a well-balanced
force for such an important sector.

Although organisational faults existed in Feurstein's dispositions,
they were largely offset by the strong natural defences and the fortifications which had been built to block the Liri Valley. North of Monte
Cassino, 5 (Mountain) Division's dispositions had not been tested, but
so difficult was the country and so few were the advantages of attacking
through it that this sector could almost be ignored. There was a road
round the back of the Monte Cairo Massif through Atina which would
have turned both the Cassino positions and the Hitler Line, but it ran
through narrow and difficult defiles, which 5 (Mountain) Division
would have little difficulty in holding until reinforcements could arrive.
In any case, for Eighth Army to attack there would be to throw away its
great superiority in tank, artillery and air support. 44 Division and 1
Parachute Division's positions above Cassino depended for their
strength on closely-knit infantry positions sited for all-round defence
along the rock-strewn ridges and spurs above the Monastery. Most of
these positions contained pillboxes, armoured emplacements, case-
mates and well-built stone sangars. They were lavishly equipped with
machine-guns and well supported by light and heavy mortars hidden in
the clefts and gullies on the reverse slopes. All buildings and ruins were
fortified and two or three Sherman tanks, knocked out and incorporated
in the German positions during the last New Zealand attack, provided
further fire power. Wherever an Allied approach seemed practicable
mines, booby traps and wire were strewn to make an assault as difficult as

possible. The closer to the Monastery, the more closely knit the defences became; in all, an infantry defender's dream and an attacker's nightmare.

The real Gustav Line fortifications, as opposed to the reinforced natural defences of Monte Cassino, started in the Liri Valley below. The fast-flowing and deep Rapido was a tank and infantry obstacle in its own right. Along its German bank there was a continuous system of barbed wire entanglements, minefields, pillboxes and deep dugouts to shelter the infantry during Allied bombardments. These shelters were reminiscent of the Somme battlefield and held the garrisons of the numerous fire trenches which had been dug and concealed amongst the growing but untended crops on every knoll or slight rise which could afford a machine-gunner a practicable arc of fire. The whole fortified zone was covered by artillery and mortar defensive fire tasks, which had been built up and continually improved upon throughout the winter. The greatest strength of the Liri Valley positions did not lie in the fortifications themselves. German artillery observers on the slopes of Monte Cassino and Monte Cairo to the north and on Monte Majo to the south could bring accurate fire to bear on any movement in the valley with a certainty of obtaining full effect from almost every round fired. An attack up the Liri Valley could not succeed unless these observation posts were taken or neutralised; the latter being virtually impossible. An attack on Monte Cassino, however, without a complementary attack up the Liri Valley to unsettle the defenders of the Monastery would be just as costly. It was quite clear to Oliver Leese and the Eighth Army staff that since an advance through Atina was impracticable for a major force and would not allow them to use their great superiority in artillery and tanks, both Monte Cassino and the Liri Valley defences would have to be assaulted simultaneously if they were to have any reasonable chance of success.

After studying the sector closely from observation posts, air photos and intelligence reports and after long discussions with Freyberg and the New Zealand staff, Oliver Leese concluded that he had four immediate tasks: first Monte Cassino must be taken or pinched out to clear observation off the valley; secondly, the defences of the valley must be breached to open up Route 6; thirdly, he must so organise his Army that he could exploit rapidly up the Liri Valley to burst through the Hitler Line before the Germans had time to man it properly; and finally he had to protect his long northern flank which would become very exposed as he advanced north-westwards. Looking at each of the Corps which had been put at his disposal for the offensive, the obvious candidates for the

Liri Valley assault were the British X and XIII Corps. They were trained and experienced in the major set-piece battle in which tanks, guns, infantry and sappers have to be welded together like a well-balanced orchestra. McCreery was the more imaginative of the two commanders, but both were sound, able organisers who knew how to control the complex machinery of a large Second World War Corps. McCreery's X Corps had been under American command since Salerno and had lost all its original divisions either for Overlord or for rest or refit in the Middle East. Kirkman's XIII Corps had been Montgomery's principal assault Corps on the Adriatic coast and still had a number of its original formations and units. Furthermore, it was freshest as it had not been in a major action since the abortive Sangro offensive the previous December. For these reasons the responsibility for launching the attack into the Liri Valley went to Kirkman who was given four divisions— General Dudley Ward's 4 (Br) Infantry and General Dudley Russell's 8 (Indian) Infantry for his initial assault across the Rapido, and General Charles Keightley's 78 (Br) Infantry and General Vyvyan Evelegh's 6 (Br) Armoured Division with which to reinforce and expand his bridgehead.

McCreery's X (Br) Corps was given the less exacting task of protecting the northern flank and so was moved from the lower Garigliano up to the mountain sector where it took over Freyberg's 2 (NZ) Division and a number of independent brigades, including one Italian Liberation Group, to form a scratch mountain force for secondary operations towards Atina.

The choice of the Corps for the assault on Monte Cassino was easier to make. It could not be Burns' Canadian Corps as its headquarters had only recently arrived and the composition of its divisions—1 (Canadian) Infantry and 5 (Canadian) Armoured—was quite unsuitable for mountain work. Anders' II (Polish) Corps with two infantry divisions was already in the mountains further north and only needed to side step over the Apennines to relieve Juin's North Africans, who were due to move to Fifth Army, and it would be in its correct starting position for an assault on Cassino. A much more important reason for the choice of Anders' Poles for this difficult task was psychological. It would give the Poles a chance to show their manhood by doing what had defied American, British, New Zealand and Indian troops. Anders describes in his memoirs his reactions when Oliver Leese invited him to undertake the task:

It was a great moment for me. The difficulty of the task assigned to the Corps was obvious, and, indeed, General Leese made it clear that he well understood all that was involved. The stubbornness of the German defences at Cassino and on Monastery Hill was already a byword, for although the Monastery had been bombed, and the town of Cassino was a heap of ruins, the Germans still held firm and blocked the road to Rome. I realised that the cost in lives must be heavy, but I realised too the importance of the capture of Monte Cassino to the Allied cause, and most of all to that of Poland, for it would answer once and for all the Soviet lies that the Poles did not want to fight the Germans. Victory would give new courage to the resistance movement in Poland and would cover Polish arms with glory.

The selection of the Poles for the assault on Monte Cassino left the exploitation task to Burns' Canadians. This was also an appropriate selection. It would be the first time that the Canadians had fought as a national Corps in a major Second World War offensive. The Corps was ideally composed for the task, having an infantry and an armoured division which should, or so it was thought at the time, give it just the right mix to reap havoc behind the German lines once Kirkham's Corps had made a breach.

After making these allotments of tasks and resources Eighth Army should have had three divisions left over. In fact, there was only one, General Poole's 6 (South African) Armoured Division, which was just arriving in the theatre and would be held as Army reserve. It had not proved possible to withdraw the two British divisions from Truscott's VI (US) Corps at Anzio, nor were there any other British or Commonwealth divisions available from the Middle East. Oliver Leese had to accept a force of ten instead of the twelve divisions which Harding had originally specified for the main striking force. This had, of course, only been a theoretical calculation which, as had always been intended, would be modified when the time came to consider the actual troops to tasks.

During planning Eighth Army issued no written orders. Oliver Leese gave his Corps commanders a short written directive on 11 April and that was all. The Army plan which was finally confirmed after Alexander's coordinating conference on 1 May, consisted of two phases:

In Phase One, Anders' Poles were to isolate Monastery Hill and Cassino by attacking from the north-east and were to dominate Route 6 from above until a junction could be made with Kirkman's XIII (Br)

Corps. The latter would assault across the Rapido between the Liri River and Cassino to secure a bridgehead and then to isolate Cassino from the west, cutting Route 6 and joining hands with the Poles on the hills above to force Heidrich's paratroopers to surrender Cassino and the Monastery.

In Phase Two, the Poles were to advance from Monte Cassino towards Piedimonte along the southern slope of Monte Cairo to gain contact with the Hitler Line and to develop operations to turn the line from the north. XIII (Br) Corps was to advance parallel to the Poles along Route

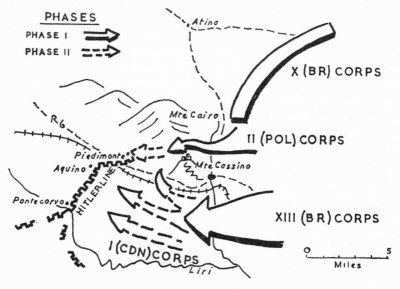

6   *Eighth Army's Plan*

6 in the Liri Valley below and was to plan its operations with a view to breaking through the Hitler Line on the Route 6 axis. Burns' Canadians were to be ready to pass through Kirkman's Corps for the advance up Route 6 to Rome. If the Germans managed to man the Hitler Line in strength, the Canadians would assault it alongside XIII (Br) Corps. During both phases McCreery's X (Br) Corps would simulate an attack towards Atina, but would be ready to release troops to the main assault Corps as the battle progressed.

In the notes used by Oliver Leese at Alexander's 1 May conference, there is a very clear picture of how he saw the battle developing. Under the heading 'Army Reserve' he lays down the general principles for the use of the Canadian Corps. It should operate to the south of XIII (Br) Corps and should not be committed until Kirkman had used his reserve infantry division—Charles Keightley's 78 (Br) Division. Oliver Leese envisaged a situation—which turned out to be extraordinarily accurate in the event—in which the Fifth Army would make progress against the less strongly held German positions south of the Liri River while Kirkman was still engaged in stern fighting around Cassino, unable to join hands with the Poles. Under these circumstances the Canadians would be told to cross the Rapido south of Sant' Angelo to operate on the left of XIII (Br) Corps. Canadian operations might take the form either of a break-through up the Liri Valley to unseat the Germans before they could settle down in the Hitler Line, or of giving help to XIII (Br) Corps by taking over half its sector thus forming a continuous front across the Liri Valley. In either case, Kirkman's sappers were to prepare bridges and tracks for the advance of the Canadian Corps through the southern half of the XIII (Br) Corps' sector.

The air and artillery support plans were carefully coordinated. The Eighth Army staff examined the German defences in great detail and came to the conclusion that the fortifications themselves were unsuitable for a heavy air strike. They were too linear and lacked any key feature whose obliteration would help the land battle. Moreover, H-hour was likely to be set for about midnight on D-day to give the sappers as much darkness as possible in which to bridge the Rapido. By dawn the forward troops should be well into and closely engaged with the German positions making pre-arranged air strikes difficult to anticipate. The Eighth Army staff examination of the German artillery dispositions gave a different picture. Oliver Leese's artillery commander had just over 1,000 guns with which to neutralise 400 German guns and *nebelwerfers* in range of Eighth Army's sector. The success or failure of Eighth Army's assault would depend largely upon the efficiency with which these German guns and their numerous mortars could be subdued. Not only had the Eighth Army gunners to keep the German gun and mortar positions under constant counter-battery fire; they had also to blind the German observation posts on Monte Cassino and Monte Cairo. It might prove possible to keep Monte Cassino blanketed in smoke as long as the wind remained favourable, but blinding observers on the much bigger Monte Cairo feature would be impossible.

The most useful service the Allied Air Forces could perform would be to help neutralise those German gun positions which were at extreme range for the bulk of the Allied artillery concentrated to support the assault. In the Liri Valley there were five groups of German guns, three of which were suitable for air attack. There was also a considerable concentration of artillery deployed in the Atina Valley which was out of range to the Allied guns in the Cassino sector. The final division of effort between the artillery and the air was quite simple. During the night of the attack all guns were to carry out a forty-minute counter-battery programme immediately before H-hour and then to switch to the close support of the corps to which they were allotted. The Poles would be supported by concentrations of fire on to known German positions, while XIII (Br) Corps would be given a barrage. When daylight came the bombers and fighter-bombers would begin attacking the German gun positions. A special fighter controller (codenamed Rover David) was to be established on the top of Monte Trocchio overlooking the whole battlefield as far back as the Hitler Line. From this splendid observation post he would direct fighters and fighter-bombers on to opportunity targets using the 'cab rank' system. As each flight of aircraft arrived over the battlefield, it would report to the Rover David controller. If he had a target immediately available, he would give the details to the flight commander as he circled overhead. If there happened to be nothing to attack at that moment, the flight would circle for ten to fifteen minutes before flying off to attack a pre-arranged target such as one of the German gun positions in the Atina area before returning to base. In addition to gun positions and providing immediate support through the Rover David controller, the Air Forces were to harass all roads and tracks beyond the bomb line, and to attack the suspected locations of a number of German headquarters.

Mark Clark's problems were more complex, but he had an easier task than Oliver Leese in casting his Corps commanders in the roles which they were to play because he had fewer options. His problems were more complex because he was to play a supporting role in the initial stages of Diadem, which meant that his actions were dependent to some extent on the successes or failures of Eighth Army which Alexander had designated as the main striking force. Moreover, Mark Clark was commanding two fronts; the southern section of the main front along the Garigliano River and the Anzio beachhead separated by some sixty miles of sea. In the later stages of the offensive, the action of his troops attacking from Anzio might be decisive in encircling and destroying most of the

German formations west of the Apennines. The timing and direction of their breakout would be critical. Alexander had reserved the final decisions on these to himself and so Mark Clark would not be an entirely free agent in handling his Army at this decisive stage of the battle. He had to have a number of contingency plans from which to choose as events unfolded. His tasks were made no easier by the difficult nature of the country through which both parts of his Army would have to operate.

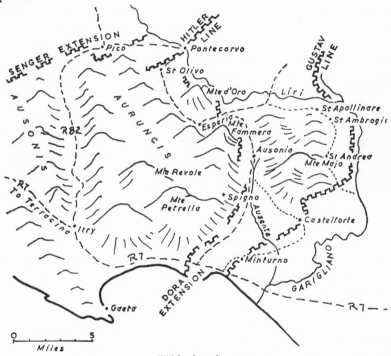

7   *Fifth Army's sector*

On the main front, he was faced with the jagged crags and escarpments of the Aurunci and Ausoni Mountains through which there were only three roads suitable for the advance of mechanised forces. There was the coast road, Route 7, which ran for the first thirty miles close under the mountains and through a number of narrow defiles between the mountains and the sea. After Route 7 emerged from the last of these defiles at Terracina it ran through the reclaimed farmland of the Pontine Marshes with deep irrigation ditches on either side. The whole area had been reflooded by the Germans, making this a singularly unattractive line of advance. In the centre of the sector there was a lesser road which wound its way through the hills from Castelforte near the Garigliano to Ausonia and Esperia and thence along the south bank of the Liri River to Pontecorvo at the southern end of the Hitler Line. This road could only be used after the mountains had been cleared either side. Its main bottleneck lay between Ausonia and Esperia in what became known as the Esperia defile. The third road was in the north of the Fifth Army's sector and was the poor road along the south bank of the Liri which eventually joined the centre road near Esperia. All three of the roads would be unusable unless the heights above them were cleared. This would be a slow and laborious business if the Germans fought as hard in this sector as they had done at Cassino.

The German dispositions on the Fifth Army front were known to the Allies with considerable accuracy. Von Senger's XIV Panzer Corps, which was holding the southern end of the Gustav Line from the Liri to the sea, had three divisions. General Wilhelm Raapke's 71 Division, which had gained a reputation for resolution in the earlier fighting above Cassino, held the northern half of the sector from the Liri River down to Castelforte. It was responsible for the defence of the Monte Majo Massif which formed the southern bastion to the Liri Valley defences and was so important to the Gustav Line defences that Raapke had been reinforced by four battalions from 44 Division. Raapke's frontage was almost ten miles long and could only be held by one division on the assumption that the country was too difficult for a major Allied offensive. General Bernhard Steinmetz's 94 Division held the rest of the sector down to the sea coast. His troops did not possess as high a reputation as Raapke's because they had been surprised and severely mauled by McCreery's X (Br) Corps in January. Their positions were only saved by the timely intervention of Kesselring's mobile divisions. Behind these two divisions, it was intended to position Rodt's 15 Panzer Grenadier Division once it had been relieved in the Liri Valley. One regiment had reached the coast near Terracina where it was made responsible for opposing any Allied landing in that area. The other regiments were, as yet, still tied down in Feurstein's sector awaiting relief. Comparing the frontages held by 71 and 94 Divisions it was quite clear that the main weight of von Senger's Corps lay astride Route 7 and along the coast back to Terracina. The area between Castelforte and the Liri was relatively weakly held though the troops defending it were experienced in holding hill country.

At Anzio, the problems were rather different but no easier to solve. The beachhead was overlooked by the German positions on the higher ground to the north from which artillery observers had been able to keep Truscott's Corps under constant harassing fire ever since the landings in January. The beachhead was like a beleaguered fortress. Everything had to be dug down for protection against shelling and heavily camouflaged to defeat the German observation posts. By day, little movement was possible, but by night the whole area came to life as

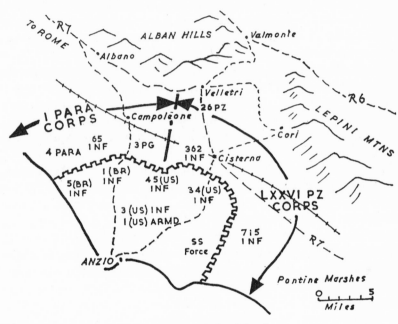

8   *The Anzio beachhead*

ammunition and supplies were rushed from the ships to the shore dumps, and from the dumps forward to the front line. It was difficult enough to maintain the existing troops in the beachhead in a defensive posture, let alone bring in more troops and build up the vast stocks of ammunition needed for a major offensive.

The dispositions of von Mackensen's Fourteenth Army surrounding the beachhead showed his considerable preoccupation with a break-out towards the Alban Hills and Rome. He had two Corps: General Alfred Schlemm's 1 Parachute Corps and General Traugott Herr's LXXVI

Panzer Corps. The former held the northern sector astride the Albano Road with three divisions: General Heinrich Trettner's 4 Parachute Division; General Hellmuth Pfeiffer's 65 Infantry Division and General Fritz-Hubert Graser's 3 Panzer Grenadier Division. While the latter with only two divisions—General Heinz Greiner's 362 Infantry Division and General Hans-Georg Hildebrandt's 715 Infantry Division —blocked the eastern sector. The Army Reserve—General Smilo von Lüttwitz's 26 Panzer Division—was disposed at the foot of the Alban Hills at Velletri. If the Allies breached the Gustav Line and von Vieting-hoff was forced to withdraw his Tenth Army to the Caesar Line, von Mackensen's 1 Parachute Corps would not have to change its disposi-tions as its divisions were only a short distance in front of the Caesar positions. His LXXVI Panzer Corps could unfold from around the eastern sector of the beachhead and fall back into its Caesar positions in the Alban Hills without difficulty as Tenth Army withdrew on Val-monte. A continuous line would then be re-established across the Italian peninsula roughly parallel to Route 5 through the Apennines to Pescara (see fig. 1).

The possible thrust lines for an Allied break-out from Anzio were, like the routes forward from the Garigliano, influenced more by hill masses than the detailed dispositions of the German divisions. To the east lay the Lepini Hills and to the north the Alban Hills, both of which barred the way to Route 6 up which Eighth Army would be advancing and along which the Germans would be struggling to withdraw. There was a gap between these two hill masses. On the map this looked the obvious thrust line for Truscott's Corps because it led directly to Val-monte on Route 6 which Alexander had suggested as the objective for the break-out, but there was a major objection to this route. It was too narrow and could only be used if the observation afforded by the Alban and Lepini Hills could be cleared. The alternative was to thrust direct towards the Alban Hills and pass the bulk of the break-out force between the hills and the sea, making straight for Rome instead of trying to cut the Germans off at Valmonte. In this way a battle for the Lepini Hills would be avoided. The Alban Hills would have to be cleared whatever plan was used.

Mark Clark had little choice in casting the roles for his three Corps. Truscott, who had previously commanded 3 (US) Division, had taken over VI (US) Corps from General Lucas when the latter had lost Mark Clark's confidence in the early days of the Anzio landing. He was a

5   (left) General Keyes, Commander II (US) Corps, being decorated by Alexander

6   (centre) General Burns, Commander I (Canadian) Corps

7   (right) General Truscott, Commander VI (US) Corps

8   (Left to right) General Anders, Commander II (Polish) Corps; General Juin, Commander French Expeditionary Corps; General Kirkman, Commander XIII (British) Corps

9 *Eighth Army's Road: the Liri Valley overlooked by Monte Cairo (the highest peak in left background) and Monte Cassino (lower spur in left middle ground with the ruin of the Monastery visible on crest). Monte Cifalco is skyline of right background. Route 6 runs along the far side of the valley close under the mountains*

10 *Fifth Army's Road: an aerial view of Fifth Army's front showing Route 7 clinging to the coast and the Aurunci Mountains blocking the rest of the front*

pugnacious and very active commander who excelled under difficult conditions. It was largely due to his forthright leadership that the beachhead had weathered so many German counter-attacks and so much harassment for so long. There was only one task that he and his corps could be given—a break-out from Anzio when ordered to do so by Alexander at the decisive moment. Keyes' II (US) Corps headquarters had fought throughout the Italian campaign from Sicily onwards but his two divisions—General John Coulter's 85 (US) Division and General John Sloan's 88 (US) Division—had only recently arrived from the United States. They should, if possible, be given a supporting rather than a key role. Mark Clark's third Corps, Juin's French Expeditionary Corps, was at that time an uncertain quantity. It had arrived during the winter battles equipped with US equipment and had done extremely well trying to outflank Cassino from the north of Monte Cairo in the direction of Atina. These operations had been in the nature of a care-fully-staged initiation against untried German troops away from the main Allied axis of advance. No one could be quite certain how these North African troops would behave when faced by first-class German troops, using all the latest weapons of war, but Mark Clark had no option as to where they should be deployed. The training of Keyes' new divisions was obviously unsuited to a mountain sector, whereas Juin's men were very much at home in such country. Juin was therefore given the northern half of Fifth Army's main front opposite the Monte Majo Massif, and Keyes was given the coastal sector.

In his memoirs Mark Clark gives his appreciation and plan very clearly in one short paragraph:

> On our sector there was but one road, Route No. 7, which ran along the coast and was under the complete domination of deep and high mountain ridges. That road was like a little gutter at the edge of a steep roof, and going up it without control of the adjacent mountains was impossible. I decided, therefore, that the Fifth Army would do what nobody expected—particularly the Germans—strike out directly over the mountains with all the strength and speed that we could muster.

He did not, however, confess that the inspiration for the plan came from Juin, as will be explained in Chapter 5.

In brief, the Fifth Army plan was for Juin to attack out of McCreery's old bridgehead over the Garigliano to take Monte Majo, while Keyes

forced his way up Route 7. Juin would then bring up a specially organised mountain force to break through the centre of the Aurunci
Mountains outflanking the German positions blocking the Esperia
Defile and Route 7. The Army objective was to be the Pico–Itri
lateral road by which the two German Corps kept touch with each
other either side of the Aurunci Mountains. If Fifth Army could fight
its way to this line, it would start outflanking the main Hitler Line and
would be through the Dora extension and up to the Senger Line.

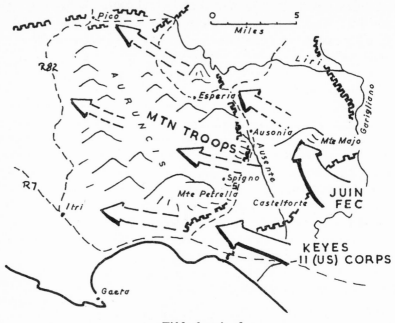

9 *Fifth Army's plan*

Fifth Army's reserve was to be General Frederick Walker's 36 (US)
Division which would be initially under command of Keyes' Corps. If
things went badly when Keyes attacked Walker would be ready to
support him, but if things went well, Walker's division would be
shipped to Anzio to strengthen Truscott's break-out force.

Kesselring's problems in preparing his theatre for the return of dry
spring weather were of quite a different order. He knew that he would
receive little help from Germany once the Russians re-opened their
offensive on the Eastern Front and the Western Allies launched their

long-awaited Second Front. He had no choice but to make the best defensive dispositions which he could devise and then await events. He had full confidence in his ability to go on holding the Gustav Line. If it were breached in the centre, the Hitler Line would seal off an Allied penetration up the Liri Valley; or if a failure occurred on the west coast, there were plenty of ideally defensible positions amongst the Aurunci and Ausoni Mountains. The Anzio beachhead perimeter seemed very secure and ideal for sealing off any attempted break-out, provided the Alban Hills were strongly held. In case things really went awry, work was in hand strengthening the Caesar and Gothic Lines. The only real problem was how to dispose his mobile divisions which he had withdrawn to rest and refit after winning the Third Battle of Cassino. There were one panzer and four panzer grenadier divisions available. 15 Panzer Grenadier Division was already being disposed behind the coastal flank of von Senger's XIV Panzer Corps near Terracina. The 26 Panzer Division was in Fourteenth Army reserve ready to pounce on any move made by Truscott. This left three panzer grenadier divisions with which to cover the long Italian coastline against Allied amphibious landings. Kesselring decided rightly that the east coast could be disregarded. There seemed to be four danger areas on the west coast: the mouth of the Tiber where a landing would threaten Rome directly; the port of Civitavecchia; the port of Leghorn; and the port of Genoa. Genoa seemed too far away from Allied fighter bases to be at all likely, but the mouth of the Tiber, Civitavecchia and Leghorn must all be guarded. Kesselring was also concerned about the possibility of an Allied parachute landing at Frosinone, a key bottleneck on Tenth Army's line of communication along Route 6 (*see fig. 1*). He, therefore, disposed his remaining panzer grenadier divisions as follows:

Ernst Baade's 90 PG Div.—mouth of Tiber with elements at Frosinone
Walter Fries' 29 PG Div.—Civitavecchia
Wilhelm Schmalz's Hermann Göring Div.—Leghorn

The Hermann Göring Division was earmarked by OKW to reinforce von Rundstedt's forces in northern France if and when the Second Front was opened in France or the Low Countries, and could not be used by Kesselring without OKW's consent.

As the Allied intelligence staffs watched these dispositions taking shape, they realised that the first part of their cover plan was working.

Kesselring was guarding his seaward flank. Alexander was now faced with the problem of how to ensure that Kesselring kept these powerful and experienced divisions coastwatching for as long as possible, and, perhaps if he were very lucky, until the decisive moment was past and Tenth Army had been defeated before they could come to its aid. It seemed unlikely, however, that such an experienced commander as Kesselring would misread the battle to such an extent once it was joined.

4 The Eighth Army's Rehearsals

'Eighth Army will break through the enemy's front in the Liri Valley and advance on Rome.'

Eighth Army's task given in Alexander's Despatches (2921)

A play is conceived, the script is written, the players are cast, and then the rehearsals begin. Nothing seems to fit; each actor has construed his part in his own way; cues which seemed easy to take when written prove awkward when spoken; and the stage with its embryo sets seems strange and unrealistic. But as the rehearsals proceed misunderstandings disappear, compromises are reached and the author's concept comes to life. So it is with military planning with one important exception: in the theatrical world the curtain rises on a first night after a blaze of publicity, whereas in the military world H-hour strikes behind a cloak of secrecy and deception.

Alexander's strategic deception plan of persuading Kesselring to look to his long, exposed western flank was seen to be working, but this alone would not be enough to ensure success unless he could achieve tactical surprise as well. There seemed little hope of this. There were only two good roads leading from Naples, his Army Group's main base, to the battle area: Route 6 to Cassino and Route 7 along the coast. There could be no hiding the build-up of ammunition, equipment and supplies along these routes from the prying eyes of German agents, or from German photo-reconnaissance aircraft flying at heights which made interception difficult. Alexander had made no attempt to disguise the move of Eighth Army across the Apennines as this was clearly impossible. For the same reason he did not attempt to hide the massive build-up for Diadem. Instead he depended for tactical surprise on disguising two other key factors which Kesselring would need to know if he were to take appropriate counter-measures; the point of attack and the date of the offensive.

The former could be disguised relatively easily by keeping activity at an even intensity all along the front from the watershed of the Apennines to the Gulf of Gaeta and within the beachhead at Anzio. Kesselring was to be given no clue as to whether the supposed holding attack would fall on von Vietinghoff's Gustav positions or on von Mackensen's Anzio perimeter while the mythical amphibious force assailed his flank and rear. A study of the dumps, hospitals, workshops and so forth would only suggest operations of equal intensity everywhere. The latter—the timing of the offensive—was more important, more difficult and its solution more subtle as it depended upon the Allies' appreciation of German strategic thinking.

The key military event of 1944 was bound to be the creation of the Second Front. All other Allied operations, in German eyes, would probably be linked with this venture. The timing of the Second Front would in its turn depend upon Soviet activity on the Eastern Front where the main summer offensive was unlikely to start before the ground had time to dry out after the spring thaw—say mid-June. The slowness with which the Western Allies had undertaken preparations for the Second Front in spite of constant Russian calls for help, and the uncomfortable experiences which they had suffered in their earlier amphibious operations at Dieppe, Salerno and Anzio seemed to suggest that they would not attempt to cross the Channel until the Russian summer offensive had drawn German reserves eastwards. The Allied Armies in Italy would clearly be called upon to mount a diversionary effort and this was most likely to come about the same time as the Russian summer offensive. If Alexander could persuade Kesselring that his preparations could not be completed before the end of May at the earliest, he would reinforce this potential train of thought in the minds of the OKW staff, and possibly catch Kesselring's divisions still in the middle of their rest and retraining programme with minimum troops in the line and many commanders still on leave or on courses in Germany. With this aim in view, the Fifth and Eighth Armies issued their divisional training and re-equipment programmes up to 21 May. Only a very few of the most senior commanders and staff officers, who had to know, were aware that Alexander intended to strike early in May. All the usual know-alls through whom the best-laid plans are so often leaked and from whom 'bazaar' gossip originates—the quartermasters, the supply depot clerks, hospital orderlies and so forth—were put off the scent by having what appeared to be an obvious pointer to the future. Since the programmes were to be completed by 21 May it looked as if something big would happen towards the end of May.

Alexander's coordinating conference on 2 April started the final phase of the preparations. In each of the five corps nominated to take part in the opening phases of the offensive there was increased activity as the orders were decentralised and more and more subordinate commanders were briefed on their parts. Most of the planning had to be done off air photos and maps. Too many strangers visiting observation posts in the forward areas would lead to gossip and possibly the chance capture of,

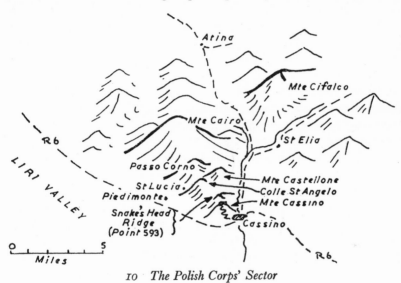

10   *The Polish Corps' Sector*

say, a Frenchman in the Garigliano bridgehead or a Pole above Cassino which might well alert the Germans to the impending offensive. The strictest orders were issued about reconnaissance and visits to the forward area were severely rationed, but even so, observation posts on the top of places like Monte Trocchio, overlooking Cassino, were crowded day after day with commanders and staff officers from the attacking formations 'having a look'. It is surprising that the Germans did not spot this activity and also failed to catch a Frenchman or a Pole in the wrong sector.

General Anders started detailed planning at his Polish Corps' headquarters on 7 April, making a personal flight over Monte Cassino in a reconnaissance aircraft and then a more detailed examination of the ground from as many observation posts as he could reach without risk of capture. Between 8 and 17 April his Poles gradually relieved the New Zealanders and 4 (Indian) Division above Cassino, the New Zealand division side-stepping to the north to take over the old Polish sector. The whole move was made to appear like a routine relief of the exhausted New Zealand and Indian troops by the fresher but as yet relatively inexperienced Polish units.

Looking at his new sector Anders found that he was faced with a classic defensive position in which strong-points at every level were mutually supporting. At divisional level the Germans held three main features which formed a triangle. Heidrich's 1 (Parachute) Division held Monte Cassino; Schrank's 5 (Mountain) Division held the eastern slopes of Monte Cairo; and Franck's 44 Division held Monte Cifalco. When he attacked Monte Cassino he would be flanked by Monte Cairo and have the whole of his artillery and rear areas overlooked by Monte Cifalco. Attacking Monte Cairo and Monte Cifalco, however, would not open up Route 6 past Cassino, nor did he have enough troops to take on all three features simultaneously. Whatever plan he used to attack Monte Cassino must take into account the German observation from Monte Cairo and Monte Cifalco.

At the next level down, the features which made up the Monte Cassino complex of rock-strewn spurs and ridges were even more closely interconnected. Resisting attacks for over three months had shown the German defenders exactly which points were important and which could be disregarded. They knew from bitter experience most of the practicable lines of attack and had constantly strengthened the artillery, mortar and machine gun defensive fire tasks blocking these approaches.

Monte Cassino, capped with the ruins of its Monastery, was at the end of a long spur which ran down from Monte Cairo in a south-easterly direction. This spur curves slightly so that the succession of false crests support each other and form the backbone of the Gustav Line in this sector. The highest defended post on Monte Cairo was at Passo Corno from which the 1st Battalion of 100 Mountain Regiment overlooked and supported the next feature, the Colle Sant' Angelo (*fig. 11*) held by the 2nd Battalion of the same regiment. Then came a deep re-entrant called the Gorge at the upper end of which lay the buildings of Massa Albanetta and above which stood the ill-famed Snake's Head Ridge crowned by Point 593. Beyond Point 593 the spur fell away and a low saddle connected it to Monte Cassino proper. The Snake's Head, Albanetta and Monte Cassino were held by Colonel Heilmann's 3 Parachute Regiment. If Anders' Poles were to succeed in their task of outflanking the Monastery and reaching positions from which they could overlook Route 6 from above, they would have to secure at least the Snake's Head Ridge or Colle Sant' Angelo. The former was supported by German positions in the Monastery, at Massa Albanetta and on Colle Sant' Angelo; while the latter was supported by the Snake's Head, Massa Albanetta and Passo Corno. Behind all four positions lay Colonel Schulz's 1 Parachute Regiment in reserve at Villa Santa Lucia on the reverse slopes of Colle Sant' Angelo, ready to reinforce or counter-attack any feature which might be endangered by an Allied penetration.

Anders consulted Freyberg at length on his experiences in the Cassino sector and was convinced that the only way to pinch out Monte Cassino was to attack at least two of its main supporting positions simultaneously. Passo Corno was furthest away and could bring least effective fire to bear. Moreover, the problem of attacking so high up the mountain presented difficult logistic problems and so Anders decided to neutralise this position by fire and smoke as far as it was practicable. So many attempts had been made to seize the Monastery itself from various directions that a further attempt seemed uninviting, at least in the initial stages of an attack. This left the Snake's Head and Colle Sant' Angelo with Massa Albanetta sandwiched between them. Freyberg had never had enough troops to take on more than one feature at a time, and then only with one brigade. If Anders attacked with two divisions thus swamping these three objectives simultaneously, he should stand a very much greater chance of success. Once these features were taken, Heidrich's garrisons of the Monastery and Cassino town would be in grave danger of encirclement and might give way relatively easily to avoid being trapped by Kirkman's Corps in the valley below.

Although II (Polish) Corps was made up of two divisions, an armoured brigade and an army group artillery, it lacked a number of units and many of those which did exist had only arrived in the theatre in March. Each division had only two brigades and so, to form a divisional reserve, the divisional commanders had to take a battalion from one of their two brigades, further weakening their attacking strength. In allotting tasks, Anders gave the capture of the Snake's Head Ridge and Massa Albanetta, and subsequently the Monastery, to General Duch's 3 (Carpathian) Division, and the capture of Colle Sant' Angelo and the exploitation to overlook Route 6 to General Sulik's 5 (Kresowan) Division. Sulik would also cover the western flank of the Corps' attack by holding Monte Castellone against interference from the Germans on Passo Corno. The boundary between the two divisions was to be the Gorge.

Duch's plan was to attack in two phases. In the first, his 1 (Carpathian) Brigade, reinforced by the divisional reconnaissance regiment, 12 Podolski Regiment, and with tanks, self-propelled guns and flame-

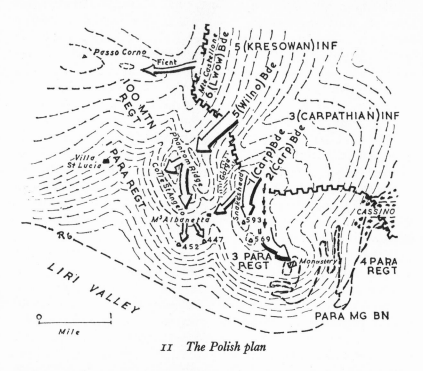

11   The Polish plan

throwers, would attack Albanetta and Point 593 simultaneously and then press forward on to the saddle between Snake's Head and Monte Cassino to clear a start line for 2 (Carpathian) Brigade. In the second phase, 2 (Carpathian) Brigade would take on the Monastery. In his orders Duch laid particular stress on the need to help 5 (Kresowan) Division's attack on Colle Sant' Angelo with flanking fire. He also stressed the need for his 1 (Carpathian) Brigade to support 2 (Carpathian) Brigade's attack on the Monastery with close-range supporting fire on to any German positions which opened up from a flank.

Sulik's 5 (Kresowan) Division would be breaking new ground. No one had attacked Colle Sant' Angelo since the original assault by Keyes' II (US) Corps had slowly died away in the bitter February weather. The crest of Colle Sant' Angelo was not visible from the forward Allied positions because it was masked by a false crest, known as the Phantom Ridge. Once on the real crest, observation into the Liri Valley was again masked by the convex nature of the ridge and so Sulik's men would have to exploit forward to Points 452 and 447 before their task was complete. This would not be easy because, dug-in close at hand on the reverse slopes, was Colonel Schulz's 1 (Parachute) Regiment in Heidrich's general reserve. Unless the Poles could consolidate very quickly, they would certainly suffer heavily from counter-attacks by Schulz's paratroopers.

Sulik's plan was to attack with 5 (Wilno) Brigade reinforced with one battalion from 6 (Lwow) Brigade, a troop of tanks and a flame-thrower detachment. Two battalions would attack the Colle Sant' Angelo frontally with an intermediate objective on Phantom Ridge. The other two battalions would then come up to exploit forward to the main crest so that the whole feature could be secured and firmly held in the face of counter-attacks. 6 (Lwow) Brigade with the men of two dismounted armoured regiments under command would cover the division's flank by holding Monte Castellone firmly and demonstrating towards Passo Corno. Sulik, like Duch, laid great stress on helping neighbouring brigades with flanking fire to counter the close mutual support of the German positions.

The II (Polish) Corps and its divisional plans were worked out in the greatest detail but there was a vital flaw in their arrangements which they could do nothing about. There could be no reconnaissance patrols to enable junior leaders to feel the lie of the land; no fighting patrols to pin-point German positions; and no overt activity of any kind within view of German observation posts. Everything had to be planned from hearsay—reports from the Indians who had held the northern extremity of the Snake's Head for so long, advice from the New Zealand staff who had tried everything they knew to beat Heidrich's paratroopers, and evidence from air photos most of which gave little away because the German positions were so carefully hidden amongst the rocks and caves which abound on Italian hillsides.

What precautions Anders' men could not take due to lack of reconnaissance, they were determined to make up for by hard work and detailed planning. Hundreds of tons of ammunition, supplies, equipment and weapons were manhandled in the dark up to the forward positions 1,500 feet above the floor of the valley. First, they ran the gauntlet of harassing fire from Monte Cifalco as the supply trucks crossed the Rapido Valley; then they used mules to carry the loads to the head of the mountain tracks; and finally men humped the heavy ammunition cases across the hillsides to the actual positions. There was a steady attrition of men, mules and trucks from the accurate German harassing fire. General Anders, in his memoirs, describes the scene after dark each night 'as if some giant ants' nest were working overtime'. Observation from Monte Cairo and Monte Cifalco meant that the Poles had to turn night into day during the weeks of preparation, but this could not happen once the offensive began; men would have to come out in the open; gun and mortar positions so carefully concealed would inevitably give their positions away by opening fire; and supply vehicles, staff jeeps and ambulances would have to run the gauntlet of the Rapido Valley in daylight. There seemed to be but one answer—smoke on an enormous scale. Special smoke detachments, using smoke generators, were organised for each Polish division and for Corps' troops to keep the Rapido Valley and the slopes on which the two Polish divisions were concentrated, under a continuous blanket of smoke. When necessary, this was to be thickened by artillery smoke shells. Some 400 tons of smoke canisters were eventually consumed on this task.

The preparations of the Polish Corps would not be complete without a mention of the feat of engineering called 'Polish Sappers' Road' which led up from the floor of the valley through the re-entrant between Monte Castellone and the Snake's Head feature almost to Massa Albanetta. It had been built originally in rudimentary form as 'Cavendish Road' by the Indian Sappers and Miners of 4 (Indian) Division and had enabled tanks to reach the Snake's Head at the time of the Third Battle of Cassino. The Polish sappers now widened this under constant harassing fire to let larger numbers of tanks and self-propelled guns reach the forward positions to support both Polish divisions in the Final Battle of Cassino.

The problems facing Kirkman's XIII (Br) Corps were very different and yet in some ways very similar to those of Anders' Poles. There were two main similarities; first, Kirkman's troops would be just as closely overlooked by German artillery observers on Monte Cassino and Monte

Cairo to the north, and Monte Majo to the south. None of these features could be taken on the first day of the offensive and so provision had to be made either to screen or just to live with this hazard. The second similarity was the fact that the German defences blocking the Liri Valley had been prepared for nearly six months and had solidified under the constant Allied pressure since the disastrous and costly failure of Walker's 36 (US) Division to cross the Rapido in January. As with the German defences opposite the Poles above Cassino, the Liri positions were so closely interlocked and mutually supporting that an attack on a narrow front was unlikely to succeed. Only by engaging as many positions simultaneously as possible would the attackers be able to prevent the defenders supporting each other. Saturation tactics seemed just as essential in the valley as upon the mountains, but here the similarities ended.

The great differences lay in the roles and tactical problems of the assault forces. Kirkman's Corps was to be Alexander's main striking force designed to achieve decisive results. Instead of the two weak divisions which made up Anders' Corps, Kirkman had three full-strength infantry and an armoured division under his command and he was closely backed by the Army reserve in the shape of Burns' Canadian Corps. The Liri Valley had been chosen as the main point of attack because only there could the full weight of Allied air, artillery and tank superiority be brought to bear; and only there would the Allies be less dependent on their infantry. But, although the Liri Valley appeared the best approach from this point of view, there was a heavy price to pay because it was also the obvious approach and had been the most heavily blocked with fixed and field defences—pillboxes, dugouts, mines and wire. And, as though this was not enough, these defences lay behind the narrow but swift-flowing and unfordable Rapido. Kirkman would have to launch the most hazardous and complex operation of war—an opposed river crossing—before trying to break through the actual Gustav defences.

In river-crossing operations there is usually a conflict between the tactical requirements of the assaulting troops and the technical needs of the sappers who have to bridge the river. In the case of the Rapido the technical factors did not limit the crossing areas. There were no proper roads down to the river in the Corps' sector. There were a few farm tracks but that was all. On the far bank there was the lateral road from Cassino southwards to the small village of Sant' Angelo which stood on

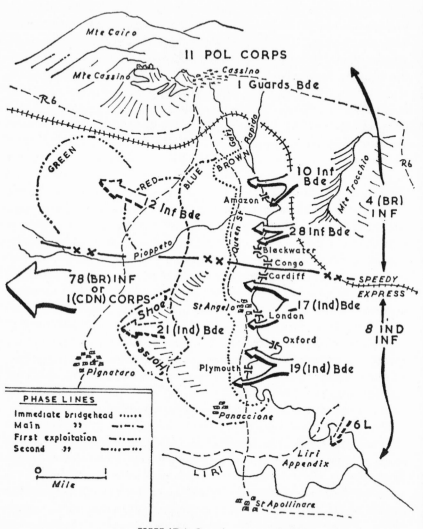

12   *XIII (Br) Corps' sector and plan*

its low bluff in about the middle of the Corps' sector with a commanding view up and down stream. Such tracks as did exist on the far bank radiated outwards from Sant' Angelo. Thus, whatever plan was made, the sappers would have to build the approaches to and away from the bridges. Technical factors would affect timing. One of the most critical factors in a successful river crossing is the early arrival of anti-tank guns and tanks in the bridgehead on the far side of the river to prevent the infantry being overrun by tank counter-attacks before anti-tank weapons can reach them. As the Rapido crossings were so closely overlooked from Monte Cassino both the infantry crossing in assault boats and the sappers' bridging of the river would need as much darkness as possible. There must be enough time after dusk for the infantry to carry their boats forward, to make their crossing and then for the sappers to build their bridges before daylight could catch them in the open exposed to observed artillery and mortar fire. Ideally the infantry needed pitch darkness to move up to the river, but the crossing itself and the bridging needed moonlight to enable the men to see what they were doing. This was one of the main factors which made Alexander choose 11 May for D-day and 11 p.m. for H-hour. On that night the moon would be just right. Everyone appreciated, however, that with the bridging equipment of those days, which was heavier and slower to build than it is today, the timings would be very tight, and so XIII (Br) Corps joined the Poles in demanding that the Monastery should be kept blinded with smoke until the bridgehead was firmly established. Elaborate smoking arrangements were made, again using canisters. The two Corps' artilleries divided the task of thickening up any weak patches which appeared—the Poles taking responsibility for the northern slopes and XIII (Br) Corps for the southern.

Kirkman's tactical plan was dictated by three features: the first was the combined fortress of Monte Cassino and Cassino town, which were so strongly held that they had to be given as wide a berth as possible; the second was Monte Trocchio, the sharp razor-backed ridge rising over 1,000 feet sheer out of the floor of the valley on the Allied side of the Rapido, dividing the Corps' sector into two; and the third was the village of Sant' Angelo and the 'horseshoe' of rising ground beyond it. Monte Trocchio dictated the inter-divisional boundary between assault divisions because its western end almost reached the Rapido just north of Sant' Angelo, allowing just enough room for one division to form up to its north and ample room for a second and a third, if necessary, to assemble under its shadow to the south. Sant' Angelo and the Horseshoe formed one mutually-supporting group of German positions which should, if possible, be dealt with by one formation.

Kirkman's plan for the initial assault was to give Dudley Ward's 4 (Br) Division the two tasks of seizing a bridgehead north of Trocchio (but as far south of Cassino as bridging and rafting considerations would allow) and then of wheeling right-handed to cut Route 6 west of Cassino, joining hands with the Poles who would be exploiting southwards from Colle Sant' Angelo. He gave the Sant' Angelo–Horseshoe task to Dudley Russell's 8 (Indian) Division which was to attack south of Trocchio. The Indians were also to clear the awkward piece of ground, called the Liri Appendix, which lay between the Liri and Rapido at their junction. This area was so dominated by the German positions south of the Liri and so constricted that it was to be left until as late as possible. The inter-divisional boundary gave 8 (Indian) Division all the ground south of the Naples–Cassino railway which had been turned into a road called 'Speedy Express'. This route would be the Indians' main way into their area and from it the Indian sappers and miners had to prepare the necessary tracks forward to the river. Where the railway skirts the end of Trocchio the boundary turned due west crossing the Rapido 1,000 yards north of Sant' Angelo.

For subsequent operations, Charles Keightley's 78 (Br) Division would be in reserve ready to reinforce or to exploit through either sector. Vyvyan Evelegh's 6 (Br) Armoured Division would be split up during the early phases of the battle. Its 1 (Br) Guards Brigade would hold Cassino town, keeping Heidrich's paratroopers quiet there, and its 26 (Br) Armoured Brigade would provide tank support for Dudley Ward's 4 (Br) Division. Tank support for Dudley Russell's 8 (Indian) Division would come from 1 (Canadian) Armoured Brigade which had worked with the Indians before on the Adriatic front. The only force left in Vyvyan Evelegh's 6 (Br) Armoured Division was a special group based on its reconnaissance regiment, the Derbyshire Yeomanry, supported by the 10th Battalion, the Rifle Brigade, which was to be held ready for rapid reconnaissance towards the Hitler Line if a break-through occurred anywhere on the front.

Dudley Ward's initial task of securing a bridgehead so close to Cassino was an unenviable assignment, made no easier by having to work from the forward slopes of Monte Trocchio in full view of the Monastery. The only good thing about it was the splendid observation afforded by Trocchio itself from which he could plan and, perhaps, control his battle. The 'perhaps' is important, as later events will show. Dudley Ward had only taken over the division on 20 April and this was to be his first battle as a divisional commander. He was a very experienced brigade commander and had fought throughout the winter commanding a brigade in 46 (Br) Division which took part in the X (Br) Corps' crossing of the Garigliano in January and stayed on in the bridgehead until Keyes' II (US) Corps took over in March. Dudley Ward's sector on the German side of the Rapido was divided by the small Pioppetto Stream which was thought to be a tank obstacle. On his own side of the river he was limited to attacking south of the junction of the Gari and Rapido, some 3,000 yards south of Cassino, by the obvious need to avoid crossing two streams. He planned to cross with two brigades up: 10 (Br) Brigade under Brigadier Shoesmith crossing north of the Pioppetto, and 28 (Br) Brigade under Brigadier Montague-Douglas-Scott south of this stream. His reserve brigade, 12 (Br) Brigade under Brigadier Heber-Percy, was to be ready to pass through Shoesmith's Brigade and to attack north-westwards to cut Route 6 west of Cassino, joining hands with the Poles advancing down the slopes from Colle Sant' Angelo. The attack was to be carried out in four phases: first, the crossing of the Rapido and securing of a shallow initial bridgehead about 1,000 yards deep (Brown Line) designed to cover the crossing places from small arms fire during darkness; second, an advance of another 1,500 yards to secure and to clear the low ridges (Blue Line) from which the Germans might be able to observe the crossings when daylight came up; third, a further advance to the main Cassino–Pignataro road, north of the Piopetto (Red Line), which would not be undertaken until the heavy bridges were complete and the leading brigades had been joined by their supporting tanks and other heavy weapons; and fourthly, the final advance to the Green Line, probably by Heber-Percy's brigade, to cut Route 6. Dudley Ward hoped to be secure on the Blue Line before dawn, but no one could estimate when he would be able to break out and secure the Red and Green Lines. The dog-fight around the bridgehead might go on for several days before a decision was reached.

The fire plan on Dudley Ward's front conformed to the overall Corps plan of forty minutes' counter-battery fire and concentrations on known German positions until five minutes before the infantry put their boats into the water, and then five minutes' concentration on the German forward positions before changing to a barrage at H-hour. The pre-arranged barrage programme was timed to continue for four and three-quarter hours. One section of Bofors light anti-aircraft guns was to fire tracer up the Liri Valley to mark the direction of advance for the infantry.

The bridging plan, on which so much depended, was in two parts. The infantry brigades themselves, using their infantry pioneer platoons and men from their anti-tank batteries, would establish assault-boat ferries and light rafts at each crossing point to ferry over essential light vehicles, anti-tank guns, machine guns and mortars into the bridgeheads. The divisional sappers would build the heavier rafts, but would concentrate most of their effort on building three bridges codenamed Amazon (forty ton), Blackwater (thirty ton) and Congo (nine ton) within the divisional sector. Amazon was the most northerly site and nearest Monte Cassino, but it was the only site to and from which passable farm tracks led on either side of the river. For this reason Amazon was the most important of the three.

General Dudley Russell's problems in the 8 (Indian) Division's sector were rather easier than Dudley Ward's because he had more room for assembly, more tracks on which to move units forward and, above all, he was further from the Monastery. On the other hand, Sant' Angelo and the Horseshoe feature behind it were strong defensive positions from which it would be difficult to unearth the Germans if they were determined to stay. Like Dudley Ward, Dudley Russell decided to attack with two brigades up: Brigadier Boucher's 17 (Indian) Brigade to the north, assaulting either side of Sant' Angelo; and Brigadier Dobree's 19 (Indian) Brigade to the south, clearing the southern arm of the Horseshoe and the village of Panaccioni. Brigadier Mould's 21 (Indian) Brigade was to be in reserve ready to exploit through either sector. The divisional reconnaissance regiment, 6 Lancers, were to create a feint crossing into the Liri Appendix to the south. The Indian attack would be carried out in three phases, coinciding with the first three phases of Dudley Ward's attack to the north. The first phase was the establishment of immediate covering positions to protect the crossing places during darkness; then the establishment of the bridgehead proper some two thousand yards from the river, and finally, the capture of the full extent of the Horseshoe. Dudley Russell made no plans for a fourth phase, matching Dudley Ward's final task of cutting Route 6. Once the Horseshoe was taken the chances were that either Charles Keightley's

78 (Br) Division or the whole of I (Canadian) Corps would be passed through for the drive on the Hitler Line. The artillery fire plan was identical to that of 4 (Br) Division, but the bridging plan was more elaborate as provision had to be made for passing the Canadians and perhaps 78 (Br) Division through the Indian sector. Four heavy bridges were to be built: Cardiff (thirty ton) north of Sant' Angelo, London (forty ton) at Sant' Angelo, and Oxford and Plymouth (both thirty ton) south of Sant' Angelo. The London bridge would become the main bridge for the advance on the Hitler Line, but as Sant' Angelo was unlikely to fall early in the assault it was not intended to bridge there before the second night.

Early in April, 8 (Indian) Division was relieved on the Adriatic coast by 4 (Indian) Division which had left Monte Cassino in March at the end of Freyberg's last attempt to take the Monastery. Mould's 21 (Indian) Brigade of 8 (Indian) Division took over the whole of the Rapido sector from Cassino to the Liri junction, while Boucher's and Dobree's brigades moved into a training area on the Volturno River where they could practise and rehearse their river-crossing drills. There they were joined respectively by 11 (Ontario) Armoured Regiment and 14 (Calgary) Armoured Regiment who were to support them during the operation. On 6 May both brigades were moved up into the sectors which they were going to assault and Mould's brigade was brought into reserve. 8 (Indian) Division was ready. Meanwhile 4 (Br) Division had a spell in the Cassino sector when Heber-Percy's 12 (Br) Brigade relieved 1 (Br) Guards Brigade of 6 (Br) Armoured Division on 22 April. After a short rest the Guards returned and relieved 12 (Br) Brigade on 4–5 May so that it could be positioned in reserve behind the other two brigades of the division whose advance parties took over their assault sectors during 8 and 9 May. During the night of 10 May the rest of the main bodies moved up and lay concealed in their assembly areas behind Trocchio. 4 (Br) Division was also ready.

On 20 April, 10 (Indian) Division, which had just arrived from Syria, started to relieve the Canadian troops on the Adriatic coast, and Freyberg's New Zealanders relieved those who had been operating in the mountains north of Cassino. Burns' I (Canadian) Corps was able to concentrate for the first time in its training areas in Eighth Army's rear area between Mignano and Venefro, about 15 miles east of Cassino. The Canadian Corps' actual whereabouts must be concealed so as not to compromise the bogus signals network set up near Salerno which was purporting to be the Canadian–American assault force training for the main landing near Civitavecchia or Leghorn. Burns could make no detailed plans as no one could foretell the outcome of the early phases of Kirkman's and Anders' battles, but he knew his primary target was the exploitation to and breaking of the Hitler Line, and so Canadian training was concentrated on tank–infantry–artillery cooperation in more open types of warfare than had been possible in Italy so far, and on breaching defences of the Hitler Line type. In the latter, Canadian experience in the close fighting at Ortona during the previous autumn stood them in good stead.

By dawn on 10 May, Eighth Army was ready for the curtain to go up. Three divisions—4 (Br), 8 (Indian) and 6 (Br) Armoured—were packed into and concealed within the small area between Route 6 and the Rapido where during the winter it had been difficult to maintain more than one division. On the reverse slopes of Monte Cassino the two Polish divisions were tucked into every hollow and re-entrant which could provide cover for them from the prying German eyes on Monte Cifalco and Monte Cairo. In the valley behind Monte Trocchio and in the few other re-entrants capable of concealing anything from the all-seeing eyes of the Monastery, stood some 500 guns of all calibres and sufficient ammunition to keep them supplied at intense rates for over a week. The ground was dry and hard, but the sky was overcast and during the afternoon it rained a little, trying the nerves of the sapper commanders who knew better than anyone else what would happen if the weather broke. Months of work would disappear overnight in the mud of the Liri Valley.

5   *The Fifth Army's Rehearsals*

'To capture the Ausonia defile and advance on an axis parallel to that
of Eighth Army but south of the Liri and Sacco Valleys.'
    Fifth Army's task given in Alexander's Despatches (2921)

To be cast in a supporting role in any great enterprise can be galling. It is
tempting to play the secondary role in such a way as to prove the pro-
ducer made a mistake in selecting his leading players. Mark Clark and
the Fifth Army staff were naturally disappointed that, after bearing the
brunt of the winter fighting, they should lose the lead to Eighth Army
whose operations on the Adriatic coast had been just as abortive as their
own. Fortunately, Fifth Army was billed to take the lead in the last act of
Diadem when Truscott's VI (US) Corps would break out of the Anzio
beachhead to seal the fate of von Vietinghoff's Tenth Army, and so
honours at Army level were even enough not to cause undue friction.
The only fear that Mark Clark and his staff nursed was that the per-
fidious British would manage affairs in such a way that Eighth Army
would enter Rome first. If there was the least sign of this happening
relations would become very strained.

At Corps level the position was rather different. Truscott was a well-
trained, non-political soldier who believed that the main purpose of all
military operations was the destruction of the enemy's main force.
Fortune had presented him with just the type of operation for which his
temperament was best suited—an American-type power drive across the
rear of von Vietinghoff's Army at the moment when it would be least
able to resist such a thrust. The only thing which irked him was the long
delay in mounting Diadem. Both sides had gone over to the defensive at
Anzio after the failure of von Mackensen's second counter-offensive at
the beginning of March, but the beachhead was far from quiet. It was not
easy to maintain morale amongst the beachhead's beleaguered garrison.
Constant German artillery harassing fire by day and by night which

reached every acre of the beachhead, and the nightly Luftwaffe raids, using both conventional high explosive bombs and the ingenious 'butterfly' anti-personnel bombs, led to a steady flow of casualties in the fighting and logistic units. Even the hospitals were not immune from these long-range attacks. Living conditions in the beachhead were infinitely worse than on the main front and lack of any obvious sign of early action did not encourage men to endure the acute discomfort of

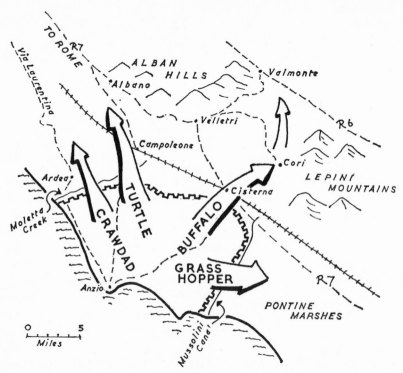

13   Truscott's VI (US) Corps' contingency plans

these conditions. Truscott, a fine commander of fighting men, did all that he could to generate enthusiasm by making plans and preparations to enable his VI (US) Corps to play a decisive part whenever it should be called upon to do so, but as the weeks dragged on Alexander and Mark Clark visited the beachhead less and less frequently and it seemed that VI (US) Corps had become a forgotten army.

During March and April Truscott directed his staff to plan for four possible contingencies, each based upon a different axis of break-out from the beachhead:

Operation Crawdad—a break-out north-westwards along the coast, crossing the Moletta Creek and taking the small town of Ardea preparatory to an advance up the Via Laurentina to Rome.

Operation Turtle—an attack up the old British centre line of the Albano road, taking Campoleone and then advancing on Rome around the western slopes of the Alban Hills, using Route 7.

Operation Buffalo—an attack up the old American centre line of the Cisterna road, taking Cisterna, then Cori at the northern end of the Lepini Hills and finally breaking through the gap between the Lepini and Alban Hills to cut Route 6, von Vietinghoff's line of retreat, at Valmonte.

Operation Grasshopper—a break-out south-eastwards across the Mussolini Canal to link up with any relieving force advancing up Route 7 through the Pontine Marshes which had been flooded by extensive German demolition of dams, bridges and pumping stations.

During April, Truscott went back to Mark Clark's headquarters near Naples and received approval of his four contingency plans, but was given no indication of which would be used. This decision was to be left open until it was clear how the operational situation developed. He was, however, told to make plans to receive the balance of Harmon's 1 (US) Armoured Division and the whole of Walker's 36 (US) Division if these were not needed on the main front.

Alexander visited Anzio on 5 May for the last time before Diadem. In his usual way he let the commander on the spot brief him on his plans before commenting himself. As was pointed out earlier, one of the essential features of Alexander's method of command was to make subordinates feel that they had thought out the problems for themselves and that the commander-in-chief was pleased with and grateful for their ideas. If the plans they presented were not what was wanted or if they did not fit the overall strategy, he would suggest various alterations on which he would ask for their opinions and views. In this way he made every officer feel personally involved with the enterprise and that he was not being dragooned into a plan in which he had no confidence. This method of command, although ideal for British troops and useful in an Allied Army Group of the type that Alexander commanded, could and did lead to misunderstandings; and, on occasions, to accusations of lack of firmness of direction. Just such an occasion occurred during Alexander's last visit to VI (US) Corps' headquarters before Diadem. After hearing the break-out plans, he suggested to Truscott that 'Buffalo' was the only one likely to achieve his, the Army Group Commander's, purpose. He also told Truscott that he, personally, would decide when VI (US) Corps was to start its break-out. Truscott must be ready to strike at twenty-four hours' notice at any time after D + 4. When Truscott reported this conversation to his Army commander, Mark Clark jumped to the conclusion that Alexander had decided to run Fifth Army for him. Nothing could be further from the truth. Alexander was letting Truscott know how he saw the battle developing—thinking aloud possibly—but certainly not going behind Mark Clark's back. In his memoirs Mark Clark suggests that it was news to him that Alexander had reserved to himself the decision as to when Truscott should break out: but this had already been laid down at Alexander's final coordinating conference on 1 May which Mark Clark attended. Alexander seems to have soothed Mark Clark's feelings by saying that he quite understood how he felt, but he left him in no doubt that VI (US) Corps was to attack towards Valmonte when he, Alexander, gave the order. Mark Clark accepted this instruction, making mental reservations about it and going as far as telling Truscott to keep 'Turtle'—the break-out towards Rome via Albano—ready for execution at short notice. And thus started the one unfortunate series of incidents which went some way towards making Diadem not quite so decisive as it might otherwise have been.

On the main Fifth Army front along the Garigliano a similar clash of ambitions was developing. Keyes' II (US) Corps was quite satisfied with its role. Although Keyes had commanded a corps since the invasion of Sicily, his 85 and 88 (US) Divisions were new and inexperienced and so could not demand the privilege of undertaking any of the key manoeuvres. The attacks which they were to make along the coast to open up Route 7 were not vital to Alexander's strategy, and should be well within their capabilities. Juin, commanding the French Expeditionary Corps, saw things very differently. Able, energetic and forthright with a marked tactical flair, he remarks in his memoirs:

> One has always seen, in an Allied Army, the principal partners criticising the conditions of their employment and making plans according to their own methods and their own wishes, even before

they receive instructions from the C-in-C responsible for the conduct of operations. The French, in this respect, are never behind in putting their imagination to work, particularly when arriving in a new sector, as was going to be the case here. Likewise, the members of my staff, a truly exceptional team, started going through my ideas with enthusiasm . . . naturally giving the FEC the most difficult part.

Juin's Corps represented France and carried with it all the deep-felt hopes of Frenchmen that sooner, rather than later, they would be able to re-establish their military reputations and the Glory of France. His French North African troops were particularly well suited to mountain warfare and his Corps had become one of the strongest national contingents in Italy, consisting of the equivalent of almost five divisions which he had organised into two *ad hoc* corps for the purposes of the Diadem offensive:

Pursuit Corps under General Larminat:
  1 (Motorised) Division (General Brosset)
  2 (Moroccan) Division (General Dody)
  3 (Algerian) Division (General de Goislard de Monsabert)
Mountain Corps under General Guillaume:
  4 (Moroccan) Mountain Division (General Sevez)
  1, 3, 4 Groups of Tabors (Goumiers)*

While Freyberg had been butting his head against the defences of Cassino, Juin's FEC had been protecting his northern flank by threatening the Germans with an advance around the north side of Monte Cairo towards Atina. He had never been allowed the full resources needed to demonstrate the real potential of this threat, but he had always been convinced that he could have outflanked Cassino by a surprise attack across the mountains, using his experienced mountain troops for this purpose. He was still advocating this policy in late March when he heard about the plan to switch his FEC to the Garigliano. He set out immediately to visit McCreery whose X (Br) Corps was holding his future sector and with him made a detailed reconnaissance by jeep, pony and on foot of the whole of his new front.

---

* A Tabor was equivalent to a battalion, and a Group of Tabors to a brigade. A Tabor was made up of a number of Goums, equivalent to a company. The three Groups of Tabors contained some 12,000 Goumiers.

On his return he set down his thoughts in a carefully worded appreciation dated 4 April. In his clear logical way he pointed out that there were only two routes along which the main Allied effort could be launched—Route 6 past Cassino and Route 7 along the coast. Both were heavily defended and Kesselring had succeeded in keeping them barred.

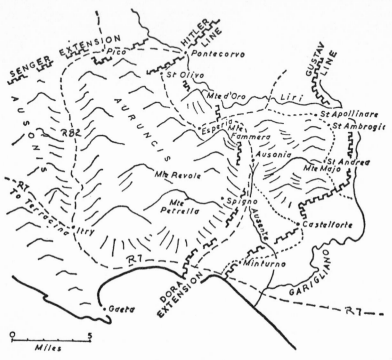

14 The Garigliano sector

Between these two routes lay the Aurunci and Ausoni Mountains which were relatively weakly held and had not been attacked in any great strength so far. If he could persuade Mark Clark and Alexander to let him strike through the centre of these hills, using his mountain troops, he would be able to outflank the Germans defending both routes. The only question to be resolved was, could it in fact be done? Juin's reconnaissance with McCreery convinced him that it was practicable. Furthermore, if he could link the break-through by Guillaume's Mountain Corps with a rapid advance by Larminat's Pursuit Corps, he should be able to bring the FEC astride von Vietinghoff's communications in the area of Ceprano–Arce (*see fig. 1 inset*), completing a classic outflanking movement based on the twin principles of using an unexpected axis of advance and depending upon the speed of execution to throw the Germans off balance.

Juin had considerable difficulty in convincing Mark Clark that his plan was sound. He was not helped by Giraud, C-in-C of the French Forces in Africa, who tried lecturing Mark Clark on tactics. Giraud had come over from North Africa to visit Juin's headquarters because he had grave doubts about the plan set out in Juin's memorandum of 4 April. Juin took him forward to look at the front for himself and convinced him that it was practicable to send Guillaume's troops through the centre of the Aurunci Massif. Giraud became as enthusiastic as Juin and promised him all possible support, including the acceleration of the shipment of French units from North Africa to Italy.

Juin's description of the negotiations which followed Giraud's visit gives the feeling prevalent in Fifth Army and particularly in his FEC at the time, and is interesting in the light of subsequent events:

The French plan now had to be approved by the senior commanders in Italy. . . . General Alexander, C-in-C of the Army Group and General Clark, Commander of the Fifth Army, to which we were attached, had already exchanged views on the next offensive, but their personal ideas, when combined, had led to a concept very different from ours.

Firstly, the British persisted in wanting the main attack to be delivered through the valley of the Liri, an attack which they intended to make entirely by themselves, after removing the two bastions which guarded the entrance, Monte Majo and Monte Cassino. The Eighth Army thus hoped to be the first to open the road to Rome, which it was anxious to do for reasons of prestige. Since the beginning of the campaign in Italy, they had indeed suffered from the disadvantage of being deployed, by chance, on the eastern flank on the Adriatic coast, where it was most mountainous, and their efforts had not received much publicity outside Italy.

Clark, for his part, fearing that his Corps on the left would face the greatest difficulties advancing northwards up the Appian Way (Route 7), wanted II (US) Corps to relieve the French in the Pico area and then, supported by the British, to march with them on Rome while the Anzio forces were being relieved.

There was no longer any question of a deep penetration via the Petrella Massif (Aurunci Mountains), the intention of which was to put constant pressure on the German right flank; we were reverting to cramped concentration which would lead, after the break-through, to the same congestion of troops which had occurred in front of Monte Cassino. The French were only to be used to make a breach in the Monte Majo sector and to open the route to Esperia to cover the flank of the Eighth Army. They were then to be squeezed out as they reached the Pico area and kept in reserve during the advance upon Rome, which was quite unacceptable.

This information had been given to us verbally on 1 April by Général Brann, head of the operations staff of the Fifth Army. This caused deep emotion in my headquarters and a discussion ensued, comparing the concept of our appreciation, which was just being completed, with that of the one presented to us.

General Brann was very upset when he left us. Later on he must have supported our point of view when reporting to General Gruenther, General Clark's Chief of Staff, and to General Clark himself, who in the end decided that the break-through, within the framework of the Fifth Army, should be carried out in accordance with the provisions of our appreciation of 4 April. This result was due to the deep respect which the commander of the Fifth Army had for the French since he had seen them in action during the winter campaign.

At Army Group level, although this decision was approved, the official instructions still maintained that the Eighth Army would be responsible for the main attack. It would, according to the terms of its mission, break into the enemy's defences, open up the valley of the Liri and press home its advantage by advancing up Route 6 to capture Rome.

I was less certain than my British friends of the success of the mission entrusted to the Eighth Army on my right. On the 27 April, 15 days before the attack was launched, I wrote the following letter to the Defence Committee of the Provisional Government in Algiers; this letter outlined my feelings on this point, and endeavoured to forecast the leading role which the FEC would be called upon to fill in the battle:

'The Eighth Army's attack in the valley of the Liri, although linked to ours, will not be extended any great distance north (of Cassino). Here, the second prong of the pincer (he refers to McCreery's X

(Br) Corps), which I have ceaselessly recommended should be directed on the Atina/Frosinone axis, will fail completely. Continually blocked by the Cassino spur, the Eighth Army will have to be satisfied with bringing up its Polish Corps . . . in order to go around Cassino the shortest way—not a very rewarding manoeuvre, as it will require an entire corps, without, in the end, ensuring the safety of the right flank of the British forces engaged in the valley.'

It is true that the British are sheltering behind the excuse of the difficulty which they have, owing to lack of troops and special equipment, in carrying out deep penetrations into mountainous areas.

It is to be expected, under these conditions, that XIII (Br) Corps, responsible for the main attack in the valley, will not succeed in advancing near us and by taking advantage of our advance. . . .

I have a feeling that, once the break-through has been achieved, it will be the FEC that will set the pace; the essential is that the Germans should be followed up, particularly on the right, in order to force the Hitler Line (if the enemy has had time to man it) in the vicinity of Pontecorvo and to enable me to put the main striking force in the Pico region.

The acceptance of Juin's ideas was grudgingly given. From Mark Clark's point of view a French success would enable Fifth Army to show that it could do just as well as the victors of El Alamein; but if Juin did not succeed, nothing would be lost because Fifth Army's real task was to hold the Germans while Eighth Army broke through and not vice versa. Alexander also seems to have acquiesced, but there is no specific mention of any great hopes being pinned on Juin's actions. Mark Clark's plan for Diadem called for a parallel advance by Keyes' II (US) Corps and Juin's FEC in what looks like a remarkably orthodox and unambitious operation with the two corps abreast.

Unambitious though the Fifth Army orders seem to have been, just the opposite was the case within the French headquarters. Juin fired his staff with enthusiasm for his ideas. Whatever the doubting Anglo-Saxons, English or Americans might think, he was determined to win the battle for them. In his letters back to his superiors in Algiers he predicted with remarkable accuracy how slow the Eighth Army would be in its battle north of the Liri and how his FEC would appear in the German rear after its surprise march over the mountains.

Juin's staff had three major tactical problems to solve. First, the existing Gustav defences had to be broken open before any grand manoeuvres of the type that Juin envisaged would be possible. Secondly, the defences of Ausonia and the Esperia defiles must be cracked before Larminat's Pursuit Corps could reach the south bank of the Liri and advance round the southern flank of the Hitler Line to Pico and thence

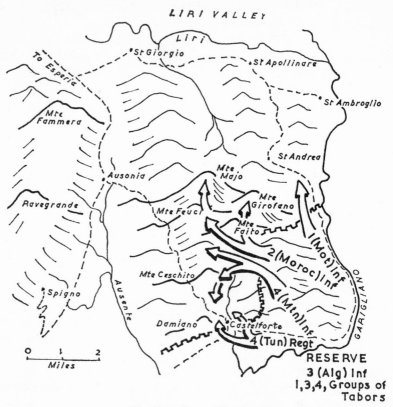

15   The first phase of Juin's plan

to the Ceprano–Arce area (*see fig. 1, inset*). Thirdly, the Dora and Senger extensions of the Hitler Line running round the eastern and western sides of the Aurunci Mountains must be broken by Guillaume's Mountain Corps if he was to cut the Itri–Pico road which was the Germans' main lateral between Routes 6 and 7 and which must be blocked to protect Larminat's flank as he advanced on Pico. Let us look briefly at each of these problems in turn.

McCreery's X (Br) Corps' bridgehead over the Garigliano in the future French sector was barely deep enough to house the two British brigades holding the line. Their artillery and supply echelons were kept on the east bank and were not housed in the bridgehead due to lack of space.

Moreover, the greater part of the bridgehead was overlooked by German positions on Damiano and Monte Majo. This would mean the greatest difficulty in assembling Larminat's three divisions which Juin believed would be needed to crack the Gustav defences in his sector. These defences ran from Damiano, a bare rocky hillock on the extreme left of the French sector, around the south side of the ruins of the hill town of Castelforte, then along the southern and eastern spurs of Monte Majo, and finally due east down to the Garigliano. The Gustav positions overlooking Juin's Garigliano sector were similar to those above Cassino—a series of interlocking and mutually supporting positions dug into the rocky hillsides and depending for their strength on the difficulty of working laboriously up the steep rough slopes under heavy defensive fire. They had not withstood the same scale of attack as the Cassino defences, but they had been subjected to constant pressure by McCreery's Corps which had revealed to the Germans most of the weaknesses that existed in their layout. The crest of Monte Majo itself was guarded by defences on a series of false crests on the spurs radiating southwards, the most important of which were Monte Feuci to the south-west, Monte Faito due south and Monte Girofano south-east. If Monte Majo and these three features could be taken, it should be possible to open up the road from Castelforte to Ausonia and a route along the west bank of the Garigliano through Sant' Andrea and Sant' Ambrogio, entering the Liri Valley at Sant' Apollinare.

Juin's plan for the first phase of his battle was to attack Majo, via Faito and Girofano with Dody's experienced 2 (Moroccan) Division which had done extremely well in the fighting north of Cassino. He would support both of Dody's flanks by directing Brosset's 1 (Motorised) Division to attack up the Garigliano Valley towards Sant' Andrea; and General Sevez's 4 (Moroccan) Mountain Division, reinforced by the 4 (Tunisian) Infantry Regiment from Monsabert's 3 (Algerian) Division, to outflank Castelforte from the north and south to clear a way through to the Ausonia road. The rest of Monsabert's division was to be in reserve behind Dody's main attack, and Guillaume's Goumiers were to be kept well back at this stage. So important did Juin consider Dody's attack on Faito and Majo that he decided to give him priority call on all the 400 guns of the FEC.

The problems of the Ausonia defile and the break through the centre of the Aurunci Mountains were closely connected and to some extent mutually supporting. Once Monte Majo had been taken it would be relatively easy to clear the hills on the eastern side of the main road to Ausonia, but the road itself would still be unusable unless the Germans

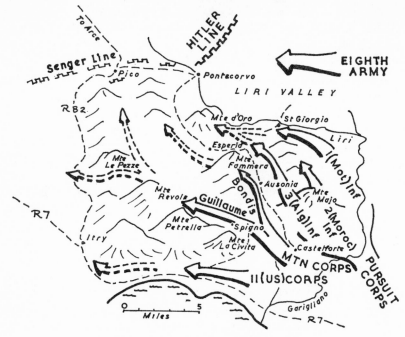

16   The second and third phases of Juin's plan

could be driven from the rudimentary defences of the Dora extension which followed the line of the Aurunci escarpment, overlooking the road from the west. This escarpment ran from Monte Fammera above Ausonia southwards to Monte La Civita just south of Spigno at the southern end of the Aurunci barrier. There were a few tortuous tracks up and through this wall but they were only suitable for mountain troops supported by pack transport. Thus, in order to break the German defences of Ausonia and to set Guillaume's mountaineers off on their drive across the Aurunci, the Fammera–La Civita escarpment had to be breached and, if occupied by the Germans, cleared as rapidly as possible although this would not be easy in such difficult country. The second phase of Juin's plan was, therefore, to give Larminat the task of clearing all the high ground east of the Castelforte–Ausonia road, using the three divisions of his Pursuit Corps, while Guillaume cleared the escarpment to the west with Sevez's 4 (Moroccan) Mountain Division reinforced by the 1, 3 and 4 Groups of Tabors of Goumiers.

For this second phase Guillaume's Mountain Corps was to be organised into three task forces, each force consisting of a Group of Tabors, supported by Moroccan Mountain infantry. Artillery support was to be provided by 69 (Algerian) Artillery Regiment organised on a pack basis, and all supply (which was to be kept to a minimum because most of the supply-dropping aircraft had been withdrawn to the United Kingdom for Overlord) would be by pack transport and porters. The Mountain Corps would be supported by about 4,000 pack animals. Guillaume himself was to command two of the task forces which were to enter the mountains at Spigno and to drive due west, making for Monte Revoli where he would establish a firm base from which he could mount operations to cut the Itri–Pico road. His task forces were the 1 and 4 Groups of Tabors supported by 1 (Moroccan) Mountain Infantry Regiment. The third task force—the 3 Group of Tabors supported by the 6 (Moroccan) Mountain Infantry Regiment—under the command of Colonel Bondis was to scale the escarpment above Ausonia, taking Monte Fammera and then advancing westwards parallel to Guillaume to outflank the German positions on the southern side of the Liri which might hold up Larminat's Corps.

While Guillaume was breaking into the Aurunci above Ausonia and Spigno, Larminat's three divisions would advance westwards as well. Monsabert's 3 (Algerian) Division would attack Ausonia in conjunction with Bondis' task force and then advance on Esperia. Dody's 2 (Moroccan) Division would probably go into reserve after taking Monte Majo, while Brosset's 1 (Motorised) Division would clear the south bank of the Liri as quickly as it could, thereby covering the Eighth Army's southern flank and also helping the British advance by outflanking the German positions on the north bank.

Juin's third phase was too far ahead to plan in detail but he hoped to bring Larminat's three divisions into the area of Pico, while Guillaume would cut across the Itri–Pico road. From this position he would be able to strike north to Arce if von Vietinghoff was still opposing Oliver Leese in the main Hitler Line, or he would advance westwards in step with

Eighth Army to the north and Keyes' II (US) Corps to the south to join Truscott near Valmonte.

Keyes' II (US) Corps' plan was designed to support Juin's break through the centre of the Auruncis. Whatever happened, Route 7 would have to be opened sooner or later to enable Keyes' divisions to supply themselves as they went forward. This task was given to Coulter's 85 (US) Division which was to attack just north of Route 7 to turn the

17 Keyes' II (US) Corps plan

German positions blocking the road itself. Keyes' second new division, Sloan's 88 (US) Division, was to attack slightly further inland but parallel to 85 (US) Division with the aim of breaking through, like the French, across the less strongly held southern spurs of the Aurunci. Sloan's first major task was to break through the Gustav defences north of Minturno to seize Spigno and Monte La Civita, through which Guillaume's mountain forces were to pass. Guillaume would move round the north side of Monte Petrella while Sloan would fight his way round the south, making for Itri. Meanwhile Coulter would have the unenviable task of launching direct assaults against the German positions along the coast, aiming for Formia. No one knew whether either division would prove up to its task, but if enthusiasm and keenness were anything to go by there would be no stopping Sloan's and Coulter's men once they were over the initial shock of battle. Keyes' third division, Walker's veteran 36 (US) Division, was in Army reserve and only on call if progress was slower than expected. It might be necessary to commit

Walker's division in Sloan's sector to ensure that an opening was made for Guillaume in the La Civita–Spigno area.

Problems of concealment, deception and build-up on Keyes' sector presented no obstacle. American troops had been on the lower Garigliano for some weeks and there was plenty of room for artillery, tanks, supply dumps and concealed concentration areas for the attacking infantry. Juin's problems were more difficult. The Germans were meant to believe that the French were still in the Apennines many miles away from Monte Majo. Those Frenchmen who had to take over forward positions all wore British steel helmets to simulate the continued presence of McCreery's X (Br) Corps. Wireless silence was maintained on the French wireless nets, the British signallers handled all French traffic. The French divisions themselves were held back in training areas as far afield as the Sorrento peninsula south of Naples, while the French logistic staff stocked the Garigliano bridgehead with all the ammunition needed for a long battle. Like the divisions of Kirkman's XIII (Br) Corps, the French divisions were not to be moved forward until the very latest moment and then only by night.

During the nights 9–10 and 10–11 May, the bridges over the Garigliano were filled with silent trudging columns of French North African infantry and their pack transport. The success of the feat of organisation achieved by Juin's staff is shown by Kesselring's plaintive comment in his memoirs when he says: 'Where and in what strength would the French Expeditionary Corps attack . . . it was sad that the Army Group could not obtain a clear picture of the American Fifth Army, and especially of the French Expeditionary Corps.' Maps captured later showed that German intelligence believed the French to have only one division in the line (correctly placed opposite Monte Majo), one at Salerno and a third unlocated. They did not know of the existence of the fourth.

By first light on 10 May, all was ready on the Garigliano sector as it was farther north at Cassino. Kesselring's commanders and troops were quite unaware how close they were to H-hour of the Allied summer offensive.

On the German side of the Rapido and Garigliano there were no doubts in anyone's mind that the Allies were preparing an offensive, but all the indications were that nothing would happen until late May. In the last week of April, Hitler summoned a number of the senior officers and men home to Germany for an investiture followed by an indoctrination course and a few days' leave. Amongst those who were away from their posts on 11 May were von Vietinghoff, the Tenth Army commander, von Senger und Etterlin, the commander of XIV Panzer Corps holding the Garigliano sector south of the Liri, and General Baade, commanding 90 Panzer Grenadier Division, all of whom were at Hitler's investiture. Kesselring's Chief of Staff was also away sick, and, to make matters worse, von Senger's Chief of Staff had been sent on leave by the deputy Corps commander. The German commanders seem to have felt that the Italian theatre had now lost all importance in the eyes of the Allies who were known to be concentrating on their preparations for the Second Front. None of them seems to have seriously considered the possibility of a major *débâcle* on the Italian front which had weathered so many storms. It would probably suffer a few holding attacks while the Second Front was being launched, but there should be no difficulty in fending these off.

As the light began to fade on the evening of 11 May the German troops in the forward positions were in an unenviable position. Above Cassino Anders' two Polish divisions would be assaulting the fronts of two German battalions—a battalion of Ringel's 5 (Mountain) Division on the Colle Sant' Angelo and a battalion of Heidrich's 1 (Parachute) Division on the Snake's Head Ridge. In the valley below, the four divisions of Kirkman's XIII (Br) Corps would be assailing only five German battalions—three from Rodt's 15 Panzer Grenadier Division and two of the Bode Group drawn from 305 Division on the Adriatic coast. South of the Liri, Juin's three assaulting divisions would be attacking Raapke's 71 Division and Keyes' II (US) Corps with two divisions would be attacking Steinmetz's 94 Division. In reserve close behind Kirkman's Corps lay Burns' Canadians and behind Keyes' Corps was Walker's 36 (US) Division. The nearest German reserves were the rump of Rodt's 15 Panzer Grenadier Division watching the coast at Terracina, part of Baade's 90 Panzer Grenadier Division watching for Allied parachutists at Frosinone and von Lüttwitz's 26 Panzer Division below the Alban Hills waiting for Truscott to try to break out. The rest of Kesselring's reserves were north of the Tiber, watching for a non-existent invasion fleet. Surprise was likely to be complete, but from bitter experience Alexander knew this was only half the battle. Kesselring's reaction would be swift once he appreciated what was really happening. The German soldiers' reactions would be equally tenacious, but they would be facing the massed artillery of the Fifth and Eighth Armies amounting to some 1,600 guns, and over their heads would be flying the whole might of the Allied Air Forces which would switch from attacking communications to giving their own soldiers unstinting air support as soon as dawn came up on 12 May. The only aircraft that the German soldiers would see over the battlefield during daylight would be wearing Allied markings. Few could appreciate what this would mean better than those Poles who had survived the Blitzkrieg in 1940 and the British who had suffered at the Luftwaffe's hands for three long years.

During the afternoon of 10 May, as the Allied troops lay huddled in whatever cover they could find in their assembly areas, Alexander's order of the day was read out to them:

SOLDIERS OF THE ALLIED ARMIES IN ITALY

Throughout the past winter you have fought hard and valiantly and killed many Germans. Perhaps you are disappointed that we have not been able to advance faster and farther, but I and those who know realise full well how magnificently you have fought amongst these almost unsurmountable obstacles of rocky, trackless mountains, deep in snow, and in valleys blocked by rivers and mud, against a stubborn foe.

The results of the past months may not appear spectacular, but you have drawn into Italy and mauled many of the enemy's best divisions which he badly needed to stem the advance of the Russian Armies in the East. Hitler has admitted that his defeats in the East were largely due to the bitterness of the fighting and his losses in Italy. This, in itself, is a great achievement and you may well be as proud of yourselves as I am of you. You have gained the admiration of the world and the gratitude of our Russian Allies.

Today the bad times are behind us and tomorrow we can see victory ahead. Under the ever-increasing blows of the air forces of the United Nations, which are mounting every day in intensity, the German war machine is beginning to crumble. The Allied armed forces are now assembling for the final battles on seas, on land, and in the air to crush the enemy once and for all. From the East and the West, from the North and the South, blows are about to fall which will result in the final destruction of the Nazis and bring freedom once again to Europe, and hasten peace for us all. To us in Italy, has been given the honour to strike the first blow.

We are going to destroy the German Armies in Italy. The fighting will be hard, bitter and perhaps long, but you are warriors and soldiers of the highest order, who for more than a year have known only victory. You have courage, determination and skill. You will be supported by overwhelming air forces, and in guns and tanks we far outnumber the Germans. No armies have ever entered battle before with a more just and righteous cause.

So with God's help and blessing, we take the field—confident of victory.

H. R. Alexander, General

May 1944   C-in-C Allied Armies in Italy.

The curtain was about to rise.

Part II Diadem

Act I The Gustav Line

'All our thoughts and hopes are with you in what I trust and believe will
be a decisive battle fought to the finish, and having for its object the
destruction and ruin of the armed forces of the enemy south of Rome.'
Churchill to Alexander, 11 May 1944

Chronology
Act I The Gustav Line
11-18 May

	Fifth Army	Eighth Army	German Army
11 May	← DIADEM Begins →		
12 May	French take Monte Faito and Castelforte	XIII (Br) Corps crosses Rapido, but Polish Corps fails on Monte Cassino	Attack on Gustav Line considered a diversion
13 May	French take Monte Majo	'Amazon' Bridge completed	90 Panzer Grenadier Division ordered forward to Liri Valley
14 May	French Mountain Corps starts advance	78 (Br) Division committed in Liri Valley	XIV Panzer Corps collapses and withdraws either side of Aurunci Mountains
15 May	French take Ausonia	XIII (Br) Corps attacks towards Route 6	Leading regiment of 90 Panzer Grenadier Division diverted to block French advance
16 May	French Mountain Corps reach Monte Revole	Canadian Corps committed in Liri Valley	Rest of 90 Panzer Grenadier Division reaches Liri Valley
17 May	French Mountain Corps shell Pico–Itri road; Esperia taken by French; Formia taken by II (US) Corps	Polish Corps' second attack on Monte Cassino; XIII (Br) Corps cuts Route 6	Kesselring sanctions withdrawal to Hitler Line; 26 Panzer Division ordered forward to block French advance on Pico
18 May	French take Sant' Oliva; II (US) Corps reaches Itri	Fall of Cassino	1 Parachute and 90 Panzer Grenadier Divisions occupy Hitler Line

6 *The First Day of Diadem*

'The tactics adopted by the Allies were thus fairly correctly estimated, yet when their attack was launched on 12 May it came as a complete surprise. This can be seen from the fact that many of the important German Commanders were away when it started.'

von Senger und Etterlin, 'Neither Fear nor Hope'

11 May seemed endless to the 100,000 Allied soldiers of the assault divisions waiting for H-hour. Dusk fell over the Italian battlefields like the footlights fading as the curtain rose on the first night of Diadem. Small parties of men began to emerge from hiding all along the front to take their places as the actors in the wings. The phase of silent preparation had begun. Above Cassino and on the lower slopes of Monte Majo, Poles and Frenchmen moved furtively out of the re-entrants and gullies on the rocky hillsides on which they had been huddled for two days and scrambled as silently as they could up the steep mountain tracks to reach their start lines. Down in the Liri and Garigliano Valleys, Britons, Canadians, Indians and Americans were moving equally silently through the deepening shadows along sunken farm tracks and battered hedgerows to reach their forming up positions. On the east bank of the Rapido, amongst the wreckage of 36 (US) Division's disastrous January attack, the men of Dudley Ward's 4 (Br) Division and Dudley Russell's 8 (Indian) Division were uncovering concealed assault boats, while their advance parties were reeling out hundreds of yards of white tape to guide the boat-carrying parties through the darkness down to the river. Further back in the many gun and mortar pits, men of all the Allied nations were checking fuse settings, dial sights, aiming posts and all the other intricacies of the artilleryman's world which go to make for success or failure in his efforts to support the infantry. The most enduring impression left on anyone who watched these last-minute preparations

was the curiously expressionless faces of the small files of infantry as they moved forward along the tracks leading to the Rapido. They seemed almost mechanical as if they were part of a machine whose purpose they did not really understand.

As darkness settled and the shapes of the hills disappeared, the routine evening shelling of Cassino started as it had done on every night since the end of Freyberg's last offensive in March. This regular bombardment was designed to cover the move of the nightly supply parties up Route 6 and into the forward positions in the ruins of the town. The shelling gradually died away and the night became quieter than usual. The Allies had no wish to alert the Germans; and the Germans, as it happened, were in the midst of one of the phases of their relief programme and had even less desire to disturb the Allies. Then quite suddenly at eleven o'clock as the first pips of the BBC time signal came over the air, the combined artillery of the Fifth and Eighth Armies opened fire with an intensity only rivalled by the barrage at El Alamein some eighteen months before. The flashes lit up the black shapes of the mountains from Minturno on the coast to Monte Cifalco north of Cassino. Keyes' II (US) Corps and Juin's Frenchmen started their assault within minutes of the beginning of the artillery programme. The infantry of Kirkman's XIII (Br) Corps began their final advance towards the Rapido at the same time, but they did not start their river crossing until forty-five minutes later as they needed the noise of the artillery to cover the rattle of their boats and rafting equipments as they carried them forward. Anders' Poles attacked later still. They needed moonlight to enable them to fight their way forward over the rough rock-strewn hillsides leading to Colle Sant' Angelo and Point 593. They also needed more time for their artillery to subdue the deeply-emplaced German strongpoints hidden amongst the rocks which dominated their lines of advance. They crossed the start line at 1 a.m. on 12 May, an hour and a quarter after Kirkman's Corps in the valley below.

The crash of the opening barrage represents the overture to any great modern battle, but from the moment the curtain rises the theatrical analogy begins to fail. Successful play-writers and generals have to be able to see their respective plots right through to the end, but the playwright contrives his characters and arranges the coincidence of events to fit the plot. Generals are faced with the harsh realities of war and must attempt to control real men and actual events with no certainty that they will succeed in reaching the finale they have planned. For the first few hours of Diadem reports reaching the headquarters of the four attacking Corps were sketchy, often contradictory and in some cases clearly inaccurate, but they all had one thing in common—there was no hint of success anywhere. Weeks of hard work, careful planning and detailed rehearsal seemed to have come to nothing. The Gustav Line appeared as impregnable as ever. Juin expressed the feeling which must have run through Anders', Kirkman's and Keyes' minds when he says in his memoirs:

> . . . the anguish which I felt . . . at the thought that the French attack, on which all depended, had not succeeded. This was the anguish felt by Montluc after the battle of Cerisoles on learning that it was only by a little that it had failed. Had I not, like him, guaranteed success before the battle and thus rallied the less courageous hearts?

To lesser men than these four Corps Commanders, the dawn reports would have spelt disaster; but they had all experienced the first days of great battles before. Nothing is ever as bad or as good as it seems at this stage of a major offensive. Success rarely comes quickly; and even if success has, in fact, been achieved it lies hidden until one side's reserves are exhausted. It is only when this moment is approaching that success or failure can be discerned. Until then a commander only knows his own losses with any certainty and that his opponent is not yet giving ground. In his pre-battle estimates for Diadem Alexander instructed his staff to expect fourteen to twenty-one days' bitter fighting before a decision would be achieved.

As events of the first night were pieced together by the four Corps' operations staffs they made a depressing picture. The two Corps of the Fifth Army had been the first to attack and had made very little progress. Keyes' two new American divisions had gone forward with great keenness but had been stopped in their tracks by Steinmetz's 94 Division without making any marked impression on the German defences along the Minturno ridge. Juin's Frenchmen had been slightly more successful. The left-hand regiment of Dody's 2 (Moroccan) Division had seized its first objective, Monte Faito, but his right-hand regiment had found its climb to Monte Girofano more difficult than expected in the dark and had been stopped short of its objective by flame throwers as well as by heavy mortar and machine-gun fire. Raapke's 71 Division had started to counter-attack early on 12 May and had inflicted serious casualties amongst both Moroccan regiments. Dody, in his turn, had beaten off these counter-attacks, which at times had verged on desperation. His success in holding the ground which he had won was largely due to the concentrations of fire laid down by the massed artillery of the whole of Juin's Corps. These German counter-attacks had so alarmed Juin that he decided to go forward to take personal command of the battle during

18   The situation at the end of 12 May

the afternoon. As he made his way forward from Dody's command post to see for himself what was happening in Monte Faito he recalls seing many of his friends being brought down the hillside on stretchers. His depression soon lifted as he watched the execution being done by the French artillery, which he describes saying 'the German reserves were literally falling apart under the chopper of my 400 guns'. Encouraged by the destruction of Raapke's infantry, he decided to renew the attack after dark that night with the reserve regiment of Dody's division which had not been committed so far. Returning to his headquarters he heard that Sevez's 4 (Mountain) Division had taken Castelforte after a day's long struggle, helped by the right-hand regiment of Keyes' Corps. Brosset's 1 (Motorised) Division in the Garigliano Valley, on the other hand, had made no significant progress and was unlikely to do so until Dody had cleared more of the Monte Majo Massif which overlooked his line of advance.

In Eighth Army's sector nothing had gone right. Kirkman's XIII (Br) Corps ran into two unexpected hazards at the very start of its assault. The mist which had started to rise in the valley towards midnight gradually thickened. Most accounts suggest that the thickening of the river mist into a dense fog was caused by the Germans deliberately firing smoke shells and igniting smoke canisters on the banks of the Rapido to confuse the attacker. This seems unlikely as the most difficult problem in defending a river is to detect where the crossings are being made. The story is probably one of those plausible myths which grow up around unfortunate events when scapegoats are needed to justify unforeseen misadventure. It is much more probable that the density of the natural valley mist was increased by the smoke of the Allied artillery barrage and of the retaliatory German defensive fire. The author, who had spent the two previous months in the Cassino sector and who waited all night near the Amazon bridge site to clear the mines on the far bank, felt that the fog was a return of the usual Liri Valley mist which had often occurred during the winter. It would not take very much additional smoke to make it very dense. Be that as it may, the fog came as a surprise and caused confusion and delay which dislocated the carefully laid plans in almost every sector of XIII (Br) Corps' front.

The XIII (Br) Corps' counter-battery programme was initially very successful. There was relatively little response from the German artillery while the troops were moving forward. Unfortunately the second unexpected hazard appeared as soon as the men reached the river and tried to launch their canvas and plywood assault boats. The Rapido's current was far faster than the streams on which training and rehearsals had been carried out. The flat, cumbersome, keelless boats were quite unmanageable in the current and, although the stream was not much more than sixty feet wide, paddling the boats across proved too difficult for many of the inexperienced crews. The current took charge and swept them downstream before they could reach the far bank. Only those units which managed to stretch ropes across the river on which to haul the boats to and fro, made anything like a successful crossing. Some did this by sending swimmers across and others by throwing grapnels over. Those who relied on paddles had little success.

It is always easy to be wise after the event. Very few of the officers concerned with planning the crossing had been able to see the stream. It could only be approached on a dark night by small reconnaissance patrols and these had to be kept to a minimum to prevent loss of surprise. Judging a river's current in the darkness is not easy as every stream appears much faster at night than it does in daylight. The result of this mis-appreciation was that many boats of the initial assault waves were swept away; others were sunk by German mortar and machine-gun fire which opened up on fixed lines as soon as activity was detected on the river; and many of those which did get across landed at unexpected points on the far bank which it was difficult to recognise in the swirling mist. To make matters worse the fog obscured the moon which the troops were relying upon to find their objectives and which had been one of the factors in fixing 11 May for the start of the offensive. It also hid the direction-keeping bursts of Bofors tracer rounds fired overhead by light anti-aircraft units specially detailed for this task.

Blinded and confused by the fog and suffering mounting casualties from German defensive fire, it was only the most determined companies which made progress that night. It was impossible to stifle the desperate feeling that the whole affair had grossly miscarried or, in soldiers' language, it was an 'unholy balls-up'! There was every excuse for the faint-hearted to dig in and to wait for dawn. It is to the great credit of the majority of the two divisions that they resisted the temptation and continued to work their way over the river in spite of the apparent failure of so many crossings. In the dry words of the official account the night's work is summed up in two lines:

Confused fighting resulted and the benefit of the barrage was soon lost. Only a shallow bridgehead had been secured by first light.

In Dudley Ward's 4 (Br) Division's sector, Shoesmith's 10 Brigade on the right, nearest Cassino, made more progress during the night than Montague-Dcuglas-Scott's 28 Brigade on the left. His two leading battalions (2 Bedfords and 1/6 East Surreys) and part of the third (2 Duke of Cornwall's Light Infantry) crossed during the night, but could get no further than 'Queen Street'—the Cassino–Sant' Angelo road about 500 yards from the river (*see fig. 12*). They cleaned out a German strongpoint in the caves and bunkers of the rocky knoll at Point 36 but were repulsed when they tried to advance into the northerly bulge of the Brown Line by Heidrich's Parachute MG Battalion holding Point 63.

Although Shoesmith's crossing had been relatively successful, the majority of his boats had been swept downstream after the initial assault wave had reached the far bank. Ferrying with the few remaining boats

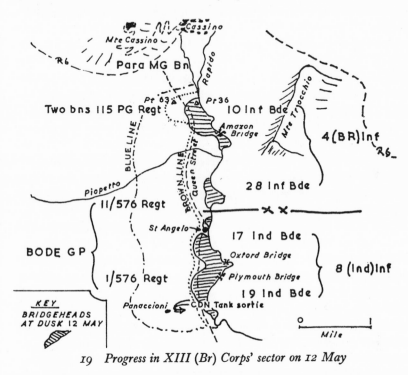

19   *Progress in XIII (Br) Corps' sector on 12 May*

was slow and frustrating, and it is fortunate that the mist stayed low in the valley well into the morning. When it did rise, all ferrying was brought to a halt by German fire. During the rest of the first day Shoesmith's men could do little more than dig in where they were and repel the German counter-attacks as they came in, hoping that the sappers would be able to bridge the river in time to give them tank support before they were overrun. Fortunately, none of these counter-attacks were supported by tanks and most were delivered in not more than about platoon strength. The Germans were not as yet ready to mount a deliberate riposte.

In 28 Brigade's sector everything seemed to have been thought of. Possibly too much had been covered, making the plan too complex and too inflexible. During the preliminary bombardment tapes had been stretched down to the crossing points; strong swimmers had fixed lines across the river; duplicated communications had been established between crossing points, boat assembly areas and battalion lying-up areas; but when H-hour came up no troops appeared. The leading battalion (1 Kings), which was to have secured both crossings in the brigade sector, had lost its way in the mist while moving down to the river and arrived thirty-five minutes late. By this time the German posts near the river had recovered from the artillery bombardment and were ready to repel any crossing. The barrage, which should have covered the brigade's advance from the river to the Brown Line, started to creep away from the Rapido before the crossing could start. Many boats were holed before they reached the river; others were hit as they were slid into the water; and some were capsized by men jumping in with heavy equipment in order to get below the level of the banks as quickly as possible to avoid blizzards of machine-gun fire which swept the open fields leading down to the river. The arrival of the second battalion (2 Somerset Light Infantry), which was to cross after the Kings, added to the confusion at the crossings. They had to wait in the taped lanes through the minefields on the home bank, suffering casualties to no apparent purpose under increasingly heavy fire. Stragglers and wounded coming back from the Kings in front repeated and embellished wild rumours that the battalion had been virtually wiped out. In spite of the confusion and apparent mismanagement men from every level—from COs down to privates—appeared, gripped the local situation and led the less stout-hearted forward. Just one example will serve to illustrate the behaviour of these men. The third battalion of the brigade (2/4 Hampshires) was responsible for working the ferries. One of the Hampshire's lance-corporals, H. Grainger, swam the river three times with ropes to keep the few remaining boats moving at the ferry sites. Between swims he stood naked on the bank for some four hours, guiding men as they came up to the ferry. Tragically, two days later he was killed in the bridgehead. Many actions of this kind enabled 28 (Br) Brigade to secure a toe-hold on the far bank, but, when daylight came and the mist was dispersed by the sun, German retaliatory fire grew so intense that all ferrying had to stop and further attempts to strengthen the bridgehead were abandoned.

While both brigades were struggling to cross, the advance parties of the sapper squadrons which were to build the bridges moved down to the river on foot. By 1 a.m. the preparation of the bank seats for the three bridges in 4 (Br) Division's sector was well advanced. As soon as the vehicles carrying the bridging equipment started to move down to the sites so that construction could start the noise attracted German defensive fire of such intensity that the sappers were driven to cover and many of their vehicles were set on fire before they could reach the river bank. When daylight came any further attempt to bridge had to be abandoned as all the sites were still under observed small-arms fire. Nothing further could be done until the bridgeheads could be deepened enough to give the sappers some immunity from aimed fire while they worked in the open, heaving the heavy Bailey bridge panels into position. The usual vicious circle of an unsuccessful river crossing set in: too shallow a bridgehead meant no bridging, and yet no bridging meant lack of the necessary strength to secure and to deepen the bridgehead. No bridges were built in Dudley Ward's sector on the first day, but fortunately the Germans failed to take advantage of the weakness of his position and launched no deliberately organised tank and infantry counter-attacks against his precarious bridgeheads.

The Indian division's attack astride and to the south of Sant' Angelo was a replica, with one important exception, of the British division's discouraging operations to the north. Brigadier Boucher's 17 (Indian) Brigade assaulted with a battalion either side of the village. They suffered relatively few casualties during their crossing, but the fog was so dense that some platoons had to advance from the river in single file with each man holding the bayonet scabbard of the man in front. As soon as the Germans located the Indian crossings the same dense curtain of fire came down and by dawn the brigade was confined to two small unconnected bridgeheads either side of Sant' Angelo. Brigadier Dobree's 19 (Indian) Brigade, like Montague-Douglas-Scott's 28 (Br) Brigade, ran into trouble before it could reach the river. It was attacking on the axis that had been used by the southern regiment of 36 (US) Division in January and this had been carefully registered by German artillery. As its battalions moved towards the river not only did they run into the pre-planned German defensive fire but they also hit an unrecorded American minefield laid in January to impede German counter-attacks after 36 (US) Division's failure. On the river itself they encountered the same difficulties as the other brigades. One battalion lost all but one of its boats in the first wave and had to resort to ferrying the rest of the battalion over in the one surviving boat.

Conditions are best illustrated by the story of 'A' Company of the 3/8 Punjab Regiment. The company lost one platoon which was swept down river at the very start of the crossing. The company headquarters and the two other platoons managed to reach the far bank with sufficient cohesion to form up and advance towards the objective. It had not gone far when it ran into a thick belt of wire and a minefield. Several sepoys were killed in the field and the noise of the exploding mines drew the Germans' attention to the position of the company in the fog. Fixed-line fire by machine guns and defensive fire from mortars killed or wounded all but fifteen men who pushed on through the fog until they stumbled on the sunken Sant' Angelo road which they crossed and dug in about thirty yards further on with their number reduced to nine. During the rest of the night they killed several Germans who tried to attack them but when dawn came there was no sign of tank support or of the other Punjabi companies and so the survivors, now down to three, were forced to surrender. The rest of the brigade was still holding a precarious bridgehead short of the main German defences pinned down by fire and unable to fight its way forward or to withdraw back across the river. In places they were so close under the German positions that the Germans could roll hand grenades down the slopes so that they burst amongst the sepoys. It was during this uncomfortable period that a nineteen-year-old sepoy—Kamal Ram of the 3/8 Punjab Regiment—fighting in his first action won the Victoria Cross. He attacked two German machine-gun posts single-handed, shooting and bayoneting the crews, and then helped his havildar to silence a third post.

The important difference between the British and Indian attacks soon began to make itself felt. The Indian Sappers and Miners were luckier than their British colleagues and had found a bridge site which was not so heavily covered by German fixed-line fire. The first of their bridges north of Sant' Angelo suffered the fate of the British bridges and work was stopped before much progress had been made. The second, just to the south of Sant' Angelo, code-named 'Oxford', was in a narrow bend in the river forming a deep re-entrant into the Indians' home bank which was difficult for the Germans to cover adequately by fire. Building started soon after midnight and was completed at 8.15 a.m. before the mist had started to rise. At their third site, 'Plymouth', at the southern end of the divisional sector, the ingenuity of Canadian tank men and Indian engineers produced a Bailey bridge carried on rollers on the back of a turretless Sherman tank which could be launched by a second tank pushing from behind. This mechanical improvisation succeeded and Plymouth bridge was open one hour after Oxford. Only four tanks managed to cross before a shell damaged the bridge, restricting its use to light vehicles. Some difficulty was also experienced in settling the ends of the bridge securely enough on its bank seats to take tanks which were unable to use it again until the following day.

The construction of these two bridges made all the difference to the course of the battle in the Indian sector. Four squadrons of Canadian tanks managed to cross Oxford during the day. Some were bogged immediately in the soft fields on the far bank, but by evening there was no doubt about the security of the Indian bridgehead. Helped by these tanks Boucher's 17 (Indian) Brigade cleared part of Sant' Angelo by dusk, and Dobree's 19 (Indian) Brigade secured the southern flank with an attack by Canadian tanks towards Panaccioni.

Reviewing the situation towards midday Kirkman appreciated that the key to the whole situation in the Liri Valley lay in the construction of more bridges over the Rapido. Unless at least one bridge could be built in Dudley Ward's sector there was a grave danger that a determined German counter-attack would destroy Shoesmith's tenuous bridgehead and Montague-Douglas-Scott's toe-hold. The Indian bridgehead was secure and might be used to help the British brigades but it was too narrow a frontage to enable Kirkman to bring the full weight of his Corps to bear. Orders were, therefore, given for a Bailey bridge to be built 'at all costs' in 28 (Br) Brigade's sector at the 'Amazon' site. 'At all costs' was meant literally and was not just a figure of speech. A special artillery programme was laid on including heavy smoke-screening of the site and an increased intensity of smoke-shelling of Monte Cassino to blind the German observers in or near the Monastery ruins. At a quarter to six that evening two field squadrons of 4 (Br) Division's sappers under Major Robin Gabbett as bridge commander started their epic task of building Amazon bridge. It was slow and murderous work carried out in the open with only the low flood bunds on the banks of the river affording any cover for the successive shifts of sappers working on the site. The whole area came under aimed sniper and machine-gun fire whenever the smoke thinned as well as from the indirect harassing fire from mortars and artillery. By the time the bridge was completed at 4 a.m. the following morning, the 7 and 225 Field Squadrons had lost three officers and eighty other ranks out of the 200 men deployed on the task, but they had the satisfaction of knowing that the building of Amazon bridge marked the turning point in XIII (Br) Corps' battle in the Liri Valley. The reserve brigade of 4 (Br) Division—Brigadier Heber-Percy's 12 Brigade—supported by the 17/21 Lancers from 6 (Br) Armoured Division crossed into the bridgehead as daylight broke on the second morning of the battle and was ready to take over the lead from the exhausted men of Shoesmith's and Montague-Douglas-Scott's brigades.

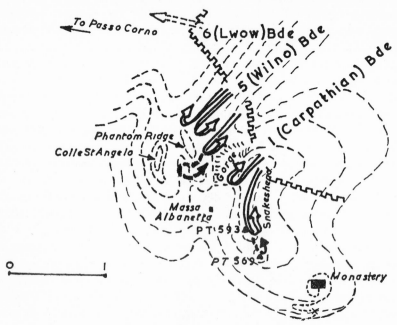

20   *The first Polish attack, 11–12 May*

Both divisions of Anders' Polish Corps attacked together at one o'clock. Before H-hour the assault troops had to be withdrawn a short distance behind their start lines for safety reasons. This was to enable the medium and heavy guns to saturate the German positions close to the Polish axis of advance. The 5 (Wilno) Brigade with four battalions under command led Sulik's 5 (Kresowan) Division's attack on Phantom Ridge. It advanced with two battalions up, leaving the third to secure the old front line as a firm base and holding the fourth in reserve to exploit to Colle Sant' Angelo. The 6 (Lwow) Brigade covered the right flank by making a feint attack towards Passo Corno half way up the mountain spur leading to the summit of Monte Cairo. The 1 (Carpathian) Brigade led Duch's 3 (Carpathian) Division's attack along the Snake's Head Ridge and upon Albanetta Farm with two battalions up and a third in reserve. The whole of his 2 (Carpathian) Brigade was in reserve ready to exploit to the Monastery.

The 6 (Lwow) Brigade's feint successfully drew German defensive fire away from 5 (Wilno) Brigade's front in the early stages of its attack but not for long enough. It was soon clear that the Allied counter-battery programme had not subdued enough of the numerous German guns, mortars and *nebelwerfers* hidden in the re-entrants on the reverse slopes of Monte Cassino and Colle Sant' Angelo. Although the German communications were badly disrupted sufficient of their guns came into action to disorganise and slow the 5 (Wilno) Brigade's advance to a painful crawl. It was not until 2.30 a.m. that the leading battalions reached the bottom of Phantom Ridge, the top of which was their first objective. They had taken twice as long as expected and, like XIII (Br) Corps in the valley below, they had lost much of the benefit of the timed artillery concentrations by being unable to keep up to their planned schedule. Casualties had been high during the advance (about one in five); both wireless and telephone communications had been disrupted; and the attack began to slip out of control. Nevertheless, both leading battalions reached the top of Phantom Ridge, but when they tried to advance over the crest they ran into intense fire from German positions which had escaped the brunt of bombardment on the steep reverse slopes. They managed to clear most of the German posts on their own side of Phantom Ridge and two companies of the left-hand battalion managed to work their way round the southern end to reach a point almost halfway between the Ridge and Colle Sant' Angelo, but finding themselves unsupported and losing heavily from German fire, they were forced to withdraw back to Phantom Ridge. Meanwhile, the reserve battalion, which had lost touch with the forward battalions and with the brigade headquarters due to loss of its communications, came up as planned to continue the advance to Colle Sant' Angelo, only to find itself adding to the congestion on Phantom Ridge and to the number of targets available for the German gunners. By now much of the damage done to the German artillery communications had been repaired, and their defensive fire increased steadily as more and more weapons were brought back into action. Soon after first light the Germans launched a counter-attack which was successfully beaten off. At about 1 p.m. the reserve battalion commander decided on his own initiative to withdraw his battalion which was losing heavily in its exposed position to no purpose. He had no means of contacting the brigade commander or of bringing down artillery defensive fire, so he gave the order to withdraw to the start line. Other troops seeing them go decided that a general withdrawal must have been ordered and fell back as well leaving the two forward companies of the two leading battalions clinging to their positions on Phantom Ridge.

The attack of Duch's Carpathian Division fared no better. 1 (Carpathian) Brigade advanced with two battalions up; the right-hand battalion supported by tanks, aiming for Massa Albanetta with the head of the Gorge as an intermediate objective; and the left-hand battalion, on the Snake's Head Ridge, attacking in succession the two high points— Points 593 and 569. Both battalions were to storm their intermediate objectives by 1.30 a.m. Just after 2 a.m. Duch heard that Point 593 had fallen and forty minutes later that some of his troops had reached the forward slopes of Point 569. The battalion attacking Massa Albanetta reported that it was pinned down short of the Gorge by fire coming from Colle Sant' Angelo and from mortars in the Gorge itself. It was not until daylight that fresh artillery concentrations enabled his right-hand battalion to reach the head of the Gorge which it found was heavily mined. The Polish sappers came forward to clear a lane for the tanks but lost eighteen men out of the twenty deployed without succeeding in clearing a safe path. In the meantime, all the tanks of the leading troop and one of the second had been destroyed by a combination of mines and anti-tank weapons. Deprived of tank support and pinned down by fire in the Gorge, the battalion suffered steady losses throughout the morning.

The battalion on the Snake's Head Ridge was no more successful. Its companies which had reached Points 593 and 569 came under heavy fire from the Monastery and its surrounding posts when daylight revealed their exposed positions to Heilmann's paratroopers. They had repulsed six determined counter-attacks by midday, but the continuous deluge of German fire, augmented by guns firing into the Poles' backs from the gun positions in the Atina area could not be sustained much longer. Point 569 was lost to the seventh parachute counter-attack and the company holding the southern slopes of Point 593 was reduced to one officer and seven men.

General Anders reviewed the position during the morning as reports came in, and proposed to renew the attack with fresh battalions in both divisional sectors provided he could have the support of Kirkman's artillery. This plan had to be cancelled because Kirkman's troops were in a more dangerous position than the Poles who did not have an un-bridged river behind them. At 2 p.m. Anders ordered a general with-drawal of all his troops back to their original defensive positions. Two hours later Oliver Leese arrived at Anders' headquarters and approved the decision. There was no point in resuming the attack until XIII (Br) Corps was in a position to cut Route 6. This was unlikely to happen before the following afternoon, 13 May; and even this timing might prove overoptimistic. Oliver Leese instructed Anders to reorganise his depleted battalions and to be ready to renew the offensive as soon as Kirkman's troops were within striking distance of Route 6. In the mean-time, he was to keep the Germans on Monte Cassino and the surround-ing spurs fully occupied by aggressive patrolling and sudden concentra-tions of artillery fire.

12 May was a day for strong nerves—physical and mental—in the Ger-man chain of command. Soon after first light Kesselring's headquarters north of Rome, von Vietinghoff's near Avezzano, and many of their subordinate headquarters were ferociously attacked by the Allied Air Forces. Von Vietinghoff's was so badly damaged that his staff had to move forward and share the communications of von Senger's XIV Panzer Corps headquarters near Frosinone to maintain touch with the battle. The Allied Air Forces flew a record of just under 3,000 sorties that day over the battlefield. The disruption of German communica-tions, the harassment of their key staffs and the sudden inability to move freely in daylight caused by the waves of Allied fighter-bombers, which attacked all movement in the rear of the German lines, led to an unco-ordinated and erratic response to the Allied offensive. It was not, how-ever, these physical discomforts which did the greatest harm to the German cause. Misjudged operational appreciations, unsound intelli-gence assessments and the consequential faulty strategic decisions taken over a long period, began to have their effect and were reflected in the short-term tactical situation.

The first misappreciation was the gullible acceptance of Alexander's deception plan. When reports began to come in during the night of 11–12 May of heavy artillery bombardments and infantry attacks all along the main front from Cassino to the sea, most of the German higher commanders jumped to the conclusion that this was the expected holding attack designed to draw their reserves away from the decisive sector. Which sector this was likely to be they did not know, but each commander in common prudence assumed that his would be the chosen field for the main Allied effort. In consequence, they all played their cards as Alexander intended—haltingly and without the usual ruthless improvisation so often displayed by German commanders in similar crises in the past. Even at Cassino there seems to have been no inclination to launch a really powerful and coordinated counter-attack by tanks, infantry and artillery against Kirkman's flimsy bridgeheads. The shortness of the Allies' preliminary bombardments seemed to lend credence to the picture of a diversionary attack on the main front to mask the real attack from the sea or from Anzio. Von Senger's deputy at XIV Panzer Corps expected 'an expansion of the battle through a landing operation' and hence was not keen to commit his only reserve, Rodt's 15 Panzer Grenadier Division, too soon. Rodt's division, in any case, had only its 104 Panzer Grenadier Regiment intact and under its own command. Its 115 Panzer Grenadier Regiment was now pinned in the Liri Valley, locked in a grim struggle with Dudley Ward's division. Its third regiment—129 Panzer Grenadier Regiment—had been split up on Kesselring's orders, and against von Senger's advice, to provide immediate counter-attack battalions close behind 71 and 94 Divisions. Von Mackensen, at his Fourteenth Army headquarters, had his eyes glued to his own sector containing Truscott at Anzio and covering the west coast from the beachhead northwards. He was convinced that the main attack would come either from the beachhead or, as Kesselring surmised, in the form of an amphibious landing north of the Tiber. Von Mackensen was so convinced that his Army was the real Allied target that, as will be seen later, he resisted Kesselring's orders to move reserves southwards when the latter at last realised the true position. There is no published record of what von Vietinghoff's deputy thought, but his views are of academic interest only because the bombing of his headquarters dislocated his means of influencing the battle in the Tenth Army area for the first twenty-four hours.

The second German misappreciation was the strength of the Allied forces which Alexander had concentrated above Cassino, in the Liri Valley, and against Monte Majo. A situation map for 12 May found in von Mackensen's headquarters after it was overrun towards the end of Diadem shows how the German intelligence had underestimated these

11   Troops of 8 (Indian) Division dug in along a sunken track in their assembly area waiting for darkness on 11 May 1944

ASSEMBLY

12   Polish troops moving up in the dusk to their start line on Monte Cassino

13 Infantry making their way through the smoke to one of the bridges over the Rapido

THE RAPIDO

14 A Canadian tank fighting its way into Sant' Angelo

Allied concentrations and bears out von Senger who says in his memoirs that the Italian front seemed to have declined in importance in German eyes because everyone felt that the Allies were concentrating their resources for the Second Front in France. They were completely unaware of the size of force that Alexander had managed to bring to bear for Diadem in spite of surrendering, during the previous autumn, seven of his most experienced divisions to Eisenhower for Overlord. Von Mackensen's map showed that the Germans had a very clear picture of the Allied troops actually in the line on 12 May, but they were hopelessly in the dark about the rest. They had plotted 85 and 88 (US) Divisions accurately on the lower Garigliano, but they did not know under whose command they were operating. 4 and 78 (Br) Divisions were placed at Termoli in the rear areas. McCreery's X (Br) Corps was shown in the Apennines but in the wrong location. Even Eighth Army headquarters was fixed twelve miles out of position and on the wrong side of the Matise Mountains.

The real mistakes, however, came in the locations of the French, Poles and Canadians. One French division was correctly identified opposite Monte Majo and another at Salerno but the other two and Guillaume's Goumiers had not been identified. Above Cassino, 5 (Kresowan) Division was correctly placed but 3 (Carpathian) Division was not mentioned and four non-existent Polish divisions were shown as located in the rear areas. The Canadian headquarters was unlocated. 1 (Canadian) Division was shown near Salerno as the Allied deception plan intended. 5 (Canadian) Armoured Division was shown under the Polish Corps north of Cassino. Some Canadian elements had been located by radio interception in their actual location near Mignano opposite the Liri Valley but no deductions had been drawn from this. 36 (US) Division was identified carrying out practice landings near Naples and, finally, a mythical 18 (Br) Division (the real one was lost in the surrender of Singapore) appears firmly located by radio intercept in the Apennines.

Thus by underestimating the strength of the Allied troops attacking the Gustav Line and by firmly resisting the temptation to commit their reserves too soon, they condemned their troops to fight against over-whelming odds for longer than even German troops could endure. Feurstein's and von Senger's Corps fought with their usual skill and resolution thoughout the night of 11 May and all 12 May. If there had been as few fresh Allied formations awaiting their turn to enter the battle as the German intelligence staffs envisaged the Gustav defences might have been held. The cumulative effect of the Allies' ability to commit a constant flow of fresh infantry and tank formations to the fight, together with the unrelenting pounding by the greatly superior Allied artillery and the round-the-clock Allied air offensive, was to create a very different situation for the German Command. As yet this was not apparent to anyone on the German side. There was no reason to believe that their well-tried battle drills would not prove adequate to meet this fourth Allied attempt to open the road to Rome.

The third misappreciation was that of timing. The German front was still in the middle of the relief programme designed to be ready for an Allied spring offensive towards the end of May. The reliefs which took place on the night 11–12 May above Cassino increased the number of German troops available to counter-attack the Poles and may· have contributed to Anders' men failing to hold their initial gains, but in the Liri Valley Kirkman's Corps hit the German defenders at a moment when there was a muddled chain of command. Ortner's 44 Division was still in the process of taking over tactical control of the Valley from Rodt's 15 Panzer Grenadier Division, and his headquarters were not fully established when the Allied attack began. Furthermore, the whole sector had been taken out of von Senger's experienced hands and given to Feurstein's LI (Mountain) Corps which had had little experience of fighting a major action in Italy. It had come down from northern Italy at the time of the Anzio landing and had taken over the quiet Adriatic sector to release Herr's experienced LXXVI Panzer Corps to command the southern half of the beachhead perimeter. Feurstein had not moved over to the Cassino sector until April and so was not fully conversant with its problems. The worst misfortune of all from the German point of view, was Hitler's summons of von Vietinghoff, von Senger and Baade to Obersalzburg and their consequent absences from their headquarters on 11–12 May.

Although the higher echelons of the German Command were making decisions on 12 May which were to lose them the battle, the picture was rather different at the lower levels. The German gift for quick tactical improvisation came to the fore at once. The Allied penetrations into their positions had to be sealed off immediately whether it was a feint attack or not. In Feurstein's Corps three sets of immediate counter-measures to reinforce the threatened front were taken. First, the alarm units of 5 (Mountain) and 114 (Jaeger) Divisions, which were not under attack in their Apennine sectors, were ordered to reinforce Ortner's units in the Liri Valley as quickly as possible. These alarm units were part of the standard operating procedures of all German divisions in Italy and consisted of reserve units of about company strength, often composed of the reconnaissance elements of regiments and battalions which could be moved quickly to the coast if an Allied landing occurred. It was these units which had sealed off the original Anzio beachhead so quickly in January. Secondly, and true to German tactical tradition, Feurstein began assembling a reserve force on Route 6 near Aquino to back up his troops in the Liri Valley and to ensure that no Allied break-through occurred along the main road to Rome. This group was formed round the reserve battalion of 1 Para Regiment and became known as Battle Group Schulz, after its commander. Later in the day, as the full extent of the Allied attack in the Liri Valley became more obvious, Feurstein took his third step when he demanded and obtained from Tenth Army the reluctant release of the leading regiment of Baade's 90 Panzer Grenadier Division which had been deployed to meet a possible Allied airborne landing at Frosinone. South of the Liri in XIV Panzer Corps' sector there was less reaction as von Senger was away. Steinmetz's 94 Division was holding its own against Keyes' II (US) Corps, but Raapke's 71 Division had to commit its reserve panzer grenadier battalion from Rodt's 129 Panzer Grenadier Regiment to try to re-capture Monte Faito from the French. No other significant measures seem to have been taken to block the Fifth Army.

If the previous battles in Italy provided any precedent, these counter-measures should have been adequate to restore the situation. Conditions, however, had changed, destroying the relevance of the earlier fighting. It was spring, not winter: the ground was hard and the Allied tanks could now move more freely; the sky was clear and the Allied Air Forces could find their targets unhindered by weather; and Alexander and his staff had set the stage for Diadem with deliberate and fascinating care to avoid another Somme or Passchendaele.

7 *The Destruction of the Gustav Line*

'There is no doubt that the Germans intend to fight for every yard and that the next few days will see some extremely bitter and severe fighting.'

Alexander reporting at 6.30 p.m. on 12 May (Despatches 2923)

There were to be two occasions during the Battle for Rome when un-expected events led to decisive results. The first occurred during 13 May, the second day of the battle. On that day the Gustav Line was fatally penetrated, but not in the Cassino sector as Alexander intended, nor by the main striking force, Kirkman's XIII (Br) Corps. The break came, as Juin had predicted, in the French sector and was made by his French Expeditionary Corps. With the benefit of hindsight it is now easier to discern why this happened, but at the time Juin's success appeared no more than a very welcome bonus after the depressing first thirty-six hours of Diadem. This was not a deliberate depreciation of the French success. It was because it came in a sector where exploitation would be extremely difficult and where German counter-measures should have been correspondingly easy to take. Within five days, however, the Gustav Line had been destroyed and Monte Cassino lay behind the Allied lines, an awe-inspiring ruin, attracting press corres-pondents and touring dignatories from every country in the Allied camp.

After issuing his final orders late on 12 May, Juin spent a second rest-less night. Would Dody's Moroccans master Monte Majo or would this battle for the southern bastion of the Liri defences follow the same pattern as the struggle for Monte Cassino, disproving all Juin's theories as to how Keyes, Freyberg and now Anders should have tackled the Cassino problem? Juin had not been allowed to make the wide turning movement through the mountains north of Cassino which he had advocated before Freyberg's last offensive. If Dody failed on 13 May,

Juin's ideas on mountain fighting would be proved no better than those of the over-mechanised Anglo-Saxons. No one would worry about this except Juin, who had written and said a great deal in criticism of the tactics employed by the Allies so far in the Italian campaign. The French would merely be confirming the general opinion held at that time that they did not understand modern warfare.

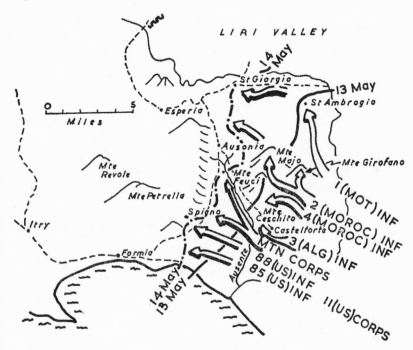

21   *Fifth Army operations on 13 and 14 May*

Dody's Moroccans attacked at 4 a.m. on 13 May and soon after dawn were firmly established on the eastern feature, Monte Girofano. Despite a number of well-led German counter-attacks, his troops pressed on in broad daylight to take the western feature, Monte Feuci, against lessening resistance. What had happened in the early hours of 13 May in 71 Division's headquarters is not recorded in any published records, but it seems that Raapke must have ordered a withdrawal to the Ausonia defile some time after the fall of Monte Girofano. When Monte Feuci fell the Moroccans found themselves opposed by only rearguards and by mid-afternoon the summit of Monte Majo was in their hands. On Juin's instructions, a specially-prepared Tricolour was hoisted on the summit by German prisoners to mark the triumph of the French Expeditionary Corps and of Free France.

The capture of Monte Girofano loosened up the German resistance in front of Brosset's 1 (Motorised) Division in the Garigliano Valley because the German artillery observers covering his axis of advance were forced to withdraw. German positions which had resisted all his efforts during 12 May began to crumble and the same German retirement, which had been noted by Dody's troops around midday, started on Brosset's front. The Germans in the Garigliano bend had further to go than those on Monte Majo to reach the new line and so their withdrawal had to be more rapid. The French operations gradually changed from attack to advance and then to pursuit as Raapke's troops gave way. By midnight Brosset held Sant' Ambrogio and his leading troops were approaching the south bank of the Liri River.

On the French western flank, Sevez's 4 (Mountain) Division and Monsabert's 3 (Algerian) Division mounted a brilliant encircling operation against Raapke's southern regiment which was trying to stop the French breaking out from the hills around Castelforte and into the Ausente Valley. Working through these hills north of the town and taking advantage of Dody's success on Monte Feuci, Sevez reached Monte Ceschito, overlooking the Castelforte–Ausonia road in the early afternoon. Meanwhile, Monsabert's 3 (Algerian) Division had broken out from the town itself and was approaching Monte Ceschito from the south. Raapke's withdrawal in this sector was too slow and by nightfall his southern regiment had lost 700 prisoners in its attempts to pull back towards Ausonia.

It is only possible to guess at the events in the XIV Panzer Corps' sector during 13 May. Steinmetz's 94 Division succeeded in repelling most of Keyes' II (US) Corps' attacks during 12 and 13 May, inflicting heavy losses on the American 85 and 88 (US) Divisions. By dark on 13 May he was able to issue an order of the day congratulating his troops on their success, saying, 'in spite of several enemy penetrations into our advanced positions the main field of battle remains in our hands'. In Raapke's 71 Divisional sector the loss of Monte Faito and Castelforte on the first day seems to have unsettled his defence. His immediate reserves were committed early in the day and the Corps' reserve in his sector, a single battalion of 15 Panzer Grenadier Division, was thrown in and decimated in the attempts to retake Monte Faito during the afternoon of the first day. By evening, Raapke seems to have appreciated that his division, which was holding a very long front, was being attacked by the whole of Juin's Corps of four divisions. Without von Senger's steadying influence at XIV Panzer Corps' headquarters, the deputy Corps commander seems to have decided that a withdrawal to a shorter line covering Ausonia was the only answer to Raapke's plea for reinforcements. If the French attacked again in force, as they did in fact on 13 May, then 71 Division would have to give up the Monte Majo salient and re-establish itself on a new line from San Giorgio on the Liri to Ausonia, blocking the French axis of advance around the northern side of the Aurunci Mountains. No provision seems to have been made to defend the tracks through the Auruncis as the area was deemed impassable for all practical military purposes. Steinmetz's 94 Division would continue to block Keyes' II (US) Corps axis around the southern side of the Auruncis.

Dody's attack on Monte Girofano at 4 a.m. on 13 May seems to have decided the issue, and by midday the 71 Division withdrawal plan was in full swing, resulting in the unexpected French successes on Monte Majo. It is interesting to speculate what would have happened if von Senger had been with his Corps instead of at Obersalzburg attending Hitler's investiture. In his memoirs he casts the blame for the *débâcle* on his deputy. He condemns, rightly, the dispersal of Rodt's 15 Panzer Grenadier Division which left no strong reserve in the Corps commander's hand. A more basic mistake was the failure to create new reserves as the existing ones were committed. Feurstein had adopted this policy in the Liri Valley when he formed the Schulz Group and demanded reinforcements from Baade's 90 Panzer Grenadier Division. If von Senger had been with his Corps south of the Liri he would also have been gathering in reserves from other sectors of the front as his own were expended. He would probably have been able to plug the gaps in his front as they occurred with the same marked tactical flair that he had displayed in his successful handling of the winter battles from Cassino to the sea. He knew the ground; he knew his troops and he knew the French whom he had stopped north of Cassino in February and March. He would certainly have held the front for two or three days longer, but in the end the weight of the French and American attack would probably have told. Juin was lucky to catch XIV Panzer Corps without its real commander, but it is hard to see how two German infantry divisions could have withstood six Allied divisions, supported, as they were, by such an overwhelming weight of artillery and air power. Apart from surprise, the factors which led to Juin's success in making the first breach in the Gustav Line were the concentration of his artillery behind Dody's attack, the cumulative effect of Allied air attacks and above all the *élan* of his North Africans, officered by Frenchmen who were prepared to sacrifice anything to re-establish the Glory of France.

The withdrawal northwards of Raapke's exhausted troops left a

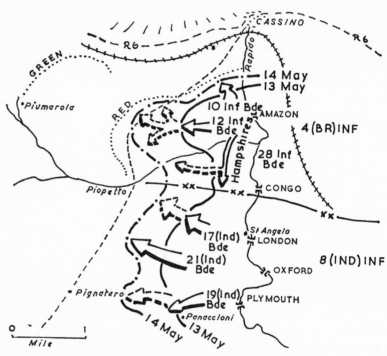

22   *Eighth Army operations on 13 and 14 May*

widening gap in the centre of XIV Panzer Corps' front—the very gap which Juin had anticipated and for the exploitation of which he had organised Guillaume's Mountain Corps. Before describing Guillaume's historic dash through the Aurunci Mountains, we must look once more at the main striking force struggling to achieve a similar decision in the Liri Valley.

The successful but costly construction of Amazon bridge in Dudley Ward's 4 (Br) Division's sector changed the whole complexion of the fighting in Kirkman's XIII (Br) Corps' sector. While the morning mist still hung in the valley, Heber-Percy's 12 (Br) Brigade, supported by Brigadier Mitchell's 26 (Br) Armoured Brigade of 6 (Br) Armoured Division, crossed into the bridgehead and started a succession of battalion attacks to widen the bridgehead. Uncertainty about the positions of the forward troops of the original assault brigades, and the difficulty of reading maps and identifying tracks and features in the mist which hung in the valley until late in the morning, made the organisation and control of these attacks slow and difficult. The superb observation from Monte Trocchio, which seemed so attractive before Diadem, was rendered useless by the pall of mist and artificial smoke which lay in the valley most of the day. The Rover David air controller also found his targets obscured and was unable to direct any strikes in close support of the infantry fighting just below him.

The Pioppeto stream, dividing 10 and 28 (Br) Brigade sectors, was found, as expected, to be a tank obstacle. This tended to canalise Heber-Percy's westward advance to the northern half of the sector. An attempt to cross the Pioppeto to clear Montague-Douglas-Scott's front from the north was held up when the tank bridge-layer, sent to make the crossing, received a direct hit before it could place its bridge over the stream. By midday, however, the main bridgehead north of the Pioppeto had been increased in depth to about 2,000 yards. It now touched the Blue Line, Dudley Ward's second objective, in a number of places. A spirited attack southwards across the Pioppeto during the afternoon by 2/4 Hampshires, the reserve battalion of 28 (Br) Brigade, carried all before it, clearing the west bank of the Rapido almost to Sant' Angelo. This enabled the sappers to start further bridges, and by evening fortune had started to turn against the German defenders who began to surrender in increasing numbers. Even the 1 Parachute Division's MG battalion, upon which Heidrich was relying to stop 4 (Br) Division's advance towards Route 6, gave up 150 prisoners to Shoesmith's 10 (Br) Brigade as it pushed its way northwards towards Cassino. The Hampshires' attack netted a further 150 in its sweep southwards.

In Dudley Russell's 8 (Indian) Division's sector progress had been faster, as there were more bridges over the Rapido across which tanks and infantry could be passed into the bridgehead. Sant' Angelo fell to Boucher's brigade during the late afternoon after prolonged and difficult fighting amongst the ruins and cellars of the village. South of Sant' Angelo Dobree's brigade, supported by Canadian tanks, made steady progress clearing the defences of the river and the Liri Appendix, but had to beat off a number of counter-attacks launched by battalions of 15 Panzer Grenadier Division which had been thrown into the battle in the same wasteful way that was occurring in the French sector south of the Liri. By dusk on 13 May Dudley Russell could report that two thirds of the Sant' Angelo Horseshoe were in his hands.

With substantial progress being made by both assault divisions, Oliver Leese decided that the time had come to make another co-ordinated Army attack to cut Route 6 and to pinch out Cassino. He ordered Kirkman to commit his reserve, Charles Keightley's 78 (Br) Division, in order to maintain the momentum of the attack in the Liri Valley in a north-westerly direction. At the same time he instructed Anders to be ready to renew the Polish attack on Colle Sant' Angelo and the Monastery. He estimated that it would take most of 14 May to bring 78 (Br) Division to within striking distance of Route 6 and so he ordered Anders to prepare his attack for the morning of 15 May.

The XIII (Br) Corps' order putting these instructions into effect was issued just before 10 p.m. on 13 May. 78 (Br) Division was to cross the Rapido, using three bridges near Sant' Angelo—Congo, London and Oxford, but at Corps headquarters no one was quite sure which bridges, if any, would be open and available. The account in Alexander's des-patches ascribes the slowness of 78 (Br) Division's appearances in the bridgehead to difficulties in crossing the Rapido. Unfortunately, many of these difficulties were staff-made and caused by inaccurate assessments of the conditions at the bridge sites and of the abilities of the sappers to overcome the dearth of approach and exit tracks which doubled the difficulties of bridging. Neither London (at Sant' Angelo) nor Congo (north of Sant' Angelo) had, in fact, been built when the Corps order for 78 (Br) Division's advance was issued. Work at London could not start until Sant' Angelo had been cleared and this did not happen until the late afternoon. As London was to be a heavy forty-ton bridge needed for the Corps centre line, it could not possibly be completed much before dawn on 14 May. Work at Congo had not started for a much simpler reason. No one had told the Commander, Royal Engineers, of 4 (Br) Division that the bridge was wanted that night. He did not hear of the requirement until the Corps order reached his divisional headquarters. With the best will in the world he could not get a field squadron to the site before midnight. It took until 8 a.m. on 14 May to build the bridge and to strengthen the approaches and exits sufficiently to take 78 (Br)

Division's traffic. The only other bridges available were Amazon, Oxford and Plymouth. Plymouth was still causing trouble but this was to be expected as it had only been intended to act as a temporary assault bridge. Amazon was needed by 4 (Br) Division to reinforce and resupply its bridgehead during the night. Oxford was similarly needed by 8 (Indian) Division to move its reserve brigade, Brigadier Mould's 21 (Indian) Brigade, into the bridgehead and to resupply the Indian infantry and Canadian tanks after their hard day's fighting. 78 (Br) Division's units had to be sent forward to these two bridges as spaces occurred in the 4 (Br) and 8 (Indian) Divisions' traffic over them. As luck would have it, Amazon bridge was blocked for three hours during the night by some ammunition trucks which had been hit and set on fire near the bridge.

The slow move of 78 (Br) Division into the bridgehead was the first of a series of errors in staff work and movement control which was to mar Eighth Army's actions in the Diadem offensive and confirm in many people's minds what Juin had been saying during planning, that Eighth Army was too ponderous and far too lavishly equipped for this type of campaign. The French Expeditionary Corps depending on pack animals and about half the amount of the transport of the British formations, moved three times as fast over more difficult country. XIII (Br) Corps made only half-hearted attempts to force units to operate on light scales and to leave behind all the mass of transport which had been needed for the mobile warfare to which Eighth Army was so accustomed. The result was that whenever reserves were ordered forward, they either arrived late or could not get forward at all. 78 (Br) Division spent a frustrating night trying to cross the Rapido by non-existent or already overcrowded bridges. Its leading brigade—Brigadier Scott's 38 (Irish) Brigade—did not start assembling in the bridgehead until the afternoon of 14 May.

Meanwhile 4 (Br) and 8 (Indian) Divisions had been getting into their stride. Two days' constant pounding from artillery and air was beginning to have its effect on the German defenders. Most of the forward positions of the Gustav Line in the Liri Valley itself had been overrun. On the German side, Feurstein hoped to send Ortner enough reinforcements to stabilise a new line along the Cassino–Pignataro road. Between Cassino and Pioppeto, Heidrich's Parachute MG Battalion still covered the southern outskirts of Cassino; then came Schulz's 'ad hoc' group based on the 3/1 Parachute Battalion, reinforced by units from 114 Jaeger Division and 5 Mountain Division whose Apennine sectors had not been heavily attacked; and finally, the remnants of 115 Panzer Grenadier Regiment blocked the line of advance along the Pioppeto. To the south of the Pioppeto 8 (Indian) Division was still opposed by the original Bode Group, reinforced by units raked up from all over the front. Feurstein intended to commit the leading regiment of 90 Panzer Grenadier Division in Bode's sector as soon as it arrived.

14 May opened on 4 (Br) Division's front with a rapid advance by Heber-Percy's 12 (Br) Brigade towards the Cassino–Pignataro road which began at 5 a.m. The leading battalion, 6 Black Watch, moving in close company with its supporting tanks of the Lothian and Border Horse and working on a compass bearing, passed undetected between a number of German positions in the thick early-morning mist and crossed the road which Feurstein had intended as his new main line of resistance. The Black Watch had just time to dig in on their objective when the mist rose and revealed their isolated position. The two other battalions of the brigade—the Royal Fusiliers on the Black Watch's right and the West Kents on their left—had not been so lucky in advancing through the German defences and were some way behind the Black Watch on either flank. 4 (Br) Division's historian comments: 'Nobody counted the counter-attacks that broke against the position during the rest of the day.' All were thrown back, but there were many anxious moments as Dudley Ward organised fresh attacks by Montague-Douglas-Scott's and Shoesmith's brigades to protect Heber-Percy's flanks which suffered constant counter-attacks by German tanks and infantry until nightfall. It was not until late afternoon that Scott's 38 (Irish) Brigade of 78 (Br) Division came up on the exposed southern flank of Heber-Percy's 12 (Br) Brigade.

After crossing the Rapido, 78 (Br) Division had run into further difficulties. Traffic congestion, soft makeshift approaches to the new bridges, shelling and mortar fire and uncleared minefields had all taken their toll as Charles Keightley's division moved into the bridgehead to take its place between 4 (Br) and 8 (Indian) Divisions and to prepare its attack northwestwards to Route 6. Any chance of mounting that attack on 14 May had gone. The most urgent need was the protection of 12 (Br) Brigade's southern flank. The morning of 15 May would be the earliest that any coordinated attack could be mounted. Consequently Oliver Leese had to postpone the Polish attack on Colle Sant' Angelo and

decided not to give a new date for its resumption until the effect of
Charles Keightley's operations on 15 May could be assessed.

In the Indian sector progress through the heavily-cultivated and
broken country around the Sant' Angelo Horseshoe was slow and
laborious. The intensive training in tank–infantry cooperation carried
out by the Indian battalions with their supporting Canadian tank regiments paid great dividends as they worked their way forward against the
Bode Group. The Liri Appendix was evacuated by the Germans during
the night 13–14 May in conformity with Raapke's 71 Division's withdrawal on the south bank of the Liri. As the Indians approached the
Pignataro–Cassino lateral German resistance stiffened as it had done in
front of 4 (Br) Division to the north. Von Vietinghoff had by now issued
instructions to both the German Corps to stabilise the front on the line
Cassino–Pignataro–San Giorgio–Ausonia–Formia to enable Feurstein's
Corps to continue the defence of Cassino. The same evening Oliver
Leese ordered General Burns to move the Canadian Corps forward
to its assembly areas ready to cross the Rapido and to pass through
the Indian division in an attempt to break through the Hitler Line
before the Germans had time to settle into its defences. Von Vietinghoff had no intention at that stage of falling back so far. He hoped to
form a new front well forward of this long-stop position, but he was as
yet unaware of the disaster which was overwhelming Raapke's 71
Division.

The German High Command suffered more acutely than usual from
the fog of war during 12, 13 and 14 May. The disruption of German
communications by persistent Allied bombing of all known headquarter
areas, the constant fighter-bomber attacks on all movement behind the
German lines, and the continuous artillery bombardment in the forward
areas which disrupted tactical communications all had a cumulative
effect. Furthermore, the German divisional and regimental commanders were kept so busy that they failed to report events to their
superiors as often or as quickly as they would normally have done.
Kesselring complained bitterly:

> it is intolerable that troops could be in fighting contact with the enemy
> for two days without knowing whom they are fighting. . . . The Army
> Group was not in possession of data on which to make a far reaching
> decision on 14 or 15 May.

So far the only mobile division to be ordered southwards was

Baade's 90 Panzer Grenadier Division. Its 200 Panzer Grenadier Regiment was approaching Pontecorvo when it received orders to move south of the Liri to help extricate Raapke's 71 Division and to stop the French advance along the south bank of the Liri. Its second regiment, 361 Panzer Grenadier Regiment, did not receive orders to move forward for a further twenty-four hours and could not reach the Bode Group in the Liri Valley until the evening of 15 May. Ortner's chances of holding Kirkman's Corps at bay on the Cassino–Pignataro line for this extra twenty-four hours were very slender indeed, but Kesselring—always an optimist—seems to have been convinced that it was still possible to hold forward of the Hitler Line.

This might have been possible if von Senger had been in command of his XIV Panzer Corps and Juin had not been commanding the French Expeditionary Corps. As early as the evening of 12 May, Juin had ordered Guillaume's Tabors of Goumiers to cross the Garigliano with their supporting mule trains and pack artillery. When Castelforte had fallen on the evening of 12 May, the Tabors had moved silently through the ruins of the town during the night and had lain concealed amongst the hills to the west of the town throughout 13 May while the fighting had been going on to clear Majo and the hills between Castelforte and the Ausonia road. On the night 13–14 May, Juin issued his orders for putting his carefully prepared plan for breaking through the Aurunci chain into effect. The conditions were just right. 71 Division was falling back north-eastwards on Ausonia, and 94 Division was being pressed back by Keyes' Corps in a north-westerly direction along Route 7 and the coast. The gap between the two German divisions was widening and in between them lay the Aurunci escarpment, almost undefended.

Juin's planning proved excellent in execution as well as concept. Monsabert's 3 (Algerian) Division took over the frontal drive on Ausonia from Sevez's 4 (Moroccan) Division so that the latter could link up with their respective Groups of Tabors to form the two mountain forces— Guillaume's 1 and 4 Groups of Tabors with 1 Moroccan Infantry Regiment and Bondis' 3 Group of Tabors and 6 Moroccan Infantry Regiment. This regrouping was completed early on 14 May and the advance of the Mountain Corps was soon under way. Progress was slow during the day, but by evening Guillaume's Group was overlooking the Ausonia road and Bondis' Group was half-way to Ausonia, only opposed by German rearguards.

In Keyes' II (US) Corps sector 14 May was a turning point. Stein-

metz, despite his optimistic order of the day on 13 May, realised that the
withdrawal of Raapke's troops on Ausonia had made his position un-
tenable on the coast and that he would have to disengage and withdraw
rapidly to the Senger Line if he was not to be surrounded and cut off on
the coast. XIV Panzer Corps authorised his withdrawal which started
before dawn on 14 May. When Keyes' divisions attacked during the day

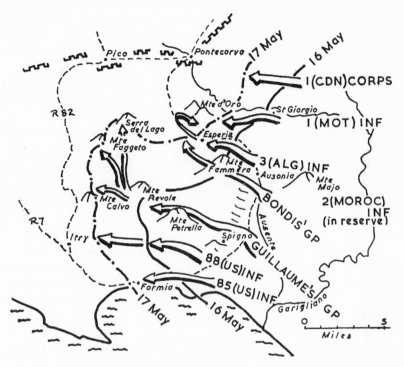

23   *Fifth Army's operations, 15–17 May*

the Germans gave ground relatively easily and by nightfall 88 (US)
Division was approaching Spigno at the foot of the Auruncis, and
85 (US) Division had cleared the Gustav defences blocking Route 7 on
the coast. Steinmetz's 94 Division, like all German infantry divisions,
depended on horse-drawn artillery and transport and so disengagement
could not be rapid. It lost over 1,000 prisoners to Keyes' Corps as it
broke contact and fell back towards Formia.

15 to 17 May was a period of sweeping and decisive movement on
Mark Clark's Fifth Army front. Led by Guillaume's Mountain Corps

which pushed its way almost unopposed through the mountains, Juin's French divisions to the north and Keyes' American divisions to the south hurled the disintegrating XIV Panzer Corps back towards the Senger Line with accelerating success.

Early on 15 May Guillaume's own force of 1 and 4 Group of Tabors crossed the Ausente and started scaling the Aurunci escarpment just north of Spigno. Guillaume divided his force into light and supporting echelons. The light echelon scaled the cliffs, while the supporting echelon carrying the heavier equipment waited until a firm lodgement had been made. The force then made its way up the tortuous mountain trails with the first echelon pushing on ahead as fast as it could to the next objective while the supporting echelon made its way up more slowly to join the first echelon before it went ahead again. No opposition was met and by early morning on 16 May Guillaume had secured a firm base on Monte Revole, some twelve miles west of the Ausente and almost within artillery range of the Itri-Pico road which was the Germans' main lateral road between their two Corps. If Guillaume could cut this road, he would make it extremely difficult for XIV Panzer Corps to reform on a new defensive front based on the Senger Line running from the Hitler Line at Pontecorvo to Pico and thence to Fondi and Terracina on the coast.

Guillaume had to use most of 16 May to allow his support echelon to catch up and to give his exhausted men and mules a rest before starting on the decisive phase of his advance. He had two objectives. Firstly, he wished to cut the Itri–Pico road. Secondly, he wished to reach the hills above Pico to forestall any attempt the Germans might make to stand on the Hitler-Senger Line. His pack howitzers reached Monte Revole during 16 May, but did not have sufficient range to reach the road along which his forward patrols could see the Germans withdrawing in front of Keyes' Corps.

During 17 May Guillaume advanced again, but this time fanning out from his Monte Revole base in three columns. One struck due west to cut the Itri–Pico road at Monte Calvo which it reached unopposed. As soon as it started to interfere with movement on the road the Germans reacted, counter-attacking with tanks and self-propelled guns from 15 Panzer Grenadier Division, but they were unable to drive the Goumiers off completely or to clear the road from French artillery fire. The other two columns struck north-westwards towards Pico and succeeded in reaching Monte Faggeto and Serra del Lago about eight kilometres from

15   *Units moving over 'London' bridge to reinforce the bridgehead*

THE BRIDGEHEAD

16   *The scissors bridge over the Pioppeto stream*

17   *Tanks and infantry waiting for the final advance to cut Route 6 on 17 May*

CUTTING ROUTE 6

18   *Infantry advancing towards Route 6 late on 17 May. (Note the quantity of smoke still being used to mask the Monastery)*

Pico, where they were forced to consolidate as they found German infantry and tanks barring their way. By now the supply position of Guillaume's force was becoming precarious. Thirty-six bombers from the Allied Tactical Air Command dropped some forty tons of mixed supplies to the force on 17 May, but increasing German resistance made a further advance beyond the protection of the mountains too risky. Guillaume's force had achieved its aim in a remarkable fashion. XIV Panzer Corps, with its front split by Guillaume's force, was quite unable to stabilise any new defensive position, and was forced to abandon a succession of potentially strong positions by his appearance on the main Itri–Pico lateral and above Pico.

Bondis' Group was just as successful. Advancing rapidly up the Ausente during 14 May in the wake of Raapke's withdrawal, Bondis reached Ausonia by nightfall but made no attempt to take the town. He left his infantry to contain it until Monsabert's Algerians could arrive on 15 May, and struck westwards into the hills with his Goumiers. Advancing through the night he scaled the Monte Fammera end of the Aurunci escarpment the following morning and started his march through the hills to outflank the next potential German position in the Esperia defile. By dawn on 17 May his Goumiers were concentrated with their supporting infantry in the hills a mile and a half south of Esperia.

Monsabert's 3 (Algerian) Division took Ausonia early on 15 May and met Dody's 2 (Moroccan) Division, which had cleared the Monte Majo Massif, just north of Ausonia. Dody's division had completed its task of breaking the southern bastion of the Liri defences and was pulled back, as Juin had planned, into reserve. Monsabert pressed on northwards hoping to hustle the Germans out of Esperia without a fight, but ran into the leading elements of 90 Panzer Grenadier Division's 200 Panzer Grenadier Regiment. The pace slowed as the French, for the first time, met rearguards provided by a German mobile division. It was not until 17 May that Monsabert was in a position to attack Esperia and Brosset's 1 (Motorised) Division had cleared San Giorgio on the Liri.

Monsabert's attack on Esperia was launched during the morning of 17 May and was completely successful, the German rearguards withdrawing before they were heavily engaged. Elements of 15 Panzer Grenadier Division brought up from the coast were identified in the area and it began to look as if the Germans might be able to stabilise the front on the extension of the Hitler Line whose fixed defences ended at Sant' Oliva three miles west of Esperia behind a stream called the Forme

Quesa. This impression was increased when Monsabert's leading regiment was successfully ambushed while pursuing the Germans withdrawing from Esperia. Caught in a well-laid trap, the French fell back to Esperia. Monte d'Oro which lies between the Liri and the Esperia–Sant' Oliva road was clearly held in strength. There were also extensive minefields laid between the mountain and the Liri which brought Brosset's advance to a halt as well. The French had reached the Hitler Line and

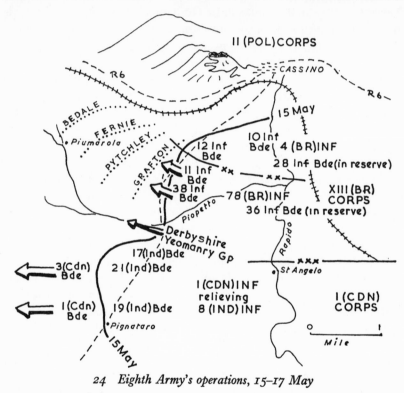

24 *Eighth Army's operations, 15–17 May*

were beginning to meet more coordinated and better equipped opponents.

Back in the Liri Valley events were moving to a climax. After the disappointing efforts of 78 (Br) Division to cross the Rapido on 14 May, its concentration was completed in the bridgehead during the night 14–15 May. New and less ambitious plans were made for it to advance on a two brigade front in a great north-westerly wheel towards Route 6. Coordination was to be ensured by using four report lines—Grafton,

Pytchley, Fernie and Bedale. The first was approximately on the line of 4 (Br) Division's third objective—Red Line—which it had almost but not quite reached. The fourth was 700 yards south of Route 6 from which any German withdrawal could be stopped. 4 (Br) Division was to conform by advancing towards Route 6 on the inner side of the wheel, and 78 (Br) Division's southern flank was to be protected by 6 (Br) Armoured Division's Derbyshire Yeomanry Group. The latter consisted of Colonel Payne Galway's Derbyshire Yeomanry, the division's armoured reconnaissance regiment, and 10 Rifle Brigade, which was the motor battalion of Mitchell's 26 (Br) Armoured Brigade. 26 (Br) Armoured Brigade itself was to provide the tank support for 78 (Br) Division.

Charles Keightley hoped to reach Pytchley by the end of 15 May, but things did not go well. Grafton, his start line, was, in fact, strongly held by the Schulz Group. In consequence both of his assault brigades—Brigadier Arbuthnott's 11 Brigade on the right and Brigadier Scott's 38 Brigade on the left—had to fight for their start lines as they moved up to their forming-up positions during the night. Grafton was not completely cleared until the following evening after a day's hard and disjointed fighting. It was then too late for 78 (Br) Division to launch its attack towards Pytchley during 15 May. The extent of the opposition on Grafton is shown by the fact that the Inniskilling Fusiliers collected 126 prisoners from the area which was to have been its start line.

During the night 15–16 May more careful preparations were made for 78 (Br) Division's attack next day. These included an artillery barrage to ensure that the attack did not again miscarry. In 8 (Indian) Division's sector progress during 15 May had been methodical but encouraging. The whole of the Horseshoe was taken and the village of Pignataro fell just before dark after a very brisk fight. 90 Panzer Grenadier Division's second regiment arrived just too late to save the town.

During the night, Oliver Leese gave Burns the 'go ahead' to pass through Dudley Russell's Indians and to start the planned advance to the Hitler Line. Burns ordered Vokes' 1 (Canadian) Division to take over the Indian front brigade by brigade on successive nights; Brigadier Spry's 1 (Canadian) Brigade would take over the southern half of the front while Brigadier Bernatchez's 3 (Canadian) Brigade would take over the northern half. Vokes himself would take command of the whole sector late on 16 May.

78 (Br) Division's much-delayed attack opened at 9 a.m. on 16 May. Its two leading brigades advanced abreast from Grafton to Pytchley

behind a barrage fired by seven regiments. By midday, Pytchley was reached, though German opposition had been as determined and German shelling as intense as ever. 4 (Br) Division on the inner side of the wheel also attacked and overran a number of the parachute MG battalion's positions, capturing some at bayonet point. Parachutist prisoners taken during this attack had only given up because there was no ammunition left in their weapon pits. No food or supplies of any kind had reached them for the last two days.

Opposition in front of the two divisions showed no signs of slackening during the afternoon. On the contrary, German positions on the outer flank of the wheel were still holding out against the Derbyshire Yeomanry Group and it took a further five hours to clear this opposition. The 10 Rifle Brigade eventually captured the German position which was causing the trouble, taking 300 prisoners and over twenty anti-tank guns. By then, it was again too late in the day to mount another formal tank and infantry attack from Pytchley to Fernie and Bedale. Oliver Leese, however, judged the moment to be right for coordinating the action of Kirkman and Anders for the final battle of Cassino.

At 10.35 p.m. Oliver Leese issued orders for Anders and Kirkman to launch a concerted attack at 7 a.m. on the following morning, 17 May, to encircle Heidrich's force on Monte Cassino and in Cassino town. 78 (Br) Division was to repeat the previous days' tactics by continuing the wheel with 11 and 38 (Br) Brigades still leading and again attacking with tanks and infantry advancing together behind a barrage from Pytchley to Fernie and Bedale. Anders' Poles would again attack with their two divisions making for the same objectives as before; but this time they had had time to patrol and get to know the German positions much more thoroughly than had been possible before their first attack on 11–12 May. They had analysed the reasons for their failure and were now ready to profit by their previous misfortunes.

At about the same time that Oliver Leese issued his orders for the final battle, von Vietinghoff was doing the same thing. In a conversation with Kesselring earlier in the evening, he had reported the penetration of the Pignataro–Cassino Line. Kesselring had by this time realised the enormity of the disaster which had overwhelmed XIV Panzer Corps. His intelligence staff had also identified the Canadian Corps by wireless intercept in the Liri Valley instead of at Salerno or at sea. He now knew where he was and could take counter-measures to restore the situation. Two things had to be done at once: Feurstein's Corps had to be withdrawn to the Hitler Line before it was too late and the French break-through round the southern flank of the line had to be stopped on the Senger extension. In his telephone conversation with von Vietinghoff, which is recorded by the Canadian official historian, Kesselring said:

. . . I consider withdrawal to the Senger Line necessary.

von Vietinghoff: Then it will be necessary to begin the withdrawal north of the Liri; tanks have broken through there.

Kesselring: How far?

von Vietinghoff: To 39 (two miles north-west of Pignataro).

Kesselring: And how about farther north?

von Vietinghoff: There are about 100 tanks in Schulz's area.

Kesselring: Then we have to give up Cassino?

von Vietinghoff: Yes.

Kesselring then authorised the abandonment of Cassino and the withdrawal to the Hitler Line. He also ordered von Mackensen to dispatch 26 Panzer Division to oppose the French south of the Liri at Sant' Oliva, instead of keeping it waiting in Fourteenth Army reserve to oppose any attempt by Truscott to break out from Anzio. Von Mackensen objected strongly to Kesselring's removal of this powerful force from his command and as a result 26 Panzer Division moved forward later than Kesselring had intended and arrived in the Pico area in a piecemeal fashion. This was one of the first arguments between Kesselring and von Mackensen which eventually led to the latter's dismissal at the end of the battle.

Feurstein's plan for the withdrawal north of the Liri was to give Heidrich charge of the northern half of the valley and Baade, the commander of 90 Panzer Grenadier Division, the southern half opposite the Canadians. Each was to provide the rearguards through which the less mobile infantry units would withdraw. Heidrich was determined not to give up Cassino a moment earlier than was necessary and in consequence decided to hold on with his parachute troops longer than was wise. Baade to the south took up a position along the small tributary of the Liri, called the Forme d'Aquino (*see fig. 27*), with his mobile troops to cover the withdrawal of Bode's scratch force of infantry into the southern half of the Hitler Line. Thus, when Oliver Leese's coordinated attack started at 7 a.m. on 17 May, Anders and Kirkman met violent resistance from Heidrich's troops while Burns' Canadians found themselves opposed only by the skilful rearguards of Baade's well-trained and experienced division until they reached the Forme d'Aquino.

The second Polish attempt to seal off Cassino was an excellent example of careful planning and coordination of all arms. In the breathing space which followed the disastrous first attack, Anders' men reorganised their shattered units and set about identifying and wearing down every German position which might oppose them when the order came to attack again. Sudden bursts of shelling, simulating the start of another Polish attack, were used to make the Germans disclose the positions of

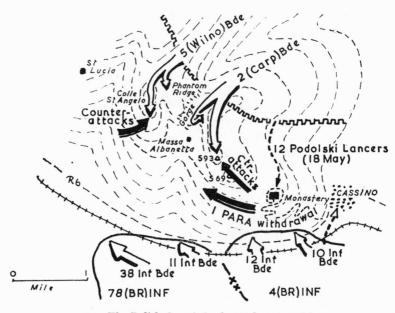

25   *The Polish Corps' final attack, 17–18 May*

their weapons and the areas in which their defensive artillery and mortar fire would be brought down. Night patrols revealed many of the hidden obstacles in the way of the Polish attack and also the fact that the Germans had not weakened their garrisons appreciably on the main Polish objectives. For the four days between the two Polish attacks Allied fighter-bombers saturated the German gun positions in the Atina Valley, and Polish artillery and mortars searched the western slopes of Monte Cassino to destroy or damage German communications and mortar positions. Polish tanks and sappers working in close cooperation managed to clear lanes through the minefield in the Gorge leading to Massa Albanetta.

In analysing the causes of their first failure the Poles concluded that it had been due to three things: by the fortuitous doubling of the German garrison by the relief which was in progress when the Poles attacked; by the overestimate of the damage likely to be caused by Allied artillery preparation which had led to the Poles preferring artillery concentrations rather than a barrage; and, thirdly, by the loss of control caused by German defensive fire rupturing Polish communications. The first was unlikely to occur again. In fact it seemed fairly certain that the three original German battalions opposing the Poles had been called upon to provide reinforcements for the hard-pressed German units in the valley below, and so they were likely to be under rather than over strength this time. The second—the overestimate of Allied artillery capability—was rectified by continued bombardment and by all units being ordered to follow much closer behind the artillery concentrations as they lifted from target to target. And the third—loss of control—was corrected by reducing distances between assembly, forming-up positions and start lines and, of course, by avoiding areas known to be subject to German defensive fire. The overall Polish Corps plan was identical to the first except for timings which were modified to take account of the greater speeds possible in daylight.

Sulik's 5 (Kresowan) Division's attack on the Phantom Ridge and then Colle Sant' Angelo was given an unexpected bonus during the night 16–17 May. A company from the leading battalion detailed for the attack on Phantom Ridge the following morning was sent out as a battle patrol to reconnoitre the ridge soon after dusk and succeeded in over-running a number of German positions on the northern end. Encouraged by this success the battalion commander sent forward the rest of his battalion in small parties. By midnight the whole battalion with artillery observers were in position on the ridge. The German garrison counter-attacked at dawn but failed to retake the position. When the Corps artillery opened fire with the planned preliminary bombardment the Polish follow-up battalion had no difficulty in sweeping forward to seize Colle Sant' Angelo. Its advance was so quick that it was missed by the German defensive fire which landed amongst the unlucky ammunition porters following the battalion. Most of Colle Sant' Angelo was cleared without much difficulty, but this was only the start of the battle. As further Polish battalions came forward to continue the attack across the remaining false crests above the Liri Valley, they came under heavy fire directed from Passo de Corno and Villa Santa Lucia. Then the German counter-attacks started. Two were repulsed but the Poles were beginning to run short of ammunition—particularly of grenades—and the third German attack regained the southern end of Colle Sant' Angelo. This was not recaptured by the Poles until they launched a further coordinated attack, preceded by artillery and mortar bombardments, just as daylight was beginning to fade. Colle Sant' Angelo was at last firmly in their hands but too late for there to be any chance of linking up with 78 (Br) Division until the next day. The Germans had suffered severely but so had Sulik's men. The only reserves left with which to continue the battle were the divisional anti-tank and anti-aircraft regiments. Little more could be done that night than bringing up these troops and reorganising the ground gained during the day ready for another effort the following morning. The German positions around Colle Sant' Angelo seemed to be held as strongly as ever.

Duch's 3 (Carpathian) Division attack was less successful. The 2 (Carpathian) Brigade was to attack with two battalions up: one battalion was to neutralise Massa Albanetta until the Kresowan division was on Colle Sant' Angelo and then to capture it; and the other was to clear the Snake's Head Ridge, taking in succession Point 593, Point 569 and finally the Monastery. Attacking at 7 a.m. the Albanetta battalion cleared the Gorge, but found lifting the remaining mines and clearing a path for its supporting tanks took longer than expected. As Phantom Ridge had fallen to the Kresowan division, Duch decided not to wait for the fall of Albanetta before launching the attack on Point 593. The attack started at 9.23 a.m. but was met with immediate German counter-attacks and it was not until 11.30 a.m. that Point 593 was in Polish hands. As in all the previous attacks, taking Point 593 was easier than holding it, and certainly easier than trying to attack from it towards Point 569 and the Monastery. Under heavy machine-gun and mortar fire the Polish battalion on Point 593 began to wither away. The reserve battalion of 2 (Carpathian) Brigade was brought up to press the attack, but towards evening it became clear that no more progress would be made until Massa Albanetta was taken. All the efforts of the battalion detailed for this task failed. Its tanks were stopped by more mines which could not be cleared in daylight. The Germans allowed the Polish infantry to come within 200 yards of their Albanetta positions and then decimated them by fire from well-hidden and heavily-protected small

19 *The Monastery after its capture by the Poles*

THE FALL OF CASSINO

20 *British patrols in the ruins of Cassino town*

21 *Castelforte nestling at the foot of the Monte Majo Massif*

THE FRENCH ADVANCE

22 *A French supply column making its way up to Monte Majo*

steel pillboxes. The Carpathian division, like the Kresowan, had been fought to a standstill and took up defensive positions for the night with only one of its objectives taken and held—Point 593. Although news from XIII (Br) Corps in the valley below suggested that Heidrich would probably evacuate Cassino and the Monastery during the night, Anders' men were too exhausted and disorganised to force a way over the crest of Monte Cassino to bring the southern slopes under fire.

In the valley, 78 (Br) Division started to attack again at the same time as the Poles. German resistance was sharp at first, but as the day wore on the effect of Feurstein's orders to start thinning out for the withdrawal to the Hitler Line began to show. German counter-attacks became less frequent and their retaliatory fire less intense. Scott brought all three of his Irish battalions into the line and pressed north-westwards meeting stiff resistance from parachute rearguards in the village of Piumarola in which the Inniskillings captured 150 paratroopers. By nightfall 78 (Br) Division had almost reached Bedale, its final objective.

Meanwhile Dudley Ward had ordered Heber-Percy's 12 Brigade to attack due north in an endeavour to cut Route 6. The leading battalion, 2 Royal Fusiliers, met surprisingly little resistance and by midday it had reached the railway just south of Route 6 and soon afterwards its leading patrols were on the road. The rest of the brigade, supported by New Zealand tanks, followed up and were firmly astride the road by nightfall. Any of Heidrich's force still in Cassino would have to scramble along the steep rocky side of Monte Cassino if they were to escape by daylight the following day. A strong-enough cordon could not be pushed up the southern slopes of Monte Cassino to cut this escape route during the dark and so the known tracks on the hillside were harassed with artillery fire all night to make the German escape more difficult. During the night small parties of Germans ran into 12 Brigade ambushes on the lower slopes, but the great majority of Heidrich's force slipped away.

At dawn on 18 May Dudley Ward sent Shoesmith's 10 Brigade into the ruins of Cassino. From cellars and dugouts small parties of Germans emerged to give themselves up and by midday the town was in Allied hands but by no means clear. Mines, traps and, in some cases, fanatical paratroopers who had not received the order to withdraw, went on taking a toll of British soldiers' lives. On the hills above the town the German rearguards still held Massa Albanetta and Point 569. It was not until midday that these were finally cleared by 2 (Carpathian) Brigade. Meanwhile, a patrol from 12 Podolski Lancers had worked its way forward and had reached the ruins of the Monastery. The few remaining Germans were mostly wounded and it did not take much to persuade the commander to surrender with his thirty survivors. The Polish standard was broken over the ruins at 10.20 a.m. on 18 May. The Final Battle of Cassino was over.

Act II The Hitler-Senger Line

'It is unusual for a beaten Army to stop at a line of entrenchment which has been dug for them in the rear unless there is another considerable force already holding this line.'

Churchill to Alexander, 17 May 1944

Chronology
Act II The Hitler-Senger Line
19–25 May

	Fifth Army	*Eighth Army*	*German Army*
19 May	Reaches original Diadem objective from Itri to Pontecorvo.	Attempts by XIII (Br) and Canadian Corps to rush Hitler Line fail.	All German troops south of Liri fall back to Senger Line; 29 Panzer Grenadier Division ordered to Terracina.
20 May	French start battle of Pico; II (US) Corps take Fondi.	Canadians prepare to assault Hitler Line (Operation Chesterfield).	305 and 334 Divisions ordered across from Adriatic coast to Pico.
21 May	French lose and retake Monte Leucio.	Canadians probe Pontecorvo with French.	26 Panzer Division counter-attacks French at Pico.
	Alexander orders break-out from Anzio and assault on Hitler Line to start on 23 May		
22 May	French enter Pico; and II (US) Corps reaches Terracina defile.	Abortive Canadian attack on Pontecorvo delays regrouping for Chesterfield.	29 Panzer Grenadier Division attempts to hold Terracina.
23 May	Break-out from Anzio starts.	Canadians breach Hitler Line.	Hermann Göring Division released by OKW for use at Anzio.
24 May	Terracina falls to II (US) Corps.	Canadian armour breaks through and reaches Melfa.	1 Parachute Division continues to hold northern half of Hitler Line blocking XIII (Br) Corps.
25 May	II (US) Corps patrols make contact with VI (US) Corps at Borgo Grappa.	Crossing of the Melfa by Canadian and XIII (Br) Corps.	Kesselring authorises withdrawal to Caesar Line.

8 The Attempt to Rush the Hitler Line

'I have ordered Eighth Army to use the utmost energy to break through the Adolf Hitler Line in the Liri Valley before the Germans have time to settle down in it.'

Alexander to Churchill, 18 May 1944

Alexander had won the first round of Diadem. The occupation of Cassino by Dudley Ward's 4 (Br) Division and breaking the Polish standard over the ruins of the Monastery symbolised the end of the Gustav Line, but only the end of the first act of the Battle for Rome. Kesselring had been deceived as to the weight and timing of the Allies' attack, and he had been fooled into withholding his mobile divisions until too late, but he was far from beaten. He had always expected a tough fight when the spring came and he had taken the precaution of building the Hitler Line to block Route 6, and of flooding the Pontine marshes to submerge Route 7. In addition he had authorised von Senger when he commanded the whole of the western sector, to plan and partially fortify the extension of the Hitler Line from Sant' Oliva via Pico, Fondi and Terracina to the sea. Von Senger's extension ran along the eastern edge of the Ausoni Hills—the next Massif west of the Auruncis. It was not much more than a line on the map with prepared positions reconnoitred and, in some cases, dug to block the roads and tracks through the line. It could, however, serve as a rallying position for divisions falling back from the Gustav Line. The country was naturally suitable for defence and so the Senger Line offered a fair chance of bringing any Allied advance to a halt whether it was fully fortified or not. As soon as Kesselring authorised von Vietinghoff to issue his orders late on 16 May for the evacuation of Cassino and the occupation of the Hitler Line, every effort was made to form a new front on the Hitler-Senger Line. Appreciating that they might have withdrawn too late from Cassino to man the new line effectively, the German staff began to refer to the whole line as the Senger Line in case it failed to live up to the Führer's name.

A withdrawal is the most delicate of all the operations of war. The balance between a planned withdrawal and a rout is very fine indeed. The first rule is to ensure that the new main position, to which a force is to withdraw, is at least partially manned by rested, if not entirely fresh, troops, before the old position is given up. More often than not when a withdrawal becomes necessary, there are very few fresh troops left in reserve and so those already fighting in the existing front line have to be progressively thinned out and sent back to occupy the new line without the attacker detecting their withdrawal. Those who are left have to make up for those who have gone back by greater activity and greater use of weapons, particularly artillery. If an army stays too long on its old position it risks being so weakened that it has too little left with which to defend its new line. On the other hand, if it does not stay long enough, there may not be sufficient time in which to organise and man the new defences. The attacker's aim is to rout the defender by breaking through the existing front before the final withdrawal is ordered so that he can beat the defender in the race back to the new line and break it before he can settle into it properly. In the case of the German Army there was a further complication. The majority of the German divisions were infantry divisions in which the troops marched and artillery and supply transport was horse-drawn. Only the panzer, panzer grenadier and parachute divisions had a mobility comparable to the Allied divisions. Whenever a battle became fluid on the Italian front Kesselring was forced to use all his mobile divisions to cover the withdrawal of his infantry. Thus one of the first moves in Feurstein's disengagement had been the withdrawal of Ortner's 44 Division headquarters and its replacement by Heidrich's 1 Parachute Division opposite Kirkman's Corps, covering the northern half of the valley, and by Baade's 90 Panzer Grenadier Division, covering the southern half opposite the Canadians. These two divisions provided the mobile troops to hold the Allies at bay while the Hitler Line was being manned.

Knowing that the Hitler Line existed, Oliver Leese hoped to achieve a sudden break-through in the Liri Valley which would allow him to rush Feurstein's new main position. Feurstein, with both Kesselring and von Vietinghoff breathing down his neck, had to ensure that such a break did not occur. Up to 17 May all had been well. The test would come on 18 May when Eighth Army ceased to be pre-occupied with the capture of Monte Cassino. Only rearguards would be facing Kirkman's XIII (Br) Corps and Burns' Canadians, but those rearguards would be provided by two of the best divisions in the German Army.

Kesselring himself had few anxieties about the Hitler Line: Heidrich and Baade could be trusted to hold it whatever happened. It was the Senger extension which caused him most concern. The French were already in front of Sant' Oliva, just south of Pontecorvo, and were astride the Pico–Itri road heading for the naturally strongest but most weakly-held centre of the line around Lenola. 26 Panzer Division had arrived in

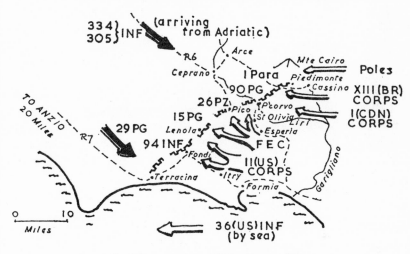

26   *The race to the Hitler-Senger Line*

the Pico area and had been committed piecemeal against the French in an attempt to give XIV Panzer Corps some new coherence. It had suffered heavy losses in its engagements with the French and from Allied air attacks and was clearly unable to stop the French mountain troops in country so unsuitable for tanks. Kesselring ordered von Vietinghoff to transfer 305 and 334 Infantry Divisions from the Adriatic sector to reinforce 26 Panzer Division in the Pico area. The remnants of 15 Panzer Grenadier and 94 Divisions were struggling to build up the southern half of the Senger Line opposite Keyes' II (US) Corps, but they too were clearly not strong enough to hold the long stretch of front from Lenola through Fondi to Terracina, and so Kesselring ordered 29 Panzer Grenadier Division south from Civitavecchia with the twin tasks of first, to block any attempted break out by Truscott from Anzio in a south-easterly direction to meet Keyes advancing up Route 7, and, secondly, to stop Keyes' advance through the Terracina defile. 29 Panzer Grenadier Division was the last of Kesselring's reserve mobile divisions except for the Hermann Göring Division at Leghorn which could not be committed without OKW's consent as it was earmarked for France.

Looking at the scene from Alexander's point of view everything had gone as he had planned, except that the Gustav Line had been broken initially south instead of north of the Liri. This was to his advantage as the French were now well positioned to break through the weak Senger Extension and to outflank the Hitler Line from the south if Eighth Army failed to breach it at its first attempt. The main decision which Alexander had still to take was when to order the break-out from Anzio. 90 Panzer Grenadier and 26 Panzer Divisions had been identified on the main front, but 29 Panzer Grenadier and the Hermann Göring Divisions were still, as far as he could tell, available to pounce on Truscott's break-out. It would be preferable not to attack from Anzio until these divisions had also been drawn southwards into the battle for the Hitler Line. There was a further factor to be considered. Keyes had not needed to ask for 36 (US) Division to be committed in his Corps' sector and so this Fifth Army reserve division was fresh and available for shipment to Anzio. This would take about four days, making the ideal time to launch the break-out about 22 May. On the other hand, if Oliver Leese managed to breach the Hitler Line and thus forced von Vietinghoff's Tenth Army into a precipitate retreat to the Caesar Line, 22 May would be too late. Truscott would have to attack without this reinforcement. The final decision on the break-out must depend on Oliver Leese's success or failure in rushing the Hitler Line. Alexander reported his intentions to Churchill on the evening of 18 May:

I have ordered Eighth Army to use the utmost energy to break through the Adolf Hitler Line in the Liri Valley before the Germans have time to settle down in it. I have also directed that the Poles push on at once to Piedimonte so as to turn this line from the north. And I have directed that the French Corps, after reaching Pico, turn north and come in behind the enemy facing Eighth Army. If these manoeuvres are successful, it will go a long way towards destroying the right wing of the German Tenth Army. If we get held up in front of the Adolf

Hitler Line, and we are unable to turn it from north or south, a full scale mounted attack will be necessary to break it.

Oliver Leese almost won the race for the Hitler Line. The Canadians had relieved the Indians successfully in the southern sector without losing the momentum of the Indian attack and had fought hard and successfully against Baade's rearguards during 16 and 17 May. By dusk they had reached Baade's main delaying position on the Forme d'Aquino. Lessening German resistance seemed to point to an imminent withdrawal into the Hitler Line. In his planning before Diadem, Oliver Leese had anticipated a break-through in the southern half of the Army sector and had told Burns to be ready to push forward rapidly for the Hitler Line as soon as the Gustav Line showed signs of collapse (*p. 43*). In consequence, Burns had planned to bring up Hoffmeister's 5 (Canadian) Armoured Division to advance abreast and to the north of Vokes' 1 (Cdn) Division to ensure that the momentum of the Canadian advance would not falter. Three things conspired to upset Oliver Leese's forecast and Burns' intentions. First of all, the congestion over the Rapido bridges and along the tracks in the Liri Valley in the Canadian Corps' sector was so bad that Hoffmeister's move forward turned out to be as difficult and exasperating as that of Keightley's 78 (Br) Division had been a few days earlier. His infantry brigade—11 (Cdn) Brigade—was due to relieve 3 (Cdn) Brigade in the northern half of the Canadian Corps' sector on the night 18–19 May but by 19 May it was only just crossing the Rapido. Vokes' 1 (Cdn) Infantry Division by this time was already in contact with the Hitler Line.

The second factor which upset the Army forecast was the difficulty experienced by all Canadian units crossing the Forme d'Aquino when Baade's 90 PG Division rearguards gave way on 18 May. This stream proved to be a tank and vehicle obstacle which had to be bridged. Before breaking contact during the night 17–18 May Baade's troops counter-attacked across the stream hitting the 48 Canadian Highlanders astride the Pontecorvo–Pignataro road. The panzer grenadiers lost heavily, but did manage, as they intended, to slow the advance of Spry's 1 (Cdn) Brigade. To the north, Bernatchez's 3 (Cdn) Brigade seized a bridgehead over the stream and by midday on 18 May had two battalions on the far bank but without vehicles or tank support. Again traffic congestion started to play its evil part in the affairs of the valley. Bridging equipment was ordered up but could not be brought forward until the tracks had been cleared of vehicles waiting to move up as the advance progressed. Unfortunately the advance could not progress until the stream was bridged and so the vicious circle was complete. A passage had just been cleared for the bridging vehicles when a column of vehicles from 6 (Br) Armoured Division appeared right outside the XIII (Br) Corps' boundary and reblocked the track. Further delay ensued and it

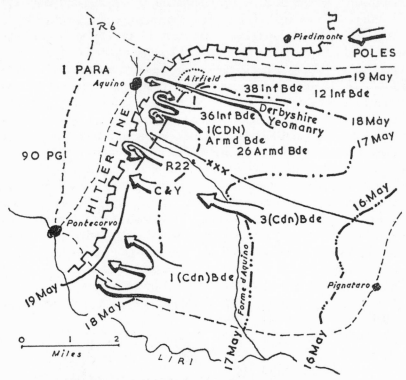

27   *Operations in the Liri Valley, 18–20 May*

was not until six o'clock in the evening of 18 May that the bridge was finally opened. By midnight, Bernatchez's brigade was reunited with its tanks and transport. By first light on 19 May both Canadian brigades were within 2,000 yards of the Hitler Line and were in the process of reconnoitring its outer defences with a view to attacking as soon as the necessary preparations could be made. By then the third factor had intervened in the form of overoptimistic reports from Kirkman's XIII (Br) Corps' sector.

Kirkman's Corps had no Forme d'Aquino to negotiate. Moreover, Heidrich's parachute troops had left their withdrawal so late that they could not afford to stay out in front of the Hitler Line any longer than necessary. They could rely on their artillery to slow Kirkman's advance because they still held superb observation over the northern half of the valley from Monte Cairo. The Poles were attacking along the southern slopes of the mountain but their progress was bound to be slow and tedious. A rapid withdrawal in the valley was unlikely to endanger Heidrich's sector of the Hitler Line which was firmly pivoted on the small mountain town of Piedimonte. Thus when Keightley's 78 (Br) Division, led by Payne Galway's Derbyshire Yeomanry Group and followed by Brigadier James' 36 (Br) Brigade, started its advance on the southern side of Route 6, it met with much less resistance than it had experienced so far in the battle. The country was far from ideal for a rapid mechanised advance: the roads were no more than cart tracks; the countryside was furrowed with numerous small streams; and most of the farms had been turned into strong points which could be used with effect by the German rearguards as they fell back. By midday, German opposition had dwindled and the British advance went almost unopposed. At six o'clock in the evening Derbyshire Yeomanry patrols had not only reached Aquino airfield, surprising and destroying a column of German transport making its way into the Hitler Line, but had managed to penetrate some of the defences which were at that time still unmanned. One troop of tanks entered the outskirts of the town of Aquino, but as it was unsupported by infantry was forced to withdraw. 38 (Irish) Brigade, supported by 26 (Br) Armoured Brigade, reached the airfield at dusk and was joined there by 1 (Canadian) Armoured Brigade which was to have relieved 26 (Br) Armoured Brigade so that it could revert to command of its own division, 6 (Br) Armoured Division, ready for a rapid advance on Rome if the Germans gave way. As things seemed to be going so well, both armoured brigades stayed forward ready for a decisive breakthrough, if it occurred.

Keightley decided to follow up his advantage and push his leading troops through Aquino during the night. The Derbyshire Yeomanry Group with 17/21 Lancers were to lead the way and were to be followed closely by 36 (Br) Brigade and 1 (Cdn) Armoured Brigade. When Payne Galway's leading troops moved forward this time they found Aquino strongly held. Moreover, the roads through the town were discovered to be blocked with rubble brought down by heavy Allied bombing during the day. The night was also exceptionally dark, making control of the mixed battle group very difficult. The only thing to do was to wait for daylight.

Fresh plans were made during the night for a more deliberate assault next morning to be carried out by 36 (Br) Brigade either side of the town supported by tanks of both armoured brigades and the divisional artillery. The usual early morning mist hung low in the Liri Valley and at first light on 19 May 5th Buffs attacked to the north and 8th Argylls to the south of the village. Steady progress was made through the mines and wire of the outer defences of the Hitler Line and it seemed as though the Line might not prove as formidable as expected. Quite suddenly the mist began to thin with disastrous consequences. The Canadian tanks supporting the attack found themselves in the open almost looking down the barrels of German anti-tank guns. These were not the normal towed or self-propelled guns either. None of the air-photo interpreters who had worked on photos of the Hitler Line before Diadem had been able to say with any certainty what was under certain blobs of camouflage visible amongst the defences. Now the ugly truth emerged. The blobs concealed Panther tank turrets mounted on concrete emplacements, covering all the likely tank approaches through the anti-tank minefields and ditches. It was not discovered until much later that these turrets were manned by a specially trained Panther Turret Company belonging to Rodt's 15 Panzer Grenadier Division—all men with considerable experience in the defensive fighting which had taken place during the winter. Within minutes many of the tanks were burning and the infantry came under heavy mortar and machine-gun fire. Three Sherman tanks of the leading troop of tanks which had approached within 100 yards of Aquino were knocked out by a single Panther turret. To meet this sudden emergency every gun within range—British and Canadian—was switched to support 36 (Br) Brigade. Under cover of this weight of artillery fire the infantry were withdrawn to the western edge of Aquino airfield, but the tanks were ordered to hold their ground while plans for renewing the attack that night were made. The high hopes of XIII (Br) Corps smashing through the Hitler Line in the Aquino area were beginning to fade, but not before they had hamstrung the attempts of the Canadians to do the same thing further south.

Bernatchez's 3 (Cdn) Brigade was ready to mount a quick attack on the Hitler Line some 2,000 yards north of Pontecorvo by 10 o'clock on the same morning. The Carlton and York Regiment and the Royal 22nd

Regiment were to attack abreast when, at the last moment, the main weight of the Canadian Corps' artillery was switched on Eighth Army orders to help 36 (Br) Brigade in front of Aquino, where it was felt a decisive break-through might be achieved if sufficient artillery fire was applied. The artillery preparation for Bernatchez's attack was thus far less than planned. Although the attack went ahead and the first objectives were overrun, it was decided to continue the attack with only one battalion, the Royal 22nd, because of shortage of fire support. The second objective was not so easily won. As the Royal 22nd came out into the open they came under accurate and sustained machine-gun fire. Their supporting tanks were effectively engaged by hidden anti-tank guns and, although the infantry tried to get forward alone, they were soon stopped by mortar and artillery fire. Greatly increased artillery support would be needed if the attack was to continue. As this was not available Vokes ordered the attack to be stopped and the force to be withdrawn to the first objective.

Neither the Canadian nor the British quick attacks 'from the line of march' had succeeded in cracking the Hitler Line. The strength of the opposition can be gauged by the losses of the two squadrons of the Ontario Regiment which supported 36 (Br) Brigade in front of Aquino. When the regiment withdrew from its exposed positions at dusk on 19 May, twelve tanks had been lost to anti-tank guns, one to mines, and the rest had all received one or more direct hits from high-explosive shells.

By evening it was clear to Oliver Leese that the Hitler Line was now too firmly held to yield to anything but a properly mounted set-piece attack. This would require time for detailed reconnaissance and planning, for the movement of troops and artillery, and for the dumping of artillery ammunition. Oliver Leese reported to Alexander that he would not be ready to attack before the night 21–22 May. He proposed to revert to his original plan for giving the task of breaching the line to Burns' Canadians. He had momentarily given Kirkman priority, but now that he had failed to break through at Aquino there was little point in continuing to attack so close under the German observation posts on Monte Cairo. Burns' Canadians, being further away, were in a better position to avoid interference from this source. Burns' task was to break through the enemy defences and to advance to Ceprano.

Meanwhile Fifth Army had continued to make rapid progress. Keyes' II (US) Corps occupied Itri and Monte Grande, the main tactical features overlooking the town, on 19 May after a brief stand by two battalions of 15 Panzer Grenadier Division. The French Corps was also making substantial but less spectacular advances than hitherto. Brosset's and Monsabert's divisions reached the Hitler Line defences in front of Sant' Oliva before the Germans could man them properly. After a brisk action with the leading regiment of 26 Panzer Division they succeeded in

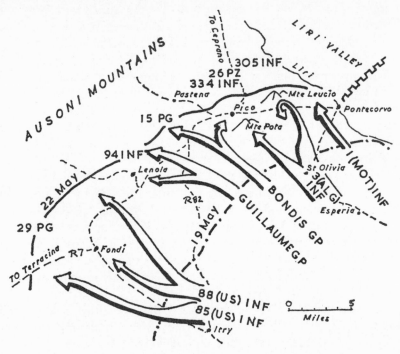

28   *Fifth Army operations, 18–22 May*

clearing the village and establishing themselves on the high ground just south of the Liri overlooking the Canadian sector of the Hitler Line around Pontecorvo. German resistance was growing stronger, but seemed to be falling back on Pico. This was in fact so. Having failed to arrive in time to hold the Sant' Oliva defences, 26 Panzer Division was preparing to stand approximately on the line of the Pico-Pontecorvo road with Monte Leucio as the northern bastion of its defences. This was a high feature which lay between the road and the Liri, commanding both. All German troops on the south side of the Liri were ordered to fall back to this line on the evening of 19 May.

It was clear to all the senior commanders on the Allied side that the decisive moment was approaching when the moves made would spell success or failure in the days ahead. Each had his own prescription for success and each felt that he should be allowed to fight the battle in his own way. The great merit of Alexander's method of command was that each felt that his solution was accepted and, in consequence, did his utmost to ensure success. Complications inevitably arose at staff level over boundaries and the mechanics of carrying out Alexander's broad directives, but he achieved his primary purpose—in spite of the national egocentricity of his subordinates—of bringing the greatest possible pressure to bear on Kesselring's experienced and well-tried formations. The country so favoured the defence and so constricted the manoeuvres of the highly-mechanised attackers that a stalemate could easily have occurred had it not been for Alexander's subtle handling of his Allied team.

Mark Clark was naturally elated by the sweeping successes of his Fifth Army. By the evening of 19 May, his troops stood on the final objective given him in the Diadem operation order. The experienced British, who had been given pride of place in the offensive, had lagged behind throughout and were now stopped in front of the Hitler Line, whereas his troops were through its first extension and were now being held back by the slowness of Eighth Army's progress. In his original Diadem planning, Clark had not expected to reach the Itri–Pico road so easily and had envisaged shipping most of Keyes' Corps round to the Anzio beachhead as soon as it was clear that little further progress was likely along the coast or through the mountains. Alexander had already authorised the move of 36 (US) Division to Anzio on 18 May and Mark Clark had earmarked Coulter's 85 (US) Division to follow, but now he had second thoughts. The success of both the French and American troops in crashing through the mountains showed that it would probably be easier to continue attacking overland to reach the beachhead rather than shipping Keyes round by sea. Staff calculations showed that 85 (US) Division and the necessary supporting Corps troops could not be operational in the beachhead much before the beginning of June. The logistic needs of the Anzio force were already taxing Allied shipping resources to the limit. An increase of one division would be tolerable, but more than that would create a quartermaster's nightmare.

The continuation of the Fifth Army attack overland could be made in one of two directions: north-west to link up with Anzio or due north through von Senger's broken Corps to cut in behind Feurstein's Corps holding the Hitler Line. As far as Mark Clark was concerned there was only one direction: north-west by the shortest route to Rome. The slower Eighth Army was in overcoming Feurstein's resistance, the better. Fifth Army was to have the honour of entering Rome and would share that honour with no one else—not even Juin's Frenchmen, though they were perhaps preferable to the British as they were sponsored and equipped by the Americans and belonged to Fifth Army.

Juin, although nominally under Fifth Army and receiving his orders through Mark Clark, was essentially an independent national-contingent commander. Unlike Mark Clark, whose mind was set on linking up with Truscott and advancing on Rome, Juin, a true soldier, had his mind, like Alexander's, fixed on the destruction of von Vietinghoff's Tenth Army. To him, the keypoint of the whole battlefield had always been the Ceprano–Arce area. If he could take Pico quickly and break through to Ceprano, Feurstein's Corps would be encircled and the glory of French arms established without any further doubt. His sensitivity on this latter point is well illustrated in his memoirs: 'Maitland-Wilson came over, followed by Alexander and Clark, to congratulate him [de Gaulle, who was visiting Juin] on the decisive success of the French Expeditionary Corps. *Evidently something had changed.*'

Oliver Leese's position was different again. He had a straightforward military task to accomplish—the breach of the Hitler Line. He did not have to worry about national pride or the honours of entering Rome. Political questions of that type, as far as the British were concerned, lay with Alexander. Oliver Leese's problem was how to smash the formidable line with least loss of life. Both Mark Clark and Juin were highly critical of the slowness of the British, but neither had to worry about manpower, nor were they faced with the strongest defences in Italy, or by best German divisions operating with the advantage of a secure flank and the excellent observation afforded by Monte Cairo. If there was a chance of avoiding a direct assault on this prepared and fully-manned position, it should be taken. British national pride was not at stake, for they had been fighting far longer than the French and Americans and needed no new or special place in the halls of fame.

There is no published record of what happened at the highest levels of command at this time. It is only possible to read between the lines of Mark Clark's memoirs. Alexander clearly irritated Clark by relaying

23 *French infantry entering Esperia*

THE PENETRATION OF THE SENGER LINE

24 *French mechanised units advancing on Pico*

25   *The ruins of Piedimonte, taken by the Poles, showing one of the Panther turrets in the foreground*

THE FALL OF THE HITLER LINE

26   *One of the Panther turrets (camouflage removed) with the hulks of two of its Churchill tank victims still lying in front of it*

instructions to him through General Lemnitzer, the senior American general on Alexander's staff, directing the Anzio break-out to start on 21 May without consulting him personally first. As was mentioned earlier in this chapter, the date 21 May was based on overoptimistic reports of the fall of Aquino on 18 May and so a new date had to be decided. Alexander visited Mark Clark next day (19 May) to discuss the position with him, and seems to have suggested, quite logically, that as Oliver Leese could not attack again before 23 May Fifth Army should try to outflank the Hitler Line from the south, as Juin wished to do, and thus make it unnecessary for Eighth Army to attack the Hitler-Senger Line at its strongest point. Mark Clark objected on the grounds that to save lives in Eighth Army would mean increased losses in his Fifth Army. In his view both Armies should attack simultaneously with maximum effort. He added that some delay would be necessary in Truscott's break-out because he needed maximum air support and the weather forecast was not good.

In the original Diadem plan the break-out from Anzio was to take place 'when a break through the enemy's second line of defence on the main front had been obtained'. Taking the feelings of Mark Clark, Juin and Oliver Leese into account, it was now clear that it might be possible to mount three attacks simultaneously on about 23 May; Juin at Pico, Oliver Leese at Pontecorvo and Truscott from Anzio. Alexander kept an open mind as to whether Fifth Army would have to swing due north to help Eighth Army by cutting in behind the Hitler Line or carry on in a north-westerly direction parallel to Eighth Army. All would depend on how Juin fared in trying to break the Senger Extension at Pico. Alexander, therefore, approved Mark Clark's plan to direct Keyes north-west on Fondi and Terracina, and Juin northwards on Pico. Truscott was to be ready to break out on 23 May, at the same time that Oliver Leese attacked the Hitler Line. All the senior commanders would be doing what they felt was right, and at the same time fulfilling the Army Group commander's overall requirements. Disagreement might arise if he had to insist on the whole of Fifth Army swinging north-wards and away from Rome because Eighth Army failed to break through the Hitler Line. This contingency might never occur, although all the indications were that Kesselring had no intention of giving up the Hitler-Senger Line unless he had no alternative.

Juin's attack on Pico proved to be a major undertaking. 305 and 334 Divisions brought over from the Adriatic were already coming into the line to support 26 Panzer Division, and orders from Kesselring made clear to all German commanders the vital importance of holding Pico to the success of holding the Allies on the Hitler-Senger Line. Juin made no changes in his divisional dispositions. Brosset's 1 (Motorised) Division was to work along the south bank of the Liri in touch with the Canadians north of the river and Monsabert's 3 (Algerian) Division was to attack Pico frontally, while Guillaume's Mountain Corps continued to work through the hills on the southern flank, keeping touch with Keyes' II (US) Corps. Monsabert opened his attack on 20 May taking Monte Leucio on the Pico–Pontecorvo road and Monte Pota overlooking Pico from the south. His success was short lived. On the following day, 21 May, 26 Panzer Division launched a series of powerful tank counter-attacks along the Liri bringing Brosset's motorised division to a halt and driving Monsabert's men off Monte Leucio. In the fighting, Canadian artillery on the north bank of the Liri supported the French and was instrumental in directing a number of air strikes on the German tanks attacking the French. The French counter-attacked four times during the day; three times they failed, but the fourth attack regained the summit of Monte Leucio by midnight. The next morning, 22 May, saw more heavy fighting in which fortunes fluctuated with the French gradually gaining the upper hand. By late afternoon they entered the ruins of Pico—too late to enable Juin to outflank the Hitler Line before Oliver Leese opened his prepared assault. 26 Panzer Division had surrendered Pico, but was still holding firm north of the town and was being reinforced by more units from the Adriatic coast.

Keyes' drive along the coast to Fondi went faster than Juin's drive on Pico. Both his divisions advanced abreast against steadily lessening resistance as the German rearguards fell back to the Senger Extension between Lenola, Fondi and Terracina. So swift was the American advance that Fondi fell on 20 May with hardly a fight and Terracina was reached, but not taken, on 22 May. An unexpected disaster had again dislocated Kesselring's attempts to stabilise the southern end of his front. He had ordered Fries' 29 Panzer Grenadier Division southward from Civitavecchia on 19 May, as mentioned earlier in this chapter, and had then set off on a tour of the front. While he was away, von Macken-sen's Fourteenth Army staff had objected to the removal of their last reserve division and an altercation had occurred between the Army and Army Group staffs. Returning to his headquarters late on 20 May, he found that his orders had not been carried out. The unfortunate 29

Panzer Grenadier Division thus lost a precious 36 hours and arrived in the Fondi-Terracina area too late to stop the American advance. Kesselring records in his memoirs:

> The division had come up too late and had offered fight in unprepared positions—with calamitous consequences. . . . An excellent defensive zone had been thrown away and the enemy handed an almost impregnable position between Terracina and Fondi, the loss of which gave the Americans the victory.

In spite of this Fries' division put up a tough fight to save the southern end of the Senger Extension and made the Americans fight for every rock and crag in the Terracina defile and the hills above, but there could be no question of stopping Keyes from eventually breaking through to the Anzio beachhead. All that 29 Panzer Grenadier Division could do was to fight long enough to enable the remnants of 15 Panzer Grenadier Division and 94 Division to escape through the mountains before the French to the north cut them off.

Thus by the evening of 22 May the stage was set for the final destruction of the Hitler-Senger Line. In the south, it could only be a matter of hours before Fries would have to give way. In the centre, Juin had taken Pico and was poised to drive north on Ceprano. In the north, Burns' Canadians were ready to crash through the Hitler Line proper north of Pontecorvo. And away to the extreme northern end of the Hitler Line on the slopes of Monte Cairo, Anders' Poles had fought a stubborn action along the mountainside and had reached Piedimonte, the northern pivot of the line, on 20 May. Although their initial attacks had cleared the outer defences, the town was still in German hands.

That evening Alexander reported that the battle had reached a critical stage. Three simultaneous attacks by British, American and French troops were planned for the early hours of the following morning which would soon show how operations were going to develop.

Scene Four: 20–25 May 1944
9 The Breach of the Hitler Line

'... according to reports received from the Commander 90 Panzer Grenadier Division, due to enemy artillery fire lasting for 14 hours, 1 Bn 576 Grenadier Regiment, 2 Bn 361 Grenadier Regiment and Battle Group Strafner must be considered as destroyed. ...'
Chief of Staff LI Mountain Corps reporting loss of units destroyed by Eighth Army artillery in the Canadian sector of the Hitler Line (Canadian Official History)

Most breaching operations are methodical affairs like sieges of bygone days. The attacker takes his time, making a very thorough examination of the defences, exploring all alternative approaches and weighing their advantages and disadvantages; and when he has decided upon his plan, he allows his subordinates time to examine every detail and to rehearse each action. He attacks at a time and in a place of his own choosing, taking elaborate steps to conceal when and where his blow will fall. The fixed defences in front of Burns' Corps were strong enough to warrant such deliberate methods, if they were fully manned. But were they? Opinion was divided. The Fifth Army's successes to the south and the losses suffered by Feurstein's Corps in the Liri Valley suggested that a prolonged stand would not be possible; and yet the preliminary attacks by the Canadian and British Corps on 18 and 19 May showed that the Germans had no intention of giving up the line without a struggle. Burns was faced with the dilemma of being accused of wasting precious time by taking the proverbial hammer to crack a nut or of sacrificing Canadian lives through inadequate preparations. Assessment of the true situation was made more difficult by the fluctuations in French fortunes south of the Liri. At one moment they were sweeping all before them, showing that a hammer would be quite unnecessary; and, at the next, they were recoiling under von Lüttwitz's 26 Panzer Division's counter-attacks around Pico and Monte Leucio which suggested that an over-hastily prepared Canadian breaching operation might prove a very bloody affair. In the event, attempts to take advantage of apparent but momentary French successes led to unfortunate complications which

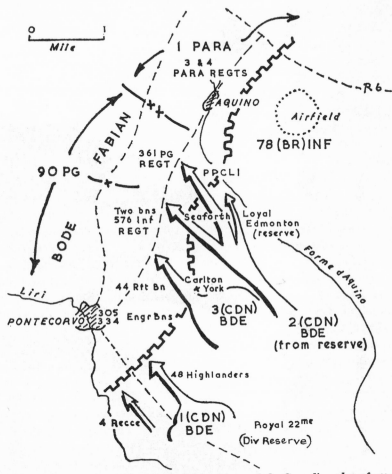

29   *The German dispositions in the Hitler Line and the Canadian plan of attack*

nearly resulted in the failure of the main Canadian breaching operation, codenamed 'Chesterfield'.

Eighth Army's pause in front of the Hitler Line to allow time for Canadian preparations gave Feurstein's Corps breathing space in which to strengthen its positions. Heidrich's 1 Parachute Division held the northern half of the Liri Valley as far south as the Forme d'Aquino with the 3 and 4 Para Regiments occupying the positions either side of Aquino. Baade's 90 Panzer Grenadier Division held the rest of the line down to the Liri itself at Pontecorvo. He had a very mixed force, consisting of the remnants of several battle groups and engineer battalions. He divided his sector into two: the northern half was held by Group Fabian and was based on two battalions of 361 Panzer Grenadier Regiment (one of Baade's own regiments); and the southern half, including Pontecorvo, was held by the Bode Group which now consisted of the remnants of two battalions of Bode's original 576 Grenadier Regiment, the remnants of Battle Group Strafner from 5 Mountain Division and the two engineer battalions of 305 and 334 Divisions whose main bodies were deployed under von Lüttwitz around Pico. In addition Baade had under his command a motley collection of 'unhorsed' tank crews, detachments of three other engineer battalions and a number of *ad hoc* units formed from supply units which had been pressed into the line to fight as infantry. Interrogations of prisoners after the battle suggests that there were not more than 1,085 actual infantry opposing 1 (Canadian) Division. How many of the engineers and other detachments were fighting as infantry is not known. The strength of the Hitler Line, however, lay in its anti-tank defences and the concentration of artillery and *nebelwerfers* which Feurstein had managed to assemble in the area of San Giovanni on the west bank of the Liri and along the Melfa River, a tributary of the Liri which could act as a long-stop behind the Hitler Line. The anti-tank defences consisted of extensive minefields closely covered by anti-tank guns and infantry positions. The former were being thickened with an extra 3,000 mines as the Canadians closed up to the line, and the engineer units responsible for laying these mines became embroiled in the fighting as infantrymen when the main Canadian attack was launched. The anti-tank gun deployment was like a series of spearheads. At the tip of each spear there was a Panther turret and echeloned back on either side were a further six towed or self-propelled anti-tank guns sited in support. All told there were some sixty-two anti-tank guns covering a front of 8,000 yards. Von Vietinghoff's assessment of the defences was:

The defence works were excellent; effective concentrations of artillery and anti-aircraft artillery, under the direct command of the Army's senior artillery commander were ready for action in the area of San Giovanni Incarico and on both sides of the Melfa; the two divisional commanders were in a class by themselves.

Burns' Corps plan was to attack with Vokes' 1 (Canadian) Division on a 2,000-yard front just south of the Forme d'Aquino. Hoffmeister's 5 (Canadian) Armoured Division would support the attack and, when Vokes' infantry had made a wide enough breach, would pass through and drive up the valley to seize the crossings of the Melfa River before the Germans had time to organise its defence. The artillery support would be provided by 810 guns of all types, including many belonging to the French to the south and Kirkman's Corps to the north. During the preparatory phase which started at midnight on 19–20 May, the defences opposite Burns' and Kirkman's Corps were to be bombarded with about 1,000 shells per hour until the attack opened. Seventy-six medium and heavy guns were detailed exclusively for counter-battery work and a further sixty-two for counter-mortar. The remaining 682 were to provide direct infantry support in the form of a three-hour barrage superimposed on which there would be a programme of concentrations on known positions likely to interfere with the advance.

Vokes' divisional plan was to attack with Brigadier Gibson's 2 (Canadian) Brigade supported by the British 25 Tank Brigade on a two-battalion front. His 1 and 3 (Canadian) Brigades, which were holding the line, were to advance as opportunities occurred. Oliver Leese considered that too few infantry were being used. Vokes accordingly modified his plan, ordering Bernatchez's 3 (Canadian) Brigade to attack on Gibson's southern flank on a one-battalion front. Vokes divided the attack into two phases. The Phase I objective was the Pontecorvo–Aquino road, and the Phase II objective was the Pontecorvo–Route 6 road on the far side of all the Hitler Line defences. Hoffmeister's armoured division would advance and break out once the Phase II objective had been taken. Spry's 1 (Canadian) Brigade would maintain pressure on Pontecorvo with the help of the divisional reconnaissance regiment—4 (Canadian) Reconnaissance Regiment—which would operate along the north bank of the Liri in close touch with the French. The Royal 22nd Regiment and the Three Rivers Armoured Regiment would be in divisional reserve. XIII (Br) Corps and the Poles would simulate preparations for attacks in their sectors and would move their tanks at appropriate times during the night before the attack to help disguise the noise of the Canadian tank and vehicle movements. To give more time for preparation, Oliver Leese agreed to the postponement of H-hour until 6 a.m. on 23 May. The artillery commander of the Canadian Corps, Brigadier Plow, remarked that 'for an attack on such a scale as this, seventy-two hours is only just sufficient'.

Planning, reconnaissance and concentration of resources were going well when, as described earlier, the French took Monte Leucio over-looking Pontecorvo and on 20 May entered the outskirts of the town on the south bank of the Liri. Next morning the 4 (Canadian) Reconnais-sance Regiment approached the main part of the town on the north bank and took twenty-two prisoners of the 44 Division Reinforcement Battalion whose poor performance and inferior fighting quality sug-gested that Pontecorvo might be weakly held. Vokes sent Brigadier Spry, the commander of 1 (Canadian) Brigade, over the river to explore with the French the feasibility of making an assault-boat crossing over the Liri, taking the defences of Pontecorvo in the rear. The French hold on the area was not as firm as the Canadians had been led to believe and was still being disputed by 26 Panzer Division. Closer observations showed also that a number of machine-gun positions on the steep banks of the Liri were covering the stretch of river which Spry's men would have to cross. The idea of an assault-boat crossing was abandoned as impractical, but Vokes asked for and received permission from Burns to mount a preliminary attack next day (22 May) with Spry's brigade directed at the apparently weak defences of Pontecorvo. This meant delaying the re-grouping for Chesterfield so that Gibson's 2 (Canadian) Brigade could remain in divisional reserve in the southern half of the sector ready to exploit any success that Spry might have. Oliver Leese seems to have been most unhappy—and quite rightly—about this variation of the Canadian plan and warned Burns by telephone 'not to get too involved in this subsidiary operation'.

Spry's attack started with an advance by 4 (Canadian) Recon-naissance Regiment and two squadrons of tanks between the Liri and the Pignataro road. Under heavy fire this force penetrated the defences to a depth of 400 yards and took sixty more prisoners from the 44 Division Reinforcement Battalion. This success was followed north of the road by an attack at 10.30 a.m. by 49 (Canadian) Highlanders and a squadron of tanks. An anti-tank ditch delayed the tanks, which suffered further losses from mines and anti-tank guns and separated them from the infantry. It was late afternoon before the tanks managed to reach the Highlanders who were within 100 yards of the town but by then their petrol was almost exhausted. Pontecorvo was obviously too strongly held to warrant committing Gibson's 2 (Canadian) Brigade, thus completely upsetting the Chesterfield plan for next day; and so the Highlanders were ordered to dig in where they were. During the day Bernatchez's 3 (Canadian) Brigade carried out a demonstration to help Spry's men and was equally unsuccessful in opening up a way into the Hitler Line. His operations did, however, give him and his battalion commanders some very useful information about the German defences which they were able to put to good purpose next day.

Kesselring was delighted with the defeat of Spry's and Bernatchez's attacks and requested von Vietinghoff to convey his appreciation to Baade and Heidrich. He added 'in their [Baade's and Heidrich's] cases one could cry with admiration; in the case of the other [von Lüttwitz] from rage'. 26 Panzer Division had failed to retake Monte Leucio and had just lost Pico.

Regrouping for Chesterfield did not start until just before dark on 22 May. This meant that Gibson's 2 (Canadian) Brigade had to move north and into its assembly area only a few hours before the main assault was due to begin next morning. The troops got little sleep that night and only battalion reconnaissance parties had seen the ground over which the brigade was to attack next morning. A message from Oliver Leese to the Canadian Corps, recorded in the Canadian Official History, read: 'I am confident that you will add the name of the Adolf Hitler Line to those epics of Canadian battle history—Sanctuary Wood; Vimy; Ortona. Good luck to you all.'

At 6 a.m. the Chesterfield artillery barrage, which was the heaviest yet used by the Allies in any theatre, opened on a 3,200-yard front with a substantial overlap of 500 yards on either side to protect the flanks of the attacking brigades. The rate of advance was to be 100 yards in five minutes during Phase I; then a pause for one hour for consolidation; and finally, a rate of advance of 100 yards in three minutes for Phase II to the final objective. Gibson's 2 (Canadian) Brigade attack was led on the right by the Princess Patricia's Canadian Light Infantry with a squadron of the North Irish Horse advancing along the southern side of the Forme d'Aquino; and on the left by the Seaforths of Canada with the other two squadrons of North Irish Horse. The Loyal Edmonton Regiment was in reserve with a squadron of 51 Royal Tank Regiment and had orders to pass through the Patricias on the first objective and to advance with the Seaforths to the second. Bernatchez's 3 (Canadian) Brigade attack was led by the Carlton and York Regiment with two squadrons of 51 Royal Tank Regiment and was to be followed by the West Nova Scotia Regiment. The third battalion of his brigade, the Royal 22nd Regiment, was in divisional reserve with the Three Rivers Armoured Regiment.

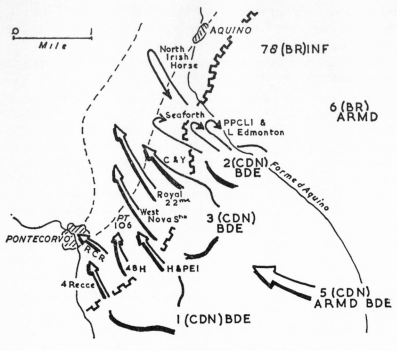

30   The breach of the Hitler Line, 23 May

A typical Liri Valley haze hung over the battlefield as the first shells of the barrage fell on the outer defences of the Hitler Line. Three minutes later the three assault battalions crossed their start lines. At first, progress in all battalions was steady and encouraging because low scrub and growing crops concealed their initial advance. As soon as the Germans realised they were being attacked they were quick to sense that a major assault had been launched and opened up with every gun and *nebelwerfer* within range, firing at intense rates. On the right, the Patricias suffered most. They were caught between their start line and the main German wire by this defensive artillery fire. Then, as their own barrage moved on, German machine-gunners came up from their bunkers to add to the general fusillade. The fire which did greatest damage and which eventually stopped the Patricias' attack came from the north bank of the Forme d'Aquino which was held by Heidrich's paratroopers. Their positions were outside the curtain of the barrage and, as they were not being attacked themselves, they could concentrate on bringing a murderous cross-fire to bear on the Patricias advancing along the far side of the valley. The squadron of North Irish Horse supporting the Patricias ran into an undetected minefield about 600 yards from the start line which was covered by Panther turrets. The infantry continued to fight their way forward without tank support, but communications began to fail and control was soon lost. Although some men penetrated to the German emplacements, the majority were stopped short of the wire. Two days later some thirty men, who had been considered lost, returned to the regiment, having gone to ground in some of the bunkers in the Hitler ·Line itself.

The Seaforths in the centre of the attack were more fortunate, as they did not have to contend with the fire of Heidrich's as well as Baade's men. Mines halted the North Irish Horse, and Panther turret crews were again presented with ideal targets at almost point-blank range. One gun is said to have destroyed thirteen Churchill tanks before an armour-piercing shell exploded its ammunition. The Seaforths, like the Patricias, pushed on alone without tank support and two hours after the start of the attack Major J. C. Allen, one of the company commanders, reported that he had consolidated on the first objective with about a hundred men, the remnants of the four rifle companies. Eleven tanks of the North Irish Horse had meanwhile managed to work their way through the Hitler Line independently on a different axis and reached the second objective, but being without supporting infantry were forced to withdraw through the line again under heavy artillery and anti-tank fire. Only four tanks survived. Altogether forty-one out of the fifty-eight tanks engaged on 2 (Canadian) Brigade's front were knocked out during the day.

Meanwhile Gibson's brigade reserve, the Loyal Edmonton Regiment, had moved forward as planned to be ready to pass through the Patricias on the first objective. The battalion and its supporting tanks caught up with the Patricias who were stopped in front of the main German wire, and could do little more than add to the targets presented to the German paratroopers and artillery observers on the north bank of the Forme d'Aquino. They did manage to breach the wire in two places but wireless communications broke down and the battalion commander had to report to brigade headquarters that he had lost control of his companies. The brigade commander thus found himself hamstrung and unable to influence the battle in his sector. His reserve had committed itself prematurely and most of his communications had been destroyed. He had nothing with which to exploit the partial success of the Seaforths and no immediate means of continuing the battle.

Bernatchez's 3 (Canadian) Brigade was much more successful. As it had been in its sector since it reached the Hitler Line on 19 May, it had been able to reconnoitre and patrol the wire and minefields, to observe the areas most frequently shelled by German guns and *nebelwerfers*. Unlike Gibson's 2 (Canadian) Brigade, it did not have to move up and regroup during the night before the attack. The Carlton and York Regiment, supported by two squadrons of 51 Royal Tank Regiment, kept up close to its barrage and suffered relatively little from German small-arms fire. German artillery and *nebelwerfers* took their toll, but could not stop the Canadian infantry taking the first objective. 51 Royal Tank Regiment, on the other hand, had to fight a grim battle with the German anti-tank gunners and with a counter-attack force of German tanks and self-propelled guns. It was 10 a.m. before they managed to fight their way through to the infantry on the objective, having lost heavily in the process. They were soon followed by brigade anti-tank guns and the follow-up battalion, the West Nova Scotia Regiment, which was to undertake the second phase of the attack.

General Vokes waited most of the morning before ordering the second phase. He had hoped that some change of fortune in 2 (Canadian) Brigade's sector might make it possible for both brigades to renew the attack together. There was a chance that the Canadian sappers might be able to clear a lane through the minefields so that the North Irish Horse could renew the attack in the Patricias' sector, but they were virtually wiped out trying to do so. As the morning wore on there became less and less chance of reorganising and restarting the attack anywhere in Gibson's sector. It was more a question of how to hold on to what had been gained by the Seaforths who were now being counter-attacked from the direction of Aquino. It was quite impossible for tanks to reach them and equally useless to try towing anti-tank guns forward through unbreached minefields under sustained German fire. It was only the weight of Canadian and British artillery fire that prevented Gibson's men from being overrun. During one of these counter-attacks the Commander Royal Artillery of 1 (Canadian) Division, Brigadier Ziegler, called for one of the rarest artillery concentrations—a 'William' target, that is to say, the concentrated fire of every gun of Eighth Army's artillery which was within range. Almost 700 guns fired some 3,500 shells (or ninety-two tons of ammunition) simultaneously at the German infantry and tanks forming up near Aquino. It was the first time this had been done, and showed the extraordinary efficiency of artillery communications as the target was engaged within thirty-three minutes of the request being made.

While Vokes waited to see whether anything further could be done to renew Gibson's attack, Bernatchez's brigade was fending off similar counter-attacks. Although Bernatchez had both tanks and anti-tank guns on the objective to defend his infantry against German tanks, his men were suffering cumulative losses in their exposed positions from harassing fire while they waited for the order to begin Phase II. Churchill tanks were ablaze in every company area, and as the pause went on, more and more damage was being done. Unless the attack was restarted fairly quickly stalemate would ensue. Shortly after midday Vokes decided that the only course open to him was to reinforce his one success and to attack again in Bernatchez's sector. With General Burns' agreement he released his divisional reserve to Bernatchez and ordered him to capture the final objective as soon as a new fire plan could be made and orders issued. The Three Rivers Regiment moved forward to replace the battered 51 Royal Tank Regiment, and the Royal 22nd Regiment advanced through the breach made by the Carlton and York Regiment ready to support the West Nova Scotias when they renewed 3 (Canadian) Brigade's attack. No major changes had to be made in the barrage programme for the second phase, but the defensive fire tasks on the objective had to be altered to cover the reduced frontage. Planning, issue of orders and regrouping was completed by 4.30 p.m. and the attack itself started twenty minutes later—eight and a half hours after the time originally planned and on a third of the frontage.

The West Nova Scotias attacked, as the Carlton and Yorks had done, 'leaning on the barrage'. Rain had started to fall and the German artillery observers seem to have been caught off guard, as they failed to bring down their defensive fire in time. Some German reserves were forming up for a counter-attack at the moment the attack started, and were caught in the open and scattered by the artillery concentrations.

Shortly after 6 p.m. the battalion was on the final objective. Baade did not give up and counter-attacked almost at once with infantry and tanks which overran one of the Nova Scotia's companies before it could dig in. The men captured did not stay in captivity long as their captors marched them by mistake straight into another Canadian position where the tables were quickly reversed. The Three Rivers' tanks were slightly delayed fighting their way forward. Their arrival on the position finally secured the Nova Scotias on their objective. Shortly afterwards, the Royal 22nd Regiment advanced into the gap between the Nova Scotias and the Seaforths to secure 3 (Canadian) Brigade's northern flank. By dark, Bernatchez's brigade was firmly established on the far side of its breach in the Hitler Line on the low ridge which lies between the two roads leading north from Pontecorvo. His losses had been remarkably light—forty-five killed and 120 wounded—in the three battalions, compared with 162 killed, 306 wounded and seventy-five taken prisoner in Gibson's less fortunate brigade.

2 (Canadian) Brigade's troubles had not ended with Vokes' decision to exploit success through 3 (Canadian) Brigade's sector. Throughout the afternoon and early evening its battalions had tried to work their way through the German defences, but the inability of the sappers to clear lanes through the minefields for the tanks and anti-tank guns under the withering German machine-gun fire left the infantry at the mercy of the German tanks. Major Allen's isolated force of Seaforths, holding the first objective, was eventually overrun by German tanks which moved up and down the Pontecorvo–Aquino road sweeping the ditches, in which many of the Seaforths were taking cover, with their machine guns. Fifty-four survivors fell into German hands, Allen himself escaping by feigning death. Relief did not come to the rest of Gibson's infantry until darkness enabled the sappers to clear lanes for the tanks and anti-tank guns to move forward.

In 1 (Canadian) Brigade's sector, in front of Pontecorvo, Spry waged a private battle outside the main attack using whatever artillery could be made available to him from time to time. The 48th Highlanders fought most of the morning for Point 106 about a mile north-east of Pontecorvo. Spry then committed the Hastings and Prince Edward Island Regiment to widen the breach and to protect the left rear of Bernatchez's brigade. The battalion commander, Lieutenant-Colonel Cameron, committed his companies in succession with great skill, gradually widening the breach with some excellent tank support. By dark, the way was open for an attack by Spry's third battalion, the Royal Canadian Regiment, on Pontecorvo itself, but this was postponed until the following morning to avoid street fighting in the dark, which might have been a very costly business.

The first part of Chesterfield was over. A breach had been made. It was now the turn of Hoffmeister's 5 (Canadian) Armoured Division to break out through the breach. Before describing the frustrations and successes of Hoffmeister's division, it might be worth considering some of the lessons of Vokes' attack about which all the Canadian commanders have been very frank. Apart from the obvious problems caused by moving so late into his assembly area, Gibson ascribed his lack of success to poor handling of reserves. The Canadian Official History quotes him as saying: 'where the ground, as here, made control and reconnaissance difficult, the reserve at company, battalion and brigade level should be held back and committed according to the development of the fight. . . .' He felt that all headquarters were too far forward for a set-piece attack and this resulted in communications being disrupted. The same applied to the tanks, most of which were destroyed before the sappers were able to clear a way through the minefields and before the infantry could deal with the covering anti-tank guns.

Mark Clark, from his distant seat in Fifth Army, was highly critical of Oliver Leese's decision to attack with one Corps, using one division only, instead of making a general effort by both Kirkman's and Burns' Corps simultaneously. In his view, Fifth Army's successes south of the Liri had been so complete that the Germans were on the point of withdrawing from the Hitler Line when Burns attacked. Had both the Eighth Army's Corps attacked the Hitler Line at the same time it would have crumpled like matchwood. This view was shared by Juin, who believed that Eighth Army's handling of the whole Liri Valley battle was faulty. He believed that as soon as the Gustav defences had been breached, McCreery's X (Br) Corps should have been reinforced so that it could fight its way through the hills north of Monte Cairo by way of Atina to appear behind the Hitler Line at Arce, thus completing the encirclement of Feurstein's Corps. There was some truth in both these criticisms; but an element of national pride, and possibly subconscious delight in debunking the over-proud Eighth Army, also played a part in French and American thinking. Feurstein's Chief of Staff telephoned von Vietinghoff's operations room at 2.50 p.m. on 23 May, when the battle was at its height, asking for directions for a possible withdrawal 'so that the Corps could make preparations that would prevent the loss of arms and equipment . . .'. It is thus clear that no withdrawal had, in fact, been contemplated by von Vietinghoff before the Canadian attack went in, and hence that much of Mark Clark's criticism is invalid. The Hitler Line had been rightly treated by Oliver Leese and Burns as a fully-prepared line of fixed defences which could not be rushed without great loss of life. An attack by both Corps would have split the artillery support, which, as the Canadian attack showed, was barely adequate for one breach, let alone two. The strength of the Hitler Line was such that Baade came very close to defeating the Canadians with just over 1,000 actual infantry soldiers holding his 5,000 yards of the line—not much more than a British or Canadian battalion at full war strength. Juin's criticism has more validity, as will emerge when the story of the second stage of Chesterfield is described.

General Burns comes nearest the truth in his own criticism of the Canadian attack. He made four points. First, the postponement of 2 (Canadian) Brigade's move to its assembly area in case Spry's preliminary attack on Pontecorvo succeeded was a mistake since it prevented Gibson's men from having a thorough look at their sector. Bernatchez's success confirmed this criticism. Secondly, the frontage of assault was too narrow as this enabled the Germans to concentrate their artillery and mortar fire with telling effect on the Canadian infantry and sappers held up in the wire and minefields. This criticism may be less valid. There is always a balance to be struck between concentration to achieve the necessary weight of supporting fire and dispersion to avoid enemy retaliation. Bernatchez's success showed what might have been possible if 2 (Canadian) Brigade had been given enough time to reconnoitre its sector. It might then have become apparent that the Patricias' axis was too exposed to Heidrich's positions around Aquino; smoke and diversionary attacks by XIII (Br) Corps could have been arranged. This led to Burns' third point: too little was done to screen the Patricias' attack with smoke and high-explosive covering fire from observation from the north bank of the Forme d'Aquino and from the more distant slopes of Monte Cairo. This is certainly valid. The 500-yard overlap of the barrage was quite inadequate for the purpose. During the battles in the Gustav Line, Monte Cassino had been kept cloaked in smoke throughout the daylight hours. Similar precautions were just as necessary in the Hitler Line. Burns' fourth point again led from the third: the barrage was far too inflexible to give the Canadians adequate

protection once things started to go wrong. The Canadian official
historian records that Burns styled a barrage 'the most inflexible form of
artillery support in the Gunners' lexicon ... never suited to the
mentality of the Canadian soldier in Italy'. In later battles in Italy, the
Canadians developed more flexible systems better suited to their mode of
fighting.

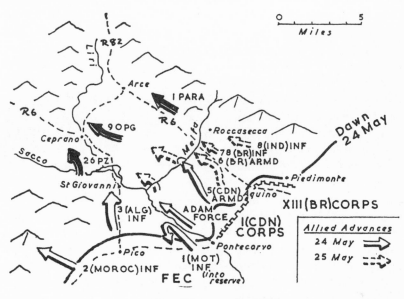

31   The advance to the Melfa

Hoffmeister watched the progress of Vokes' battle closely during 23
May and by 5.30 p.m. concluded that the situation was about to become
favourable enough for an armoured break-through. His plan was to
advance with Brigadier D. B. Smith's 5 (Canadian) Armoured Brigade
in the lead, with orders to seize a crossing over the River Melfa which was
the next obstacle upon which Feurstein might try to stand once he lost
the Hitler Line. Brigadier T. E. d'O. Snow's 11 (Canadian) Infantry
Brigade would pass through the armoured brigade on the Melfa and
continue the advance to seize the crossings over the upper Liri, thus
opening up the road to Frosinone and Rome. General Burns agreed with
Hoffmeister's reading of the battle and authorised him to start moving
forward from his concentration area east of the Forme d'Aquino near

Pignataro. The move did not go well. In the first place, Bernatchez's breach was further south than the planned axis of advance of the armoured brigade which had been reconnoitred through Gibson's sector. This meant a new route forward, a new forming-up position and a new start line. The rain, which had begun during Bernatchez's second attack, had turned the approaches to the Forme d'Aquino bridges into quagmires and made them almost impassable. To make matters worse, the leading Canadian tanks ran into the tanks of the 25 Tank Brigade as they pulled back to rearm and replenish after their hard day's fighting. Traffic control became a nightmare, and by 8.30 p.m. Hoffmeister had to report to Burns that no break-out would be possible before dawn.

Feurstein had as yet received no orders to plan a methodical withdrawal, and so when daylight returned on 24 May, Heidrich was still holding Aquino and Piedimonte, and Baade, with the remnants of 90 Panzer Grenadier Division, was trying to create a new containing line around the Canadian breach some two miles behind his old position. When Smith's leading armoured regimental group advanced at 8 a.m.— two hours later than planned—it was met with heavy shelling but only scattered resistance from tanks and infantry. By chance Smith's brigade had hit the boundary between Baade's and Heidrich's divisions and in consequence had little difficulty in breaking out into the open and advancing north-west behind the Hitler Line. It was not until about 10.30 a.m. that any significant German opposition was encountered. Some Panther tanks, the first to be met in a western theatre, appeared and in the ensuing fight the Canadians destroyed three of these new tanks and captured several self-propelled guns together with ninety prisoners from Heidrich's parachute force. A second tank action developed during the afternoon as Smith's leading tanks approached the Melfa. While this was in progress, a reconnaissance troop of light tanks from Strathcona's Horse found a crossing over the river and established three of its light tanks on the far bank, forming a small but immensely valuable bridgehead over the river. Shortly afterwards, one infantry company of the Canadian Westminster Regiment under Major J. K. Mahoney moved forward through the tank battle to reinforce the Strathcona's Horse troop on the far bank. This was the start of the epic action at the crossing of the Melfa which earned Mahoney a very well-deserved Victoria Cross.

About mid-afternoon the German tanks and self-propelled guns disengaged and fell back over the Melfa, taking up positions ready to prevent any further crossings and to eliminate Mahoney's small bridgehead. Attempts by Smith's brigade to push more troops across the wide bed of the Melfa, which was stony and fordable in several places, were stopped by artillery and anti-tank fire. At about five o'clock the rest of the Westminsters reached the river and tried to cross both north and south of Mahoney's position. The southern company failed to reach the river bank as it was stopped in the open by heavy fire, but the northern company managed to cross only to find itself unable to reach Mahoney along the far bank. The latter had meanwhile driven off two tank attacks, using Piat bombs and by firing every weapon in his small bridgehead force to give the impression of a much larger force. After dark, the other companies of the Westminsters were brought round and infiltrated across the river into his bridgehead, hauling with them their six-pounder anti-tank guns to make the position secure when daylight came.

While Hoffmeister's armoured division was exploiting north-west-ward, Vokes assembled a force under his reconnaissance regiment's commander, Lieutenant-Colonel F. D. Adams, to follow up Baade's withdrawal from Pontecorvo along the north bank of the Liri. This consisted of his own regiment, the 4th Canadian Reconnaissance Regiment, three squadrons of tanks and the Carlton and York Regiment from 3 (Canadian) Brigade. Adams set off during the morning of 24 May and engaged Baade's rearguard in a running fight all day, halting for the night about two miles short of the junction of the Melfa and Liri. The Canadian Corps was thus almost up to, and in one place over, the Melfa by the end of the day, and had every reason to be satisfied with their success. It was the first time that the 5 (Canadian) Armoured Division had been in action as a division and the first time that an armoured division of any nationality had been employed in the classic break-through role in the Italian campaign. Unfortunately, the position in the rear of Hoffmeister's division was not so flattering.

The greatest confusion and congestion reigned on the inadequate tracks behind the Canadian advance. The traffic jams were so bad that it was difficult either to consolidate or exploit the armoured brigade's success. Throughout the night his bridgehead over the Melfa was out of effective range of the bulk of the artillery allotted to his support. Not only was it difficult to move the guns forward, but vital items like engineer bridging vehicles and bulldozers, without which tracks could not be improved, were jammed in the chaotic conditions on the tracks through the Hitler Line. The track which had been used by Smith's brigade in his break-out was to have been clear of all Canadian traffic by 2.30 p.m. on 24 May so as to allow 6 (Br) Armoured Division of XIII (Br) Corps to advance round the south of Aquino to deal with Heidrich's men blocking Route 6 and then to advance in parallel with Hoffmeister's division on Ceprano. Burns' description of the situation runs:

> Returning to HQ at 12.30 hours, I found the Army Commander and Lieutenant-General Kirkman, Commander of 13 Corps, waiting, and it was requested that 'Heart Route' should be cleared as soon as possible for the 6th British Armoured Division to pass through in order that they could move forward on the right of 5 (Canadian) Armoured Division . . . thus securing the right flank of 5 (Canadian) Armoured Division for the move forward. Orders were given to do this and it was estimated at the time by the GSO I Canadian Armoured Division that the road could be clear for the advance of 6 (Br) Armoured Division by 1430 hours. However, the rest of the afternoon and evening, due to difficulties caused by bad roads and stream crossings, congestion and unexplained delays occurred and 5 (Canadian) Armoured Division did not get clear until about 2100 hours.

As a result of these delays, XIII (Br) Corps could not advance during 24 May. 78 (Br) Division was occupied with Aquino and the Polish Corps, supported by 8 (Indian) Division, with Piedimonte. At last light on 24 May Heidrich was still in possession of both. Kirkman appreciated that a German withdrawal must be imminent and so he instructed Evelegh to move his 6 (Br) Armoured Division round the south of Aquino at first light on 25 May and to come up on the right of the Canadians on the Melfa. Keightley's 78 (Br) Division would clear Aquino from the south and then advance along Route 6, repairing the bridges as it went, to make it Eighth Army's centre line along which the logistic traffic would be passed to support the advance. Whichever of these two divisions crossed the Melfa first was to advance up Route 6 to Arce.

Early on 25 May patrols reported Aquino and Piedimonte had been evacuated by the Germans. 6 (Br) Armoured Division, led by the Derbyshire Yeomanry Group, set off on its intended route round the south of Aquino and ran almost at once into unexpected trouble in the form of an extensive minefield across its path. The Canadians had bumped the same field but had changed the route to another line further south. This information had never been passed to the Derbyshire Yeomanry and so the whole division, which was already committed to this particular line of advance, was held up until the sappers managed to clear a way through some five hours later. 78 (Br) Division was luckier. By a stroke of good fortune the Germans had omitted to blow the two small bridges over the Forme d'Aquino within the ruins of Aquino, and these were found to be just strong and wide enough to take tanks and

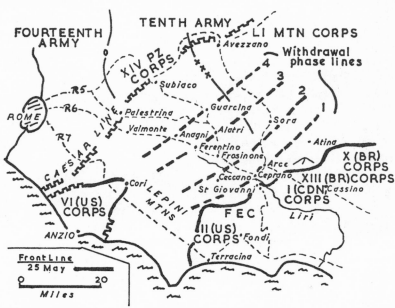

32   Tenth Army's withdrawal plan

self-propelled guns. Up on the mountainside above Aquino, the Poles had entered Piedimonte and were then withdrawn into reserve for re-organisation and rest. Their casualties had been so heavy that it would take them some time to absorb reinforcements, retrain and re-equip. Their place on the north side of the Liri Valley was taken by 8 (Indian) Division which emerged through the ruins of Piedimonte to continue the advance over the southern spurs of Monte Cairo alongside the other two divisions of Kirkman's Corps. By about 1 p.m. all three divisions were advancing in parallel towards the Melfa, which they reached in the late afternoon and succeeded in crossing during the night.

Feurstein's LI Mountain Corps was now in a chaotic condition. He had intended to make the Melfa the long-stop behind the Hitler Line to which he could withdraw when its continued defence became impracticable, either because it had been outflanked by the French or, and this seemed less likely, it had been breached by Eighth Army. So sudden had Burns' break-through been and so rapid his advance to the Melfa, that Smith's Canadian Armoured Brigade was on the river before Heidrich received Feurstein's withdrawal plan. The 1 Parachute Division was still a fighting formation, but Baade's 90 Panzer Grenadier Division was in a sorry state and was barely capable of forming effective rearguards. Only the arrival of reinforcements from 44 Division in the mountain sector enabled him to show any front at all. Feurstein's only way of delaying Eighth Army was to depend upon his artillery, which was still relatively strong, and upon his engineers, who could be relied upon to put a methodical demolition and mining plan in action. Each obstacle created by his engineers blowing bridges and culverts would be watched by artillery observers, and, when possible, would be covered by a few tanks or self-propelled guns. In this way he could make the Allies halt at every blown bridge and every minefield, thus gaining time for the creation of new delaying positions in the rear. The country was ideal for such tactics if only he and the other German commanders at tactical level could persuade the High Command to authorise a slow methodical withdrawal of this type.

Persuading the German High Command was no easy task because at the highest level, Hitler had already espoused the doctrine of 'no withdrawal' as an article of Nazi faith. At midday on 25 May, when Smith's tanks were already over the Melfa, von Vietinghoff was relaying Kesselring's instructions to Feurstein:

> I would like to emphasise that according to the Führer's orders the Melfa Line must be held for several days. An early withdrawal is out of the question. Enemy elements that have crossed the river must be thrown back. . . .

Feurstein rightly objected, saying that he would not bring back many men if he held on at all costs. Von Vietinghoff in his turn tried to impress upon Kesselring the hopelessness of the situation on the Melfa, with little success. He was told that the Führer absolutely demands that any withdrawal be carried out step by step and with the consent of the Army Group. If at all possible, no withdrawal should be made without the personal concurrence of the Führer.

By the end of 25 May there could be no doubt in German commanders' minds, either at the highest strategic or lowest tactical level, that von Vietinghoff's Tenth Army was in a very dangerous position. Von Mackensen had failed, as will be seen in the next chapter, to hold Truscott's break-out from Anzio. The 29 Panzer Grenadier Division had been overwhelmed by Keyes' II (US) Corps at Terracina, and Keyes' advanced patrols had made contact with patrols from the Anzio beachhead. Juin's Frenchmen, after three days' hard fighting, had driven 26 Panzer Division back from Pico and over the Liri into Eighth Army's sector, entering San Giovanni as Adams' Force of 1 (Canadian) Division crossed the Melfa. Kesselring's last reserve mobile division, the Hermann Göring Division, had been ordered south to help von Mackensen. The Hitler Line was now some miles behind Eighth Army's leading troops. There could be only one decision which Kesselring could take. Withdraw, whether Hitler liked it or not, to the Caesar Line.

Hitler grudgingly gave his approval for a 'methodical and economical' withdrawal. Von Mackensen was to hold firm in the Alban Hills while von Vietinghoff withdrew slowly into the Caesar Line, nursing and saving his troops while gaining as much time as possible for the occupation and improvement of their new main line of resistance covering Rome. 94 and 71 Divisions were to be brought back into the line after reinforcement from Germany, and a fresh division would be brought in from Yugoslavia to release 356 Division garrisoning Genoa, to strengthen the Caesar Line. In issuing his orders to his Army commanders, Kesselring stressed that the immediate object was not to reach the Caesar Line as soon as possible. It was to hold designated delaying positions so stubbornly that casualties inflicted on the Allies would be heavy enough to break their fighting potential before they reached the Caesar Line. Construction work on the line was to be accelerated by impressing local labour as well as using garrison troops and the Todt organisation. The delaying positions were to be:

1 Ceprano–Arce on the upper Liri.
2 The Frosinone watershed between the Liri–Sacco basin and the Roman Plain on the line Ceccano–Ripi.
3 Ferentino–Alatri.
4 Anagni–Guarcino.

A prolonged stand was to be made on the fourth line before withdrawing into the Caesar Line at Valmonte. The Italian countryside was ideal for delaying actions and the Germans were very adept at delaying tactics. The Germans had a very fair chance of success, given reasonable luck. Kesselring had always been a lucky commander and was at his best when he was forced to improvise. He had lost the battles of the Gustav and Hitler Lines, but he was now determined to recoup by winning the battle of the Caesar Line.

Act III The Caesar Line

'At long last all our forces were reunited, and we began to reap the harvest from our winter sowing at Anzio.'

Churchill, '*The Closing Ring*'

Chronology
Act III The Caesar Line
23 May–5 June

	Fifth Army	*Eighth Army*	*German Army*
23 May	Break out from Anzio starts	Canadians assault Hitler Line	Hermann Göring Division released by OKW
24 May	Cisterna surrounded	Canadians reach Melfa	Hermann Göring and 92 Divisions ordered to Valmonte. Moves to be made in daylight
25 May	Cisterna and Cori taken; Allied Air Forces destroy German reinforcing units; Mark Clark orders change of direction to north-west	Melfa crossed by Canadians and XIII (Br) Corps	Kesselring authorises Tenth Army withdrawal to Caesar Line
26 May	VI (US) Corps changes direction; Artena surrounded	Advance to Upper Liri; 6 (Br) Armoured Division stopped at Arce	Hermann Göring Division reaches Valmonte
27 May	VI (US) Corps checked by Caesar defences at Lanuvio	Attempts to cross Upper Liri and to clear Arce	Withdrawal of Tenth Army to Frosinone Line authorised
28 May	Preparations to breach Caesar Line west of Alban Hills	Bridging failure prevents crossing of Upper Liri	1 Para Corps settles into Caesar Line west of Alban Hills
29 May	VI (US) Corps renews assault on Caesar Line; Campoleone taken but attacks on Lanuvio fail	Advance resumed on Frosinone	Arce abandoned

	Fifth Army	Eighth Army	German Army
30 May	36 (US) Division plans to exploit Monte Artemisio gap; II (US) Corps takes over Valmonte thrust	In contact with German second delaying line south of Frosinone	Tenth Army authorised to abandon Frosinone
31 May	36 (US) Division capture Monte Artemisio	Frosinone entered; infantry divisions take the lead	Hermann Göring Division fails to retake Monte Artemisio
1 June	Fifth Army opens final drive east and west of Alban Hills	Ferentino reached	
2 June	Velletri taken and Route 6 cut near Valmonte	Anagni reached	Fourteenth Army start withdrawal from Caesar Line during night 2–3 June
3 June	Valmonte and Lanuvio fall	Canadians meet French and II (US) Corps at Colleferro	4 Parachute Division forms rearguard for Fourteenth Army
4 June	Leading troops reach Tiber bridges in Rome	Eighth Army east of Rome	Rome evacuated
5 June	a.m. Rome in Allied hands p.m. Overlord is launched		

10 The Break Out from Anzio

'0545! There was a crash of thunder and bright lightning flashes against the sky behind us as more than a thousand guns, infantry cannon, mortars, tanks and tank destroyers opened fire. That first crash settled into a continuous rumbling roar. Some distance ahead, a wall of fire appeared as our first salvos crashed into the enemy front lines, then tracers wove eerie patterns in streaks of light as hundreds of machine guns of every calibre poured a hail of steel into the enemy positions.'

Truscott's description of the openings of the break-out battle
('Command Missions')

The beginning of the third and last act of Diadem overlapped the climax of the second. On 21 May Alexander had directed his two Army commanders to reopen their respective offensives early on 23 May—Oliver Leese to breach the Hitler Line as already described and Mark Clark to break out from Anzio. This gave Truscott less than the three days' warning which he had asked for during planning, but, as he had been able to anticipate events and had already been alerted on 18 May for a possible break-out attempt on 21 May, this shortness of notice proved no problem to the VI (US) Corps staff. 36 (US) Division was arriving in the beachhead and would be concentrated in time to back up the offensive. Moreover, the weather forecasts, though not good, had improved and were now sufficiently promising to give a fair chance of full air support over the beachhead on 23 May.

Truscott's offensive was much more like an orthodox breaching operation than Burns' attack on the Hitler Line. VI (US) Corps had been waiting for almost three months for this battle; planning, developing breaching techniques, reconnoitring the obstacles in their path and training hard in the tasks which they expected would occur when Alexander eventually gave the order to attack. During those three long dispiriting months many novel devices had been invented to overcome the German defences. Unlike the Hitler Line, the German containing perimeter did not include large numbers of concrete bunkers nor any of the lethal panther turrets. It depended for its strength on three other factors: higher ground from which artillery observers could overlook all the likely Allied axes of attack; well-dug field defences which grew in numbers and depth as the weeks passed; and extensive belts of mines and wire. Several of the devices developed at Anzio to breach these defences have since become standard military equipment. There was the 'snake' which was very like the infantry 'bangalore torpedo' of the First World War but very much bigger—about 400 feet long—and pushed by a tank instead of infantrymen. Snakes were made of six-inch diameter, galvanised-iron pipe filled with explosive to which was fixed a rounded nose to guide it through wire and other obstacles. The last ten feet of the tube were filled with sand to protect the tank when the snake was detonated. Having pushed the snake through the minefield, the tank was uncoupled, reversed and then exploded the device by firing its machine gun into a target detonator on the rear end of the snake. The explosion cleared all wire and most—the emphasis being on the word 'most'—of the mines in its path to a width sufficient for tanks to move through the gap. A similar device for infantry consisted of a light explosive-filled hose or a rope of detonating cord carried across anti-personnel mine-fields by a grapnel fire from a mortar. This produced a furrow just wide enough for infantrymen to run along in single file with a fair chance of not hitting an unexploded mine. Another device to help the infantry which has not withstood the march of time so well, was an armoured sledge towed behind a tank in which the tanks' supporting infantry could lie with some protection in the early stages of an attack. Tanks draw all kinds of fire, making riding on them or walking beside them a hazardous way of advancing. The Anzio battle-sledges could be hooked together and six could be towed behind each tank, giving its infantry an uncomfortable but less vulnerable way of moving with it.

With so much time in which to think, there was a danger that VI (US) Corps' plans would become over-complex and impractical. Truscott was too experienced a soldier to let this happen. Most of the ingenious ideas thought up in the beachhead served to boost morale during the long dreary weeks of waiting rather than to increase tactical efficiency during the actual offensive. Truscott depended for success on simplicity of concept, on meticulous planning to ensure the most effective use of artillery and air support, and on a carefully thought out deception plan. The last was based on concealment of troop concentrations and on deceptive use of artillery. The actual attack was to be supported, as on the Gustav and Hitler Lines, by a barrage after a short period of preparatory fire. Truscott realised that the preparatory fire would alert the Germans to the imminence of the attack which they knew must come sooner or later at Anzio and so he decided to make the preparatory part of the programme a routine daily occurrence. From the beginning of Diadem until the actual break-out morning the VI (US) Corps artillery fired a short but intense harassing programme at varying times between 5.30 and 6.30 a.m. every morning. At first there was a strong German artillery reaction, showing Truscott's observers where the German defensive fire would fall. As the days went by, the Germans paid less and less attention to these early-morning fireworks which they began to treat as a daily waste of ammunition by the thriftless Americans. The timing of the real attack was further concealed by setting it for 6.30. This would catch the Germans just as they relaxed after the usual dawn stand-to, feeling that the day was to be much the same as any other in the beachhead—frightening because of the constant American artillery harassing fire and air attacks, and yet boring through its monotony and repetitiveness.

On paper the two sides were very evenly matched, and as neither had engaged the other seriously since the beginning of March they had both had time to prepare for the ultimate trial of strength. Von Mackensen had originally deployed five divisions (*see fig. 3*) in the line with Baade's 90 Panzer Grenadier Division and von Lüttwitz's 26 Panzer Division in reserve close behind the beachhead, making a total of seven divisions to contain Truscott's six. Alexander had succeeded in drawing the two German reserve divisions into the Liri Valley cauldron. For a time von Mackensen had been given Fries' 29 Panzer Grenadier Division from Civitavecchia, but this too had been drawn south to Terracina against his personal advice. Kesselring had promised him Schmalz's Hermann Göring Division and the recently formed but only half-trained 92 Division from Civitavecchia, if the Allies tried to break out from Anzio. Kesselring was convinced that von Mackensen had adequate resources with which to beat back any attack which Truscott might launch against the German containing perimeter; and so he had, even though he did not know that Truscott's force had grown to seven divisions in the last few days. Seven to five was not a large margin of superiority for a successful attack against deep defences prepared with German thoroughness on higher commanding ground.

The weakness in von Mackensen's position did not lie in inferior numbers or equipment; it lay in a false appreciation of Truscott's intentions. Von Mackensen was convinced that when the break-out came it would be northwards towards Albano and the Alban Hills (*see fig. 13*), and would probably be launched from the western half of the beachhead up the old British axis of attack along the Albano road through Campoleone. This was the direct road to Rome and to the Alban Hills whose seizure would be essential to any Allied advance on the capital. If Truscott did in fact attack from the eastern half of the beachhead towards Cisterna or over the Mussolini Canal it would either be a diversion to draw German reserves away from the Alban Hills or an attempt to link up with Allied troops advancing from the south-east. It was much less important to stop a break-out here than it was to hold the road to Rome. Moreover, the western sector of the beachhead and the Alban Hills were all part of the Caesar Line which gave an added reason for giving the west priority over the east. Basing his defence on this thinking, von Mackensen had deployed General Alfred Schlemm's 1 Parachute Corps with 4 Para, 65 Infantry and 3 Panzer Grenadier Divisions to hold the western sector and to block the direct road to Rome. General Herr's weaker LXXVI Panzer Corps had been given the task of holding Cisterna and the eastern sector with two infantry divisions—Heinz Greiner's 362 Division in Cisterna and Hans-Georg Hildebrandt's 715 Division on the Mussolini Canal. Neither of these divisions were of particularly high quality, whereas Schlemm's divisions could be trusted to defeat almost any attack which the Allies cared to mount. The very name of the Corps was sufficient to ensure a ruthless defence.

Von Mackensen's false appreciation of Allied intentions did not escape Kesselring's notice. He felt that von Mackensen was far too parochial. In his memoirs he says that he decided to open von Mackensen's eyes to the true situation by shifting Fourteenth Army's boundary to include the Pontine Marshes and the Lepini Mountains, thus forcing him to watch his south-eastern flank. This change of boundary had little effect other than causing a further deterioration in the relationship between the Fourteenth Army and the Army Group 'C' staff, and the weakening 3 Panzer Grenadier Division from which von Mackensen detached a regimental group to help slow the French advance through the Lepini Mountains. Liaison between von Vietinghoff's retreating Tenth

Army and von Mackensen's headquarters seems to have been very tenuous.

Truscott's plan 'Buffalo', which Alexander had insisted was the only one worth using, was directed at Cisterna and would fall almost entirely on Herr's weaker Corps. The offensive was to be in three phases. In the first phase, which would be the break into Herr's defences, Truscott's old 3 (US) Division, now under John O'Daniel, was to attack Cisterna

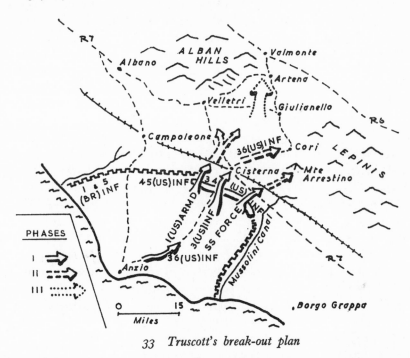

33   Truscott's break-out plan

itself with Harmon's 1 (US) Armoured Division supporting his left and Robert Frederick's 1st Special Service Force supporting his right. 3 (US) Division would attack through Ryder's 34 (US) Division which was holding the line in the Cisterna sector and was also charged with clearing gaps through the German minefields before O'Daniel's attack started. In the second phase, Walker's 36 (US) Division, fresh from its sea trip, would pass through 3 (US) Division and head for Cori on the extreme northern end of the Lipini range. Harmon's armour would drive up the valley between the Alban and Lepini Hills to protect 36 (US) Division from a German counter-attack which seemed likely as long as elements of 26 Panzer Division remained in the area. Although they had all in fact moved south before Truscott's attack took place, he had no means of knowing that this would happen. The Special Service Force would protect the southern flank by taking the hills above Cori. In the third phase, the whole Corps was to press forward towards Artena and its ultimate objective—Route 6 at Valmonte. The two British Divisions—1 and 5 (Br) Divisions—would protect the northern half of the beachhead and ensure that the 1 Parachute Corps did not interfere with the break-out. Eagle's 45 (US) Division would act as a link between the British and the attacking American divisions. Its main task was to keep 3 Panzer Grenadier Division quiet on the northern flank of the attack. To ease Truscott's problems the British divisions were placed under direct command of Fifth Army headquarters.

Mark Clark moved to his advanced command post at Anzio on 22 May. At a news conference given to war correspondents in the cellars of the Villa Borghese, which served as Fifth Army's headquarters for the battle, he laid great stress on Fifth Army taking Rome. Rome and only Rome mattered; and it was going to be Fifth Army which took the city—no one else. The correspondents had noted the transfer of the two British divisions to Fifth Army command and quite unfairly attributed this to political motives. In fact, there were very good operational and administrative reasons for doing this. Truscott had to concentrate all of his and his staff's attention on the break-out in the Cisterna area. If any counter-attacks developed, as they well might do, on the northern flank, it was far better that someone else should deal with the situation there. Mark Clark's staff had the capacity and was ideally placed to do so.

Dawn on 23 May broke at Anzio at 0538. A light drizzle was falling and at 0545 the usual American early-morning bombardment began, though with greater intensity than on previous days. The Germans had just had another active night of patrolling and probing to assess whether an American attack was coming or not, but they could report nothing unusual and so settled down to routine tasks. This time the American shelling seemed to go on longer; it seemed much heavier and more weapons were firing over a wider front than usual, but this was not significant enough to cause undue alarm. At 0625, however, waves of fighter-bombers appeared and started attacking targets in and around Cisterna. The intensity of the artillery bombardment increased to a crescendo and five minutes later died away and was replaced by the steadier roll of a creeping barrage. The American tanks and infantry loomed up out of the smoke all along the front from Carano in the west to the Mussolini Canal in the east. Tactical surprise was complete. Many of the Germans were caught in their bunkers, often with their equipment off, as they attended to their morning business after dawn stand down. The targeting of the American preliminary bombardment had been based on weeks of careful detection work piecing together clues obtained from

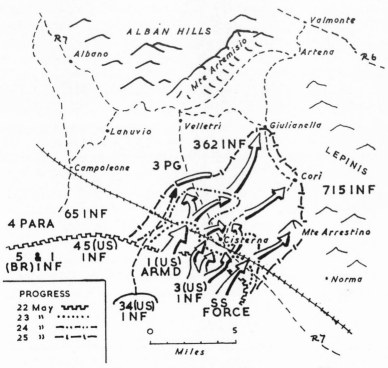

34 *The development of Truscott's offensive, 23–25 May*

air photography, front-line observation, patrol reports, interrogation of prisoners and so forth. So successful had their work been that most of the vital German communications and command posts were obliterated in the sharp forty-minute preliminary bombardment. This resulted in the German defenders reacting more slowly than usual. Their artillery defensive fire came down too late and was too halting to stop the Americans overrunning most of their forward positions in the first rush. After this initial setback the German defence never fully recovered.

The fighting was hard and brutal for the next three days, but there was little doubt that Herr's Corps had been beaten and would be compelled to withdraw or disintegrate. During 23 May all three American divisions fought their way over the railway west of Cisterna; O'Daniel's 3 (US) Division came within a mile of the town itself; and Frederick's Special Service Force succeeded in cutting Route 7 east of the town. Greiner's 362 Division fought back with typical German tenacity, but by the end of the day had surrendered over 1,500 prisoners. The American losses had been just as heavy. O'Daniel's division alone lost 950 men, and the attacking force as a whole lost over 100 tanks and self-propelled guns to German mines and anti-tank guns. American losses might have been much heavier had it not been for the magnificent support given to the VI (US) Corps by the Allied Air Forces which flew nearly seven hundred bomber and fighter-bomber sorties during the day. Most of these were against German artillery positions which had been so accurately located before the offensive that the air strikes produced a much more noticeable reduction in German artillery fire than they had done in the Liri Valley battles.

The 24 May is best described as a fierce dog-fight. Harmon's 1 (US) Armoured Division attacked in two directions. His Combat Command 'A' advanced up Route 7 towards Velletri to protect the northern flank of Truscott's breach in the German defences. It soon ran into stiffening resistance from Schlemm's Parachute Corps and was forced on to the defensive to repel a number of tank and infantry counter-attacks. His Combat Command 'B' had an extremely successful day. It broke through the crust of the hastily improved German line of anti-tank guns and mines west of the Cisterna–Cori road and advanced three miles behind the town. In Cisterna itself 956 Grenadier Regiment of Greiner's 362 Division fought a stubborn battle with O'Daniel's division. In spite of a severe pounding by American heavy artillery and by Allied aircraft, O'Daniel's men could find no way of penetrating the town's defences. His attacking regiments had crossed Route 7 either side of the town by nightfall but there was still no sign of a German withdrawal from the town itself. Further south, in the Special Service Force sector, Hildebrandt's 715 Division had mounted a series of rather uncoordinated counter-attacks and was now withdrawing in some confusion towards the Lepini Hills to avoid being cut off.

During the night 24–25 May, Truscott made his preparations for a decisive break-through. He brought up elements of Ryder's 34 (US)

Division to take over Harmon's task of protecting the western flank of
the breach, thus releasing his armour for an armoured drive towards
Valmonte; Frederick's Special Service Force made ready to dash for
Monte Arrestino above Cori; and O'Daniel's division prepared to
liquidate the defenders of Cisterna and to push on to Cori. On the German side, conditions in Herr's Corps sector were chaotic. 715 Division
was struggling to withdraw by way of Norma in the Lepini Mountains;
parts of 362 Division were grimly holding Cisterna without much hope
of relief; and the leading elements of the Hermann Göring Division and
a regiment of 92 Division were moving into the Cori–Giulianello area to
plug the gap between Herr's and Schlemm's Corps. So desperate had the
German situation become that they were forced to move units in daylight in spite of Allied air superiority.

25 May was a grim day for the German Fourteenth Army. The
movements of the Hermann Göring and 92 Divisions were spotted by
Allied airmen who lost no time in inflicting serious damage on both
divisions. Particularly heavy movement was seen in the Valmonte–
Giulianello–Cori areas. Every available fighter and fighter-bomber was
diverted from planned sorties to take advantage of this unexpected
target. By dusk the Air Forces claimed over 600 vehicles destroyed and
another 450 damaged. Such figures cannot, of course, be checked, but
evidence found on the ground in the next few days as the Americans
advanced, corroborated the airmen's claim to have carried out one of the
most damaging air operations of the campaign. The whole valley between
the Alban and Lepini Hills was strewn with twisted burnt-out hulks of
German tanks, self-propelled guns and vehicles.

Events on the ground were no less disastrous for Herr's LXXVI
Panzer Corps. Harmon's division broke through and reached Giulianello. Frederick's Special Service Force reached the summit of Monte
Arrestino. Combat Engineer patrols from the beachhead, pressing
forward in the wake of 715 Division's withdrawal from the eastern flank
of the perimeter, met fellow Combat engineers leading Keyes' advance
from Terracina at Borgo Grappa (*see fig. 33*) in the Pontine Marshes.
And in the centre O'Daniel finally crushed the defenders of Cisterna
after a day-long fight in the ruins of the town. At 7 p.m. the commander
of 956 Grenadier Regiment at last capitulated. Cori had by then fallen
to other units of O'Daniel's division which had by-passed the town and
so there was no way out.

In three days Truscott had broken von Mackensen's containing

perimeter. Herr's Corps was on the point of collapse. 2,640 German
prisoners had been taken at heavy cost to 1 (US) Armoured and 3 (US)
Divisions, and Truscott had not yet had to commit Walker's 36 (US)
Division. He now held a firm base from Cisterna through Giulianello
to Cori from which he could develop his attack on Valmonte to cut von
Vietinghoff's line of retreat. There was very little that von Mackensen
could do to stop him. The Americans were tired but elated by victory
and had plenty of reserves in hand. 26 May could have been the decisive
day of Diadem. Mark Clark and not von Mackensen or Truscott deci-

35   *The alternative axes for 26 May*

ded otherwise. It can be said that overnight he threw away the chance
of destroying the right wing of von Vietinghoff's Tenth Army for the
honour of entering Rome first.

Events in the higher echelons of the Allied command on 25 May will
always be the subject of controversy and endless speculation because the
arguments are finely balanced and the events cannot be replayed to prove
or disprove the various courses of action. Too much has probably been
made of this incident because journalists are apt to magnify differences
of opinion amongst senior commanders as they make more interesting
reading than stories of smooth, harmonious cooperation. There was,

however, a genuine dilemma in operational policy which was interesting even if the political gloss had not been added. There are two schools of thought about the correct directives which should have been issued on 25 May. For shorthand purposes, the football cliché of playing the ball rather than the man serves as an apt analogy. Churchill, Alexander and Truscott wished to play the ball. They wanted to destroy von Vietinghoff's Tenth Army by continuing the attack towards Valmonte. Mark Clark, Gruenther—his chief of staff—and Lemnitzer, the senior American officer on Alexander's staff, possibly out of loyalty to their master, wanted to go for the man—the political objective of seizing Rome—which would in their view be attained quicker by changing the axis of attack to the west side of the Alban Hills (i.e. changing to the 'Turtle' Plan).

If we discard all the emotional motives of going down in history as the latest conqueror of Rome or of ensuring that America and the world knew how much the American Fifth Army had done towards winning the war, Mark Clark's change of plan on 25 May had many sound military advantages. Unfortunately these are masked by the tone of his own memoirs which suggest that emotion rather than military logic was the dominant force that made him order the change of plan from Buffalo to Turtle. Let us, for a moment, weigh both sides of the argument from the military point of view. Alexander, it should be noted, loyally makes no mention of the controversy in his despatches and takes full responsibility for Mark Clark's change of plan.

Looked at on a black and white map, showing towns, roads, railways and only a generalisation of the hills, the attack towards Valmonte appears like a classic encircling movement which, if successful, would cut von Vietinghoff's escape routes and pin his Army against the mountain backbone of the Italian peninsula. Eighth Army's slowness in forcing von Senger's and Feurstein's Corps out of the Hitler Line could be looked upon as a positive advantage. If, however, the detailed contours of the hills are shown on the map, even the armchair strategist might have his doubts about the efficacy of the encircling move. Truscott's Corps might cut Route 6 but this would still leave Route 82 to Avezzano and the Subiaco road to Arsoli through which Feurstein and von Senger could withdraw to take up their allotted positions in the Caesar Line. Between Valmonte and Avezzano lie a series of hill and mountain ridges which would have barred Truscott's advance to cut these escape routes. Moreover, if he did attempt such an operation he would be committing the classic military sin of making a flank march across the front of an undefeated enemy force. Not only would he be vulnerable to a counter-attack from Velletri or Valmonte by Schlemm's Parachute Corps or Schmalz's Hermann Göring Division, he would also be vulnerable to strong concentrations of German artillery directed by observers on the Alban Hills and would suffer the same harassing fire as Kirkman's Corps endured advancing along Route 6 in the Liri Valley while overlooked by Monte Cairo. There were thus two very good reasons for doubting the correctness of continuing the thrust towards Valmonte.

The case against changing to Turtle in mid-stream is equally strong. A breach had been made. Herr's Corps was utterly defeated and the leading elements of the Hermann Göring Division which had been ordered to hold Valmonte were already in disarray. The Valmonte thrust line was wide open provided VI (US) Corps did not hesitate and allow Herr to recover his balance. The Turtle axis on the other hand, which ran from the town of Campoleone west of the Alban Hills was not only blocked by Schlemm's unbroken Corps but by a strongly-prepared section of the Caesar Line as well. The chances of a break-through here were slender because it was the obvious and most heavily-defended route to Rome. It would only be practicable to use this axis if and when von Mackensen was forced to detach units from Schlemm's Corps to reinforce other more threatened sectors of the Caesar Line. The attack towards Valmonte, if it did not cut off von Vietinghoff, might force von Mackensen to weaken his western flank sufficiently to give Truscott a chance of breaking through by a sudden switch of plan.

The balance of advantage from the strictly military point of view lay with continuing Buffalo at least until there was concrete evidence to suggest that Schlemm's hold on the Turtle axis had been critically weakened by detachments. No immediate change of plan would be needed and hence maximum pressure could be maintained on Herr's shaken Corps. Even if the capture of Valmonte to the north did not seal von Vietinghoff's escape it would reduce the number of routes open to him and so increase the chances of the Allied Air Forces inflicting greater damage on his retreating units in the narrow Subiaco and Sora valleys. The arrival of the Eighth Army at Valmonte would be the moment for Fifth Army to switch to the Turtle axis. A simultaneous attack by both Armies at that moment might have spelt the destruction of Kesselring's Army Group. Eighth Army might have driven rapidly past

27   *A typical German rearguard action; leading reconnaissance vehicles of Eighth Army caught in German artillery fire*

ADVANCING UP ROUTE 6

28   *A tank destroyer trying to dislodge the German rearguard holding a village blocking Route 6*

29   *The fall of Cisterna: prisoners from 365 Division being searched in the ruins*

THE BREAK-OUT FROM ANZIO

30   *3 (US) Division entering Cori*

Rome and up the Tiber Valley, as Alexander had originally intended, and Fifth Army would have occupied Rome and advanced up the west coast before von Mackensen could recover. The full weight of Alexander's Army Group would have been brought to bear instead of, as actually happened, only two Corps of Fifth Army.

The military factors were, unfortunately, not the only ones considered by Mark Clark. Emotion swayed the day, making him determined to secure Rome for his Army even though Alexander's operational directives before and during Diadem never suggested that anyone else would enter Rome. In his despatches Alexander says nothing about the altercations with his American Army Commanders and the Fifth Army Staff. He explains quite simply that by 25 May he had Kesselring exactly where he wanted him:

> To use an old-fashioned military parlance, I was now employing the 'oblique order' beloved by Frederick the Great, with my left advanced *en potence* and my right, 5 Corps, refused. In my centre I had a very strong and concentrated force, 1 Canadian and 13 Corps under Eighth Army, with which, while my left held the enemy by forcing him to fight for Rome on whose retention he set much value, I intended to drive forward on an axis parallel to the extension of my left, break through the enemy's centre thus weakened and pursue up the centre of the Peninsula, east of Rome. This would enable me to carry out the classical manoeuvre of parallel pursuit, for at the same time Fifth Army would continue to press hard against the extreme right flank of the enemy forcing back his seaward flank. There were, therefore, topographically considered, two objectives: to capture Rome and to pass a force east of Rome up the axis of the Tiber where it flows southwards from the Mountains of Umbria. These two objectives I allotted to the two Armies, the former to General Clark and the latter to General Leese. This allotment of tasks had, in fact, been made before the battle began and the operation proceeded so closely according to my original plan that there was no need to change it.

Truscott records that he discussed the possibility of changing direction with Mark Clark during the evening of 24 May. His description of the conversation runs:

> Late that afternoon, I returned to the Command Post at Conca to meet General Clark. He wanted to know whether or not I had

considered changing the direction of the attack to the north-west, toward Rome. I replied that it had occurred to me that continuing our attack might alarm the German command to the danger to their line of communications and cause them to concentrate all available reserves in the Valmontone Gap to oppose us. I thought that we should certainly find the Hermann Göring Division, which was then en route from northern Italy, in that area; and it was possible that the German command might withdraw the 3rd Panzer Grenadier Division, or the 4th Parachute Division, or both, from the beachhead front, to oppose us there. Any such concentration might delay us at Valmontone long enough to permit the German main forces to escape. If there was any withdrawal from the western part of the beachhead, I thought that an attack to the northwest might be the best way to cut off the enemy withdrawal north of the Alban Hills. My staff was already preparing plans to meet this contingency. Clark agreed with my analysis and asked that I keep the plans up to date.

Next evening, 25 May, Truscott arrived back at his command post to find one of the Fifth Army operations staff with orders for VI (US) Corps to change direction to the north-west. Truscott would not accept the order at first. There was no evidence of 3 Panzer Grenadier or 4 Parachute Division moving towards Valmonte which was the prerequisite for any successful thrust west of the Alban Hills. On the contrary, only the reconnaissance elements of the Hermann Göring Division lay between O'Daniel and Route 6. This was no time to switch to the north-west when the Germans were still strong and while there was a chance of cutting at least one of von Vietinghoff's withdrawal routes. Truscott tried to confirm the order personally with Mark Clark, but he had already left the beachhead and had returned to his main headquarters after being photographed at a restaged meeting of the II and VI (US) Corps' patrols at Borgo Grappa for publicity purposes. Truscott had to accept the order and set his staff to work on the complex task of regrouping on the new thrust line.

The speed with which VI (US) Corps arranged the change of axis reflects great credit on this very experienced Corps headquarters. It had commanded the American sector at the Salerno landings; it had fought in the early battles during the approach to Cassino; and it had executed the Anzio landing, thereafter defeating two major German counteroffensives. The switch from Buffalo to Turtle was perhaps its greatest feat of intricate high-speed staff work. The divisional commanders received their orders at 11 p.m. on 25 May and the new offensive started exactly twelve hours later at 11 a.m. on 26 May, a performance that Eighth Army had every reason to admire after its own cumbersome movements in the Liri Valley.

Regrouping during the night consisted of pivoting VI (US) Corps upon 1 (Br) Division opposite the Factory on the Albano road. 45 (US)

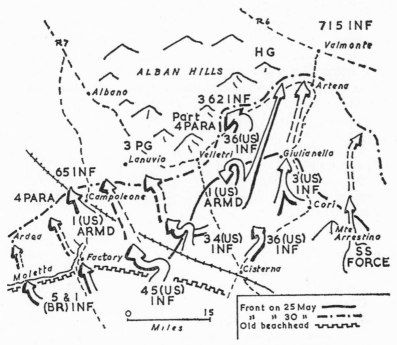

36   VI (US) Corps' regrouping on 25–26 May

Division, which had been protecting the western side of the American salient, prepared to attack north-west to Campoleone station. On its right, 34 (US) Division, which was still scattered across the front, forming a firm base for Harmon and O'Daniel, had to concentrate and form up ready to attack towards Lanuvio. 1 (US) Armoured Division, which was facing towards Valmonte, covering O'Daniel's left flank, turned due north towards Velletri. Only O'Daniel's 3 (US) Division continued with its original thrust towards Artena and thence to Valmonte. Anticipating the eventual need to withdraw Harmon's armoured units to refit, 36

(US) Division was ordered to be ready to take over its sector opposite Velletri.

Back in Caserta and in London there were immediate misgivings about this change of front. Alexander visited Gruenther at main Fifth Army headquarters to obtain his assurance that Mark Clark was not abandoning the Valmonte thrust. Gruenther was able to give this with a clear conscience as O'Daniel was still attacking in that direction although the main emphasis of the attack had changed. Alexander in his usual way of handling situations of this type let Mark Clark have his head. There were several ways of fighting the battle. No one could say which would prove right in the end, so there was no point in creating friction in his multi-national Army Group by rigidly imposing a particular method on a reluctant American Army Commander. Such an attempt could only sow dissension and hence disaster in an Allied team.

In London, Churchill's reaction was less charitable. He signalled to Alexander:

At this distance it seems much more important to cut their line of retreat than anything else. . . . A cop is more important than Rome, which would anyhow come as its consequence. The cop is the one thing that matters.

As the days passed Churchill became more and more irritated with Mark Clark's handling of the battle. It seemed to him that opportunities were being lost which could never recur.

When Truscott's offensive reopened at 11 a.m. on 26 May it met with immediate success. O'Daniel's 3 (US) Division, with its left protected by a specially-constituted task force from 1 (US) Armoured Division under Colonel Howze and its right covered by Frederick's Special Service Force, exploited his previous days' successes by sweeping forward with great *élan* towards Valmonte, in spite of some unfortunate attacks on his troops by Allied aircraft. By dusk he had surrounded Artena, only three miles from Route 6. The town fell next day and from then onwards his artillery observers could cover the road and some of his tanks could bring direct fire upon it. It looked momentarily as if he might be able to sweep across it and cut off von Vietinghoff's escape route, but by then the tide was already turning against him. The bulk of Schmalz's Hermann Göring Division—weakened by running the gauntlet of Allied fighter-bombers in its rush southwards but still a very reliable force—had arrived in the Valmonte area, taking under its wing the remnants of

715 Division and other units retreating in front of the French. Schmalz's instructions were to keep the routes through the Valmonte gap open for at least three days to enable von Senger's Corps to reach its allotted sector in the Caesar Line. Two sharp counter-attacks by his infantry and tanks soon made it clear that O'Daniel's force was not strong enough to go beyond Artena until fresh troops were available to protect 3 (US) Division's lengthening and very exposed flanks. The Valmonte thrust died, temporarily at least, through lack of support at Mark Clark's level.

Immediately to O'Daniel's left, Harmon's armoured division made scant progress in front of Velletri. The country was most unsuitable for tanks, enabling detachments of the 4 Para Division, brought over from the seaward flank of the beachhead, to play havoc amongst 1 (US) Armoured Division's units. Hastily-laid minefields, well-sited anti-tank guns and a fanatical determination to stop the American armour, enabled these paratroopers to discourage any further effort in the Velletri sector. Harmon's division was withdrawn during the night 26–27 May and replaced by Walker's 36 (US) Division with instructions to contain Velletri while maintaining a link between O'Daniel at Artena and Truscott's new main effort towards Lanuvio and Campoleone.

The new VI (US) Corps thrust with Ryder's 34 (US) Division making for Lanuvio and Eagle's 45 (US) Division for Campoleone made rapid progress during 26 May. It was soon clear that they were being opposed only by the rearguards of Schlemm's Corps which fell back as the Americans advanced into the prepared positions of the Caesar Line. On the western side of the Alban Hills, which are a crumpled mass of extinct volcanoes, the Caesar defences were cleverly sited to make the greatest use of the ridges formed in ancient times by the flow of lava running down from the hills towards the sea. Each ridge had steep, scrub-covered sides with a flat crest capped with open wheatfields which afforded ideal fields of fire for machine and anti-tank guns. The line chosen by the Germans ran from in front of Velletri round the base of the hills to Lanuvio, which stood on one of these prominent lava spurs, and thence down to Campoleone and on to the sea coast. As the American attack progressed, its divisions, which were echeloned back to the west, came up against the German main line of resistance in succession. Harmon's armour had been the first to reach the line and had been stopped dead and withdrawn into reserve on 26 May; Ryder came next

and was abruptly halted in front of Lanuvio on 27 May; and Eagle
suffered the same fate slightly later. The German defences presented no
solid line and, in fact, were formed by very effective improvisation.
'Alarm units' were created in each of the three divisions holding the
front and these were rushed from point to point to plug gaps as they
occurred. The ingenuity with which Schlemm's Parachute Corps used
the natural strength of the countryside rivalled Heidrich's and Baade's
defence in the earlier battles of Cassino.

Truscott soon appreciated that German resistance close in around the
foot of the Alban Hills was unlikely to break easily. As in the Liri
Valley, the German artillery observation over his attacking divisions was
too good. If any success was to be won it would probably occur furthest
away from the observation of the Alban Hills on the extreme left in
Eagle's sector. He, therefore, alerted Harmon's 1 (US) Armoured
Division which was still resting and directed it to attack through the
left-hand half of Eagle's sector on 29 May, hoping thereby to achieve an
armoured break-through.

The break-through never came. Ryder's men launched a series of
abortive attacks against Lanuvio suffering heavy losses in the process.
Harmon's and Eagle's renewed attacks progressed well at first. The tanks
initially by-passed many enemy strong-points which stopped the infantry
and separated them from their tank support. The tanks themselves then
ran into an anti-tank screen and, being unsupported by infantry,
suffered heavy losses. Campoleone station was in American hands by the
end of 29 May, but there was little sign of the Germans giving way
except on the extreme western flank where the two British divisions had
pushed forward in step with the American advance and were meeting
only sporadic resistance. They crossed the Moletta Creek—the old
beachhead line—on 29 May and took Ardea on 30 May.

Further heavy fighting during 30 May only confirmed the impression
gained during the previous days. Schlemm's Corps was not going to
give way easily. The Caesar Line west of the Alban Hills was congealing
very satisfactorily from the German point of view. From the Allied point
of view, Mark Clark's switch of plan had brought nothing but heavy
casualties and had allowed von Mackensen to close the dangerous
Valmonte Gap. Fifth Army had been stopped in its attempt to bounce the
Caesar Line in the same way that Eighth Army had been stopped in
front of the Hitler Line. It was time to bring up fresh troops and to re-
open the offensive against the Caesar Line on more deliberate lines.

Keyes' II (US) Corps and Juin's French divisions were closing in rapidly from the south. Moreover, Oliver Leese's Eighth Army might soon be level ready to attack at Valmonte in conjunction with Fifth Army—and possibly share the honours of taking Rome with the Americans.

11 *The Destruction of the Caesar Line*

'Walker told me that his reconnaissance had just found a gap in the enemy lines east of Velletri through which his engineers were sure troops could reach the crest of Colle Laziali (the Alban Hills) back of Velletri. . . . After talking with the engineer who made this reconnaissance I told Walker to go on with the effort . . . this was the turning point in our drive to the North West.'

Truscott's memoirs, 'Command Missions'

Mark Clark's first attempt to break the Caesar Line had failed. His premeditated change of direction had achieved little and had cost Truscott heavy losses. It had also given von Mackensen three precious days in which to strengthen the Valmonte defences and von Vietinghoff the time in which to turn a rout into a methodical withdrawal. There was still a chance that Schlemm's Corps might suffer some unforeseen disaster and give way in front of Truscott's hammer blows, but this was becoming increasingly unlikely as each new American attack was brought to a costly halt. Plans had to be made to bring greater weight to bear and these were already in hand at Army and Army Group level.

When Gruenther assured Alexander that Mark Clark would continue to press towards Valmonte, he did so with a clear conscience because he was already issuing orders for the transfer of most of Keyes' II (US) Corps to the beachhead via Route 7 as soon as the Fifth Army engineers could open a passage overland to the beachhead. Keyes himself was to move ahead with his headquarters to take over the Valmonte thrust. His 88 (US) Division was to follow immediately to join O'Daniel's 3 (US) Division in front of Artena. As soon as mopping-up in the coastal plain was complete, his 85 (US) Division would move to the beachhead as well, to add further weight to the Valmonte thrust. The residual tasks of Keyes' headquarters would be taken over by General Crittenberger's IV (US) Corps which had just arrived in Italy. These plans

came to fruition when Keyes took over the Valmonte sector on 29 May.
The leading elements of 88 (US) Division reached the line on the following day.

The two other sources of reinforcement were Juin's French Expeditionary Corps and Eighth Army. Mark Clark was keen to bring the
former into the line, but hoped that the latter would appear too late to
play any decisive part in 'his' battle for Rome. Alexander and Harding
could not consider such factors. Their task was to destroy as much of
Kesselring's forces as they could. Rome was the magnet which might
enable them to do so; otherwise it had little significance. The capital of

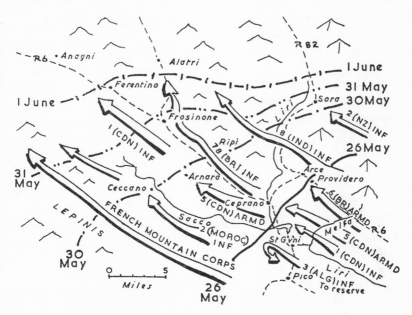

37   Operations in the Liri–Sacco Valleys, 26 May–1 June

Italy was the man and not the ball—to continue the football analogy—
the ball was Kesselring's Army Group 'C'. If all went well Kesselring
would over-commit his resources trying to fend off Mark Clark, and
would leave his centre too weakly held to resist the main striking force—
Oliver Leese's Eighth Army—as it appeared at the head of Route 6
deployed ready to launch a decisive break-through and to exploit the
breach with three armoured divisions, creating havoc in the rear of both
German Armies. If this strategy was to work Route 6 must be kept clear

for the rapid advance of Eighth Army. Clark and Juin, who were only concerned with shorter-term problems, thought otherwise.

After forcing von Lüttwitz's 26 Panzer Division back north of Pico, Juin's advance on the south side of the Liri and Sacco valleys remained twenty-four to forty-eight hours ahead of the British and Canadians on the north side. This was inevitable because von Vietinghoff was pulling back von Senger's XIV Panzer Corps as fast as possible to extricate it from the trap between the two converging Allied Armies. To do this he had to oppose Eighth Army's advance as strongly as possible to keep open Route 82 and the Subiaco road while he extricated his troops as quickly as possible from in front of the French. Juin became increasingly critical of the slowness of Eighth Army's operations, tending to say, 'I told you so'. This would not have mattered had there not been some truth in his criticism of Oliver Leese's handling of his Army, which made it all the more irritating. By 28 May it was clear that Juin's French Corps was being squeezed out of the line and, if he did nothing about it, his troops would be withdrawn into reserve like Anders' Poles had been while the British and Americans swept on into Rome. He put his case to Mark Clark, requesting that he should be allowed to advance on Ferentino on Route 6, and thereafter use Route 6 to come up on Keyes' right at Valmonte. In his view, Oliver Leese could be directed in a more northerly direction up Route 82 and the Subiaco road, if he ever managed to draw level at all.

At a conference at Alexander's headquarters the following day, the suggestion that Juin should advance on Ferentino was accepted as a means of helping Eighth Army forward against the very tough opposition which it was meeting. Whether the use of Route 6 was discussed is not clear. Mark Clark, in his memoirs, assumes that Alexander's agreement to the French advance on Ferentino carried with it his assent to the French use of Route 6 to Valmonte. Alexander had intended no such thing. He had welcomed the French assistance to Eighth Army, but Route 6 was to stay within Oliver Leese's boundary otherwise he would not be able to move forward quickly enough to smash the German centre when von Vietinghoff's rearguards finally gave way and fell back, as they would inevitably do, once the bulk of the German troops had reached their allotted places in the Caesar Line. Mark Clark records that there was 'quite an argument', but the most he could persuade the Army Group Commander to accept was that, if Fifth Army took Valmonte, then the French could be brought up by Route 6 and Oliver

Leese would be directed, as Juin had suggested, to switch his centre line further north. In the meantime Juin must continue to fight his way through the Lepini Mountains on whatever tracks he could find. Mark Clark summed up his feelings in his diary by saying:

My French Corps is being pinched out. A more gallant fighting organisation never existed, yet any offer to have it attack Ferentino was promptly turned down, unless the French then agreed to withdraw to the south over the roads they had come forward on.

I am throwing everything I have into the battle, hoping to crack this key position, which will make it necessary for Kesselring to withdraw both his Armies to the north of Rome. If I do not crack this position in three to four days I may have to reorganise, wait for the Eighth Army, and go at it with a coordinated attack by both Armies.

From the tone of the last sentence of this entry he seems to have seen himself as the Army Group Commander.

Juin had naturally been disappointed with this decision, but was still determined to be in at the kill. He had withdrawn Brosset's 1 (Motorised) Division and Monsabert's 3 (Algerian) Division into reserve after the fall of San Giovanni during the Canadians' battle for the Melfa, and had continued the advance with Guillaume's Mountain Corps pushing through the centre of the Lepini Mountains and Dody's 2 (Moroccan) Division, which had been resting since it took Monte Majo at the beginning of Diadem, advancing along the south side of the Liri–Sacco Valleys. Dody, however, had not made the progress expected of him and had reached Ceccano opposite Frosinone on 30 May only a few hours ahead of the Canadians.

Eighth Army's tale during this period is one of frustration and miscalculation; some of it caused by the hard-fought rearguard actions of von Senger's Corps and some—possibly the greater part—of its own making. We left Eighth Army in the last chapter with both leading Corps fighting for bridgeheads over the Melfa on 25 May, the day that Mark Clark decided to change direction. The Eighth Army plan was to continue the advance with the Canadian and XIII (Br) Corps abreast, because, in this way, Oliver Leese believed he could bring the greatest and most continuous pressure to bear upon von Vietinghoff's Tenth Army. Unfortunately, there were two flaws in this plan: first, there was not enough room in the narrowing Liri and Sacco Valleys; and secondly, his divisions were wrongly constituted for the type of country. The three armoured divisions, as Harding had suggested during Diadem planning, became more a road-blocking liability than a hard-hitting asset.

The Liri Valley, whose wideness attracted Harding in his original appreciation as the best approach to Rome for the main striking force, narrows and becomes tortuous and broken after the Melfa is crossed. By the time the junction of the Liri and Sacco Rivers is reached, it could be hardly less like good tank country. From the line Ceprano–Arce to the head of the Sacco Valley at Ferentino it is difficult to find more than about three reasonable centre lines for regimental groups, let alone divisions. Route 6 was thoroughly blocked by German demolitions and mines, and by Allied bombing of towns like Ceprano, Frosinone and Ferentino. The side roads were so narrow and steep-sided that it was difficult to deploy off them, even with tanks, which meant that most advances could only be made on a one-tank front. And yet Eighth Army tried to advance, at first, with five divisions up. Even when this proved impracticable there were rarely less than three divisions jostling for space as they struggled forward over roads quite unfit for the weight of traffic. To make matters worse, Eighth Army seemed to have a propensity for passing formations through each other at just the wrong moment, thereby doubling the confusion and congestion behind the leading troops, while at the same time allowing von Senger to break contact and slip back to his next delaying line almost unmolested.

On the German side von Vietinghoff was putting into effect Kesselring's order for a methodical and economic withdrawal to the Caesar Line. The phase lines for this operation are shown in figure 32 (*p. 165*). Von Senger's XIV Panzer Corps was to be responsible for the withdrawal up Route 6 and would cover Tenth Army's southern flank as it escaped northwards up Route 82 and the Subiaco road. He would have under his command all Tenth Army's mobile divisions—Baade's 90 Panzer Grenadier, von Lüttwitz's 26 Panzer, Rodt's 15 Panzer Grenadier and Heidrich's 1 Para Divisions. Feurstein would revert to his old task of covering the mountain sector with his LI Mountain Corps and would command his original 114 (Jaeger), 5 (Mountain) and 44 Divisions. He was to pull back up Route 82 holding McCreery's X (Br) Corps at bay, while von Senger used Route 6 and the Subiaco road. Von Senger would not be able to use Route 6 right back to Valmonte, which was within Fourteenth Army's area, and would have to work his way northwards through Palestrina.

During 26 May both of Eighth Army's Corps advanced towards the upper Liri between Ceprano and Arce with a total of four divisions up. On the Liri itself, Adams' force of 1 (Canadian) Division pushed ahead rapidly with the assistance of the French on the south bank, hoping to capture a bridge over the river intact at San Giovanni. They were unlucky and found the bridge already demolished, leaving a yawning 120-foot gap which the Canadian sappers started to bridge. In the centre, 11 (Canadian) Brigade—the infantry brigade of Hoffmeister's armoured division—made for Ceprano. Progress was slow through the sunken lanes in the face of long-range harassing fire and a plethora of German mines and booby traps which had been left to delay the Allied advance. By dark the main body of the brigade was still a mile short of Ceprano. It had overrun a number of rearguard positions and had captured men from Baade's, Heidrich's and Ortner's divisions, suggesting that the Germans were still in some confusion.

XIII (Br) Corps made even slower progress. Evelegh's 6 (Br) Armoured Division advanced across the Melfa with the Derbyshire Yeomanry Group in the lead on Route 6. Russell's 8 (Indian) Division covered the northern flank by continuing its advance along the lower slopes of the Monte Cairo massif. Keightley's 78 (Br) Division was to follow the armoured division when it was clear of the Melfa. 6 (Br) Armoured Division soon ran into country quite unsuitable for an armoured formation. Route 6 runs through the narrow and heavily wooded defile at Providero a few miles east of Arce. The defile is commanded by two prominent hills—Monte Grande and Monte Piccolo—which Heidrich's rearguard had chosen as its defensive position to cover Kesselring's first delaying line. The position could not have been better suited for a delaying action and Evelegh's division worse constituted for tackling it. Although 1st Guards Brigade—6 (Br) Armoured Division's infantry brigade—was brought up during the night 26–27 May, Heidrich's men held the division at bay for another thirty-six hours and did not evacuate Arce until the early hours of 29 May. They were forced to pull back, not by the presence of Evelegh's infantry and tanks, but by a wide outflanking movement by Russell's Indians which threatened their escape route from the north-east.

In the meantime the Canadian Corps had established and reinforced its bridgeheads over the Liri. Von Lüttwitz, whose 26 Panzer Division had crossed to the north side of the valley and was opposing Burns' Corps, reported that the Canadians were well established over the Liri and that it would only be a matter of time before the bridges were completed and a large body of Canadian tanks, which could be seen on the far bank, broke through his meagre defences. He asked for and received authority to pull back to the second withdrawal line during the night 27–28 May. Nothing could have been more embarrassing for the XIV Panzer Corps' staff than the failure of the Canadian armoured onslaught to materialise on the following day, but much to their surprise nothing happened. As the Canadian Official History records, the German Tenth Army staff claimed the efficiency of the German minefields as the reason for their misappreciation of the Canadian speed of advance but in fact, it was due to difficulties in bridging the Liri and the usual traffic problems. More haste less speed was the undoing of the Canadian sappers whose Bailey bridge buckled and collapsed into the river while being launched, preventing any major advances during 28 May. By the time the bridge was reconstructed Eighth Army headquarters had given XIII (Br) Corps priority over it to enable Keightley's 78 (Br) Division to outflank Heidrich's block at Arce and to re-open XIII (Br) Corps' advance along Route 6. It was not until 29 May that the Canadian Corps set off westward to drive von Lüttwitz's force from the German second line covering Frosinone.

The delay at Arce and Ceprano enabled the Germans to get into the rhythm of a methodical withdrawal. As the two Corps of Eighth Army advanced from the Liri they met demolitions every few miles with all the possible diversions on either side blocked with mines. Those demolitions which could be covered by the fire of German rearguards, and they were the majority in this type of country, caused several hours' delay while the leading Canadian and British units worked their way round and forced the German artillery observers or rearguard tanks covering the demolitions to withdraw. Even supply columns, well to the rear of the advance, were not immune to long-range harassing fire, and a number of senior officers were killed or seriously wounded when their jeeps inadvertently pulled off the centre of the road to pass a column only to strike mines buried in the verges. The advance became a sapper's headache and a traffic controller's nightmare.

Under these conditions the speed of advance was dictated by the initiative and bravery of the few reconnaissance officers, tank commanders and sapper subalterns who were leading on each road. The rest of both Corps were unable to do much to increase the speed of advance. In many ways things would have gone much faster if the main bodies had been grounded and the battle left to the advance guards and sapper mine-clearance and bridging teams. The Germans did not abandon their second line and Frosinone was not entered until 31 May. By this time the final strategic decisions in the Diadem offensive were being taken and the final dispositions made for the breach of the Caesar Line.

As the news from Truscott's Corps gave little hope that the Caesar Line would crumble under his assaults, both Armies started to make their preparations for a combined assault on the German line. Eighth Army placed an additional division under command of each Corps and

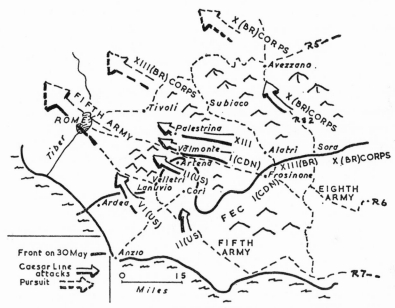

38   Plans for the combined assault of the Caesar Line

each Corps brought its infantry divisions into the lead. Burns was given the 6 (South African) Armoured Division and Kirkman was given Dudley Ward's 4 (Br) Division which had not been in action since the fall of Cassino. In the Canadian sector Hoffmeister's armoured division was relieved by Vokes' infantry and in Kirkman's sector 78 (Br) Division advanced ahead of 6 (Br) Armoured Division. In the event of a major assault being necessary the Canadians were to attack on the axis of Route 6 and XIII (Br) Corps on the axis of the Alatri–Palestrina road. X (Br) Corps would advance on Avezzano up Route 82. Once a breach

had been made, Kirkman's and McCreery's Corps would pursue the
German withdrawal east of the Tiber and the Canadians would be
withdrawn into reserve.

Fifth Army's plan was to continue the attack with Truscott's Corps
round the west side of the Alban Hills, while Keyes struck round the
eastern side through the Valmonte Gap. There was clearly an overlap
between the two Army plans. Keyes and the Canadians were both heading for Valmonte, but Keyes was only a few thousand yards from the

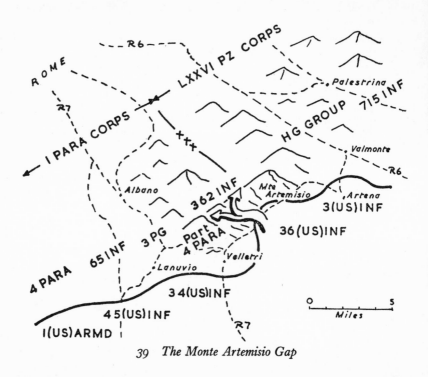

39   The Monte Artemisio Gap

objective while the Canadians were still twenty miles away. If Keyes
failed, the old Army boundary would be restored, giving the Canadians
priority on Route 6 as Alexander had always intended. For the time
being the problem was academic. Fifth Army should clearly keep up
their pressure until Eighth Army arrived, but it seemed increasingly
unlikely that there would be any break-through. Then quite suddenly a
random coincidence of events occurred and the unexpected began to
happen.

31   Monte Artemisio towering above Velletri

THE CAESAR LINE

32   Clearing Valmonte

33 *88 (US) Division entering the outskirts of Rome opposed by rearguards of 4 Parachute Division*

THE FALL OF ROME

34 *Generals Mark Clark (front, left) and Lucian Truscott (front, right) mounting the steps of the Capitol on entering Rome*

Truscott had decided as early as 28 May to relieve Ryder's 34 (US) Division, which had suffered heavily in front of Lanuvio, with Walker's 36 (US) Division. Walker's task at that time was to contain Velletri and act as the link between the Valmonte and Lanuvio thrusts. The prospect of another frontal assault did not appeal to Walker or his staff. They had suffered severely in the Salerno landing and again on the Rapido through taking part in such assaults. A third frontal assault at Lanuvio had no attractions, and so he started looking for an alternative way of unseating the German defenders. One obvious way to deal with Lanuvio was to find a way round through the barrier of the Alban Hills, but was this practicable? Walker wondered. The south-eastern face of the Alban hill mass is steep and forbidding, rising some 3,000 feet to the summit of Monte Artemisio. Most of the mountainside was steeply terraced and covered with vineyards and fruit trees. There was no obvious route up to the top which would be practicable for military vehicles, but air photos and observation from the ground showed no signs of German activity there either. Was this central sector of the Caesar Line unguarded? Walker decided to find out by ordering reconnaissance patrols to push through the German positions at the foot of the mountain. These patrols reported that they had found no German defences. If there were no Germans there, was it, in fact, impracticable to scale this face of the Alban Hills with an effective force? The Germans had presumably had time when reconnoitring the line to decide whether or not Monte Artemisio need be held. If they were not holding it, could Walker emulate Juin's feat in the Aurunci Mountains, or Wolfe before the battle of the Heights of Abraham? Only one man could answer this; his divisional engineer, Colonel Oran Stovall. Stovall's own patrols suggested that it would be practicable to bulldoze a way for tanks and supporting vehicles up the line of a farm track and on to the summit of Monte Artemisio. On this advice Walker decided to ask Truscott to let him try this approach instead of relieving 34 (US) Division for another bloody direct assault on Lanuvio. His opportunity to do this did not occur until Truscott visited his headquarters at noon on 30 May to discuss details of the Lanuvio operation. Truscott did not approve the attempt until he had cross-questioned Stovall very thoroughly, but when he was convinced he overrode the objections of his own VI (US) Corps' Engineer and reinforced Walker with an extra engineer regiment for the operation which was to start as soon as darkness fell that night— 30 May.

In the German camp, Kesselring had spotted the gap in von Mackensen's dispositions and had ordered its closure, but nothing had been done about it by the Fourteenth Army staff. Monte Artemisio lay on the boundary between Schlemm's Parachute Corps, fighting the Lanuvio–Campoleone battle, and Herr's LXXVI Panzer Corps, holding Valmonte with a mixed force based on the Hermann Göring Division and containing elements of several divisions including 334 Division from the Adriatic and the newly formed 92 Division from Civitavecchia. General Schmalz, the sterling commander of the Hermann Göring Division, who had made his name as a regimental commander in Sicily, realised the gap existed but had no reserves to fill it. All he could do was to send an artillery observation party and an engineer platoon, acting as infantry, to close the two-mile gap. His requests to Fourteenth Army for help went unheeded, and so the ground-work for the second decisive moment in the Diadem offensive had been laid—again in an 'impassable' mountain sector, this time opposite an American instead of a French division.

During the night 30 May Walker infiltrated two infantry regiments up on to Monte Artemisio. As the silent columns made their way up through the vineyards, the Luftwaffe made one of its sporadic night raids on the beachhead. Its flares lit up the mountainside, but no one spotted the crouching American troops who waited until the raid was over before continuing their climb. Dawn came before they reached the top but they were unchallenged and managed to seize the summit in broad daylight, capturing the German artillery observation party—one of whom was having his morning bath. Not a shot had been fired. Behind the infantry column, the American sappers were soon opening up a rudimentary one-way road. The German engineer platoon, on the other hand, mistook the size of the American force which it could only see in the distance and so did not report the seriousness of the situation until the Americans were firmly established. During the afternoon of 31 May Schmalz counter-attacked with the only panzer grenadier battalion left in his reserve but it was no match for two American regiments. By dusk Walker's division was too firmly established on the heights to be shaken by Schmalz. He was now supported by tanks and could threaten the rear of the whole of Schlemm's Corps from Velletri to Lanuvio. He could also bring observed artillery fire to bear on the rear of Schmalz's force defending Valmonte.

The news of this success electrified Fifth Army. All its divisions were tired, but the similarity between the seizing of Little Round Top at the Battle of Gettysburg and the fall of Monte Artemisio was clear to every American commander. One more concentrated American power drive should topple the Caesar Line. There was no time to wait for Juin or Oliver Leese. Mark Clark ordered an all-out offensive by Truscott, Keyes and the two British divisions in the coastal sector for next morning, 1 June.

The news also affected Eighth Army. The chances of a set-piece assault, for which it had been changing its dispositions as it advanced, suddenly faded. A pursuit and not a breaching operation would be needed. Burns was ordered to bring 6 (South African) Armoured Division into the lead on the Canadian axis and Kirkman was to pass 6 (Br) Armoured Division through his infantry when the break came. This regrouping unhappily caused one of the worst traffic jams of the whole advance. The 5 (Canadian) Armoured Division was pulling back into reserve to let 1 (Canadian) Infantry Division take over the advance on the old plan of closing the Caesar Line with infantry divisions in the lead when it met the tanks of 6 (South African) Armoured Division moving up to be ready to take the lead. To add to the tangle, the guns of the 1st Army Group Royal Canadian Artillery, which would have been needed for a major assault on the Caesar Line, were also still on their way forward and completed the dislocation of the traffic plan. Much of the trouble was caused by a combination of the temporary diversion round demolished bridges breaking up, by vehicles being blown up by uncleared deeply-buried mines which had not been located by the sappers' mine detectors, and by roads giving way under the weight of military traffic for which they were never intended. It was also caused by over-optimistic staff officers allowing too many units on to the roads at a time, poor traffic discipline within units and a weak traffic control organisation. All these factors enabled von Senger to break contact once more with Eighth Army and to withdraw at his own speed to the third and then the fourth withdrawal phase lines, covered only by the lightest rearguards.

As he withdrew north-westwards from Frosinone, von Senger had been uncomfortably conscious that the country around Ferentino was much more open and suitable for armoured operations. If Hoffmeister's armoured division had remained in the lead von Senger's Corps might have suffered serious losses, but the change in the countryside had not been appreciated in time by Eighth Army and Vokes' infantry division had been committed at the very moment that the armour might have had a chance of speeding up the advance. Poole's 6 (South African) Armoured Division took over from Vokes too late to affect the issue. Von Senger was safely into the hills again. Eighth Army was not going to be in at the kill.

Mark Clark's final drive started on 1 June, when Oliver Leese's leading troops were still short of Ferentino. For two days the fighting was intense. Keyes' II (US) Corps attacked with its three divisions in a

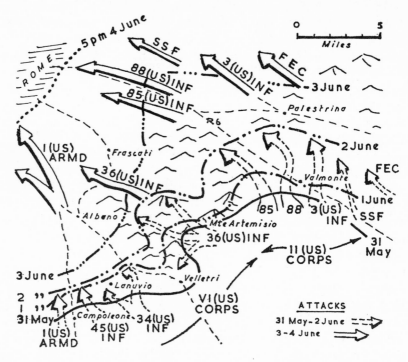

40   *Fifth Army's final effort, 1–4 June*

northerly direction: O'Daniel's 3 (US) Division attacking Valmonte and 88 and 85 (US) Division attacking the north-eastern face of the Alban Hills, overlooking the Valmonte Gap. During 1 June, Schmalz's resistance was extraordinarily stubborn and, although Keyes' men cut Route 6 and reached the top of the Alban Hills, there was as yet no sign of a German withdrawal. Truscott's VI (US) Corps assailed the southern end of the Alban Hills. His engineers worked all-out to widen the track up on to Monte Artemisio and while this was going on Walker fought his way round the back of Velletri. Fighting was just as intense here on the vine-covered terraces as it was at Valmonte, but by evening 36 (US) Division had forced its way into the town and had taken a large part of the garrison prisoner. The state of improvisation to which the Germans had been reduced and their extraordinary ability to reconstitute broken units is well illustrated by these prisoners who were found to come from over fifty different companies.

On 2 June the situation began to swing in Mark Clark's favour. The build-up of forces on Monte Artemisio had reached the point where Walker could start pressing forward aggressively, outflanking the German positions in front of Lanuvio in the plain below. He could also help Keyes' Corps by bringing accurate fire to bear on the rear of Schmalz's force still trying to hold the Valmonte gap. By the end of 2 June Valmonte itself had fallen and a general German withdrawal had begun. Von Mackensen was still ordering a last-ditch defence, but Herr's LXXVI Panzer Corps had reached the limit of its endurance and was pulling back towards Tivoli, east of Rome. Schlemm's Parachute Corps was forced to conform or be cut off from its escape routes by Keyes' advancing Corps. Ordering Trettner's 4 Parachute Division to cover his withdrawal, he too put a hastily-improvised withdrawal plan into action. Fourteenth Army headquarters had lost control and its units began to scramble back to the Tiber as fast as it was possible to disengage without the loss of too many men.

3 June was a day of exhilarating advance against failing German resistance. Keyes' Corps went forward astride Route 6 with its open flank and rear protected by Juin's Frenchmen who were now authorised to use Route 6. Truscott still had to fight hard to cut his way round the western side of the Alban Hills. By dusk the advance of Fifth Army was general right across the front. Only German rearguards stood between Mark Clark and Rome. During the night both American Corps formed up flying columns of tanks, motorised infantry and engineers with bridging equipment with which to rush the Tiber bridges next day before the Germans could destroy them.

At first light on 4 June the pursuit of von Mackensen's beaten Fourteenth Army began. Kesselring declared Rome an open city and forbade the demolition of the bridges within the city, but those either side of the city were to be blown up before the Allied advance guards could reach them. In the outer suburbs of the city, the rearguards of Trettner's 4 Parachute Division reinforced by Ritter von Pohl's anti-aircraft units, using their guns in the ground role, fought a strenuous rearguard action to hold the two American Corps at bay while the evacuation of the city and the passage of the beaten Fourteenth Army over the Tiber was completed. It was late in the afternoon of 4 June before the leading American units started to push their way into the city itself. Even then they were still subjected to sniper fire and sudden ambushes by German rearguards. The population stayed out of sight. Mark Clark drove down Route 6 to follow Keyes' leading units into the city, but only reached the first road sign marking the entrance to 'Roma'. Posing with Keyes and Frederick for photographs under the sign, he and his party were suddenly forced to jump for the nearest ditch when a sniper opened fire, riddling the signpost above their heads. He would not be entering Rome that day!

Men of both Corps did, however, reach the centre of the city as darkness was falling and found that Kesselring had kept his word, making Rome an open city. None of the bridges within the city had been destroyed but there were one or two sharp fights as the American advanced guards tried to rush them before the Germans were ready to leave.

It was not until the following morning that the people of Rome appeared in the streets—at first cautiously, and then in hysterical masses. As the Fifth Army history records 'what the Germans had never been able to do, the solid masses of the Roman throngs had accomplished: they stopped our tanks.'

Rome had fallen to its latest conqueror and had been taken only once before by an invader advancing from the south.

12 The Triumph of Diadem

'I congratulate you on the great victory of the Allied Anglo-American forces—the taking of Rome. The news has been greeted in the Soviet Union with great satisfaction.'
Marshal Stalin to Churchill, 5 June 1944

Mark Clark drove into Rome the following morning, 5 June, with a small column of staff jeeps. He was accompanied by his chief of staff, Al Gruenther, and General Edgar Hume who had been the first Military Governor of Naples and had some experience in taking over a great city. There was no ceremonial reception by the City Fathers or other dignitaries awaiting them. They lost their way several times trying to find the Capitoline Hill which had been selected as a suitable place for the latest conqueror of Rome to give his orders to his Corps commanders. At about ten o'clock the party was eventually assembled—Truscott, Keyes, Crittenburger and Juin. The Stars and Stripes, the Union Jack and the Tricolour were run up beside the Italian flag. Speaking to a small crowd of Italians who had gathered around him Mark Clark made his only official speech—one sentence:

This is a great day for the Fifth Army and for the French, British and American troops of the Fifth Army who made this victory possible.

He had achieved his ambition. No one else had shared his Fifth Army's triumph. The full blaze of world press publicity momentarily played upon him, but that evening the darkened hulls of Eisenhower's invasion fleet weighed anchor in English harbours, Allied bombers rose from English airfields and heavily-loaded parachute aircraft, many towing gliders, set course for Normandy. Churchill caught the feeling of the hour in the House of Commons next morning:

At noon on June 6 I asked the House of Commons to 'take formal cognisance of the liberation of Rome by the Allied Armies under the

Command of General Alexander', the news of which had been released the night before. There was intense excitement about the
landings in France which everyone knew were in progress at the
moment. Nevertheless I devoted ten minutes to the Campaign in
Italy and in paying my tribute to the Allied Armies there. After keeping them on tenterhooks for a little I said:

'I have also to announce to the House of Commons that during the
night and early hours of this morning the first of the series of landings
upon the European Continent has taken place. . . .'.

And so the limelight lifted off Fifth Army and the rest of Alexander's
Army Group, never to return with real brilliance even though the
campaign went on until the end of the war and achieved its essential
purpose of holding down an average twenty-five German divisions
which Eisenhower could ill afford to see appearing on his front in north-
west Europe.

Alexander's achievements, unsung though they were at the time, were
real and substantial. His timing, the scale of his victory and the success
of his diversionary effort were as near perfect as success in battle can ever
be. Kesselring had tried to stand south of Rome, obeying the demands of
Hitler's 'no withdrawal' policy. He had been beaten, because he had
been forced to dance to Alexander's tune. His mobile divisions, which
had in the past stopped every Allied offensive, arrived too late and were
committed piecemeal with disastrous results. It is not too much to
claim that the root cause of Kesselring's failure lay in the concept and
execution of Alexander's deception plan which stands out in marked
contrast to the inept efforts of the Allied High Command to achieve
surprise on the Western Front in the First World War.

As Fifth Army made its way through Rome, the two German Armies
fell back as fast as the speed of their infantry divisions would allow.
Von Mackensen's Fourteenth Army was in a rout as its staff had lost
control of the withdrawal. Von Mackensen himself was relieved of his
command and replaced by General Joachim Lemelsen who had commanded Tenth Army temporarily during the previous winter. Von
Vietinghoff's Tenth Army had recovered its balance in the good defensive country amongst the Apennine foothills east of the Tiber and, now
that the Caesar Line could not be held, was able to continue its retreat
north-westwards, fending off Oliver Leese's pursuing troops without
much difficulty. Alexander, in his evening situation report quoted in his

despatches (2928), complained 'If only the country were more open we would make hay of the lot. However, you may rest assured that both Armies will drive forward as fast as is physically possible.'

Kesselring had lost three major defensive lines in less than a month—the Gustav, Hitler–Senger and Caesar. There was only one prepared position left before the Alps—the Gothic Line between Pisa and Rimini, based on the great east-west sweep of the Northern Apennines. His chances of imposing much delay south of the Gothic Line were very poor indeed unless he received substantial reinforcements. His six mobile divisions had been seriously mauled and had lost a high proportion of their tanks, assault guns and artillery. Even Heidrich's 1 Parachute Division was in a sorry and depleted state. Four infantry divisions had ceased to exist as fighting formations. Three of these had to be withdrawn from the line to re-form in northern Italy, and the fourth was disbanded. Every other division in Army Group 'C' had suffered heavy losses, including those which had not been heavily engaged on the Adriatic sector because they had been steadily milked of units and individual reinforcements to prop up the other badly battered divisions trying to stem the Allied offensive west of the Apennines. OKW surprisingly leapt to Kesselring's assistance in spite of the imminence of the invasion of Normandy. They sent him four fresh divisions from elsewhere in Europe, three divisions' worth of individual reinforcements and a steady flow of replacement tanks and guns, including a battalion of the new Tiger tanks—all at a time when they should have been concentrating every available man in north-west Europe.

Alexander's intelligence staff had received warnings of these German reinforcements being earmarked for Italy well before Rome fell. He had signalled Churchill on 30 May:

> You will have heard of fresh enemy divisions which are on their way here. I hope our tap will not be turned off too soon . . . and prevent us from gaining the full fruits of our present advantageous position.

Alexander felt that if only the Combined Chiefs of Staff would let him keep all the troops which he had under command when Rome fell, he could make the Italian theatre a decisive factor in the war in the west. Signalling Maitland Wilson on 6 June, he said:

> Morale is irresistibly high as a result of recent successes and the whole Army Group forms one closely articulated machine capable of carrying out assaults and rapid exploitation in the most difficult terrain.

Neither the Apennines nor even the Alps should prove a serious obstacle to their enthusiasm and skill (Despatches 2931).

His pleas were of little avail. American determination to invade southern France robbed him of Truscott's and Juin's experienced Corps. The momentary numerical superiority, which he had devised for Diadem, disappeared and he was once more faced with the thankless task of pursuing offensive operations with numerical inferiority in country ideally suited for defence. The story of his continued success in holding down German divisions in Italy does not belong to the Battle for Rome. It is the theme of the Battles for the Gothic Line which did not end until April 1945. It is, however, worth considering for a moment how it was that in such country it proved possible to fight and win the Diadem offensive less than thirty years after the disastrous battles of the Somme and Passchendaele. It is in this comparison that the true greatness of Alexander and his fellow commanders in the Italian campaign really lies.

The German Army in the spring of 1944 was still far from beaten. It may be said to have been in much the same state as Falkenhayn's forces on the Western Front in the middle years of the First World War. The country which Kesselring was defending was more suitable for defence than the rolling country of northern France. The Gustav Line had congealed into just as strong a position as the German trench system on the Western Front; and the Hitler Line was no less formidable than the Hindenburg Line of 1918. And yet the Somme cost both sides over half a million men whereas the whole Italian campaign cost the Allies 312,000 and the Germans 536,000. These figures show a further remarkable feature; the attacker lost less than the defender. Why was this so? What was the secret of Alexander's success?

The basic equipment used by both sides was not very different from that used in Flanders. The tank was by now a much more efficient machine, but in Italy it could not be used with the same decisive effect that it had achieved in Poland, France, Russia or the Western Desert. The main weapons used in Italy were the machine gun, mortar and conventional artillery. Anti-tank guns and mines together with the broken nature of the country neutralised the tank; and the perfect artillery observation afforded to the defender by the hills and mountains neutralised any increased efficiency in the attacker's artillery. The Italian campaign should have become a stalemate in front of Cassino as it showed every sign of doing in February and March. There were, however, two great differences between the two wars: air power and generalship. The overwhelming air superiority of the Allied Air Forces was undoubtedly a potent factor in weakening the German ability and the will to resist. It brought the German soldier quicker to the point of moral and physical exhaustion than any of the older means could achieve, but it was not decisive. The German divisions did not go short of ammunition or supplies during Diadem because of air action. Many of their units were without food for several days at Cassino but this was due to intense artillery fire preventing supply parties moving forward. The fact that Kesselring managed to recover his balance in July and August and held the Allies to a draw on the Gothic Line as soon as Alexander lost his slender margin of superiority suggests that it was not air power alone which made the difference. Superb generalship was the root cause of success.

At the Somme or at any of the other great battles of the First World War tactical surprise was occasionally achieved, but the Germans were always able to seal the breach by moving their reserves in time to meet or to contain the attack. In the Battle for Rome Kesselring and the German High Command were surprised in the most effective way. Not only were they persuaded to hold their mobile reserves too far away from the battlefield, but they were also deceived into holding these reserves back for too long and then committing them piecemeal when it was already too late.

Brilliant though Alexander's deception plan proved to be, Diadem could not have succeeded without his inspired handling of his very mixed Allied team and his ability to maintain a predetermined strategy while at the same time keeping as many options as possible open so that he could profit by sudden and unexpected changes of fortune. Each subordinate commander was handled in a different way. Each felt he was contributing decisively to the success of the operation and that he was doing it in his own particular way; and yet all these diverse efforts were blended by Alexander into a coherent pattern, leading to the success of Diadem.

No battles are ever perfect. Writers will always argue the rights and wrongs of Mark Clark's change of direction, the reasons for the slowness of Eighth Army's advance up the Liri Valley, the rightness of Juin's views and so on. But these are minor facets of the Battle for Rome compared with its exact achievement of the directive issued to Alexander by the Allied Governments. As history distils the campaigns of the Second World War into their bare essentials, Alexander's Diadem will emerge as one of the great masterpieces of generalship.

The Diadem Orders of Battle, 11 May 1944

ALLIES

FIFTH ARMY
Main front

II (US) Corps
85 (US) Inf
88 (US) Inf

FEC
1 (Fr) Motor Inf
2 (Moroc) Inf
3 (Alg) Inf
4 (Moroc) Mtn

Army Troops
36 (US) Inf

Anzio Beachhead
VI (US) Corps
1 (Br) Inf
1 (US) Armd
3 (US) Inf
5 (Br) Inf
34 (US) Inf
45 (US) Inf

EIGHTH ARMY
Main front

XIII (Br) Corps
4 (Br) Inf
6 (Br) Armd
8 (Ind) Inf
78 (Br) Inf

X (Br) Corps
2 (NZ) Inf

1 (Cnd) Corps
1 (Cdn) Inf
5 (Cdn) Armd

II (Pol) Corps
3 (Carp) Inf
5 (Kres) Inf

Army Troops
6 (SA) Armd

Adriatic Sector
V (Br) Corps
4 (Ind) Inf
10 (Ind) Inf

Total of Allied Divisions: 25

GERMANS

FOURTEENTH ARMY
Anzio Beachhead

LXXVI PZ Corps
715 Inf
362 Inf
26 PZ

I Para Corps
3 PG
65 Inf
4 Para

Army Reserve
29 PG
92 Inf

OKW Reserve
HG

TENTH ARMY
Main front

Western Sector
LI Mtn Corps
5 Mtn
44 Inf
1 Para

XIV PZ Corps
71 Inf
94 Inf
15 PG

Adriatic Sector
Gruppe 'Hauck'
305 Inf
334 Inf
114 Jaeger

Army Reserve
90 PG

ARMY GROUP VON ZANGEN
Northern Italy
162 (Turco) Inf
356 Inf
278 Inf
188 Mtn

Total of German Divisions: 23

List of Abbreviations and Codewords used in the text and on the sketches

1 On the sketch maps the following conventions are used:

 Allied Divisions   German Divisions

2 Formation and unit titles are abbreviated as follows:

Size of formation:

Corps	Corps	Gp	Group
Div	Division	Regt	Regiment
Bde	Brigade	Bn	Battalion

Type of formation:

Armd	armoured or tank	Para	parachute
Arty	artillery	PG	panzer grenadier
Engr	engineer		(i.e. German mechanised unit)
Inf	infantry	PZ	panzer
Mtn	mountain		(i.e. German tank unit)

Nationality:

Br	British			Ind	Indian	
Cdn	Canadian			NZ	New Zealand	
Fr	French—Alg	Algerian		Pol	Polish—Carp	Carpathian
	Mot	Motorised			Kres	Kresowan
	Moroc	Moroccan		SA	South African	
	Tun	Tunisian		US	United States	

Thus 4 (Tun) Mtn Div is the 4th Tunisian Mountain Division and 5 (Br) Armd Bde is the 5th British Armoured Brigade. On sketches 'Div' is usually omitted to reduce the amount of lettering, but 'Bde', 'Regt', 'Gp' and 'Bn' are always included to distinguish these smaller formations.

No nationality suffix is included in German formations e.g. 362 Inf=362 German Infantry Division and 26 PZ=26 Panzer Division.

3   Code names, codewords and other abbreviations:

Amazon The most northerly bridge over Rapido in 4 (Br) Division's sector

Anvil Allied plan for amphibious assault on French Riviera

Army Group 'C' Kesselring's Army Group in Italy

Bedale Final objective of 78 (Br) Division in its attack below Monte Cassino

Blackwater Most northerly bridge over Rapido in 8 (Indian) Division's sector

Blue Line Second objective of 4 (Br) Division at Cassino

Brown Line First objective of 4 (Br) Division at Cassino

Buffalo VI (US) Corps plan for break-out from Anzio via Cisterna and Valmonte

Cab rank Fighters or fighter-bombers flying over the battlefield awaiting calls from ground troops to engage targets

Caesar Line German defences covering Rome, based on the Alban Hills

Cardiff Most southerly bridge site on Rapido in 4 (Br) Division's sector

Cavendish Road Track constructed secretly to bring tanks up on to the hills above Cassino

Chesterfield Code name for Canadian assault on Hitler Line

Congo Bridge site in 4 (Br) Division's sector on the Rapido

Crawdad VI (US) Corps plan for break-out from Anzio along coast to the north-west

Diadem Codeword for Allied spring offensive

Dora Line Extension of Hitler Line round the eastern side of the Aurunci mountains

Fernie Third report line of 78 (Br) Division in its attack towards Monte Cassino

Grafton First report line of 78 (Br) Division in its attack towards Monte Cassino

Grasshopper VI (US) Corps plan to break out from Anzio eastwards

Gothic Line German defensive line in northern Apennines; also known as the Green Line

Green Line Final objective of 4 (Br) Division in battle of Cassino; also alternative name for Gothic Line

Gustav Line Main German defence line based on Cassino

HG Division Hermann Göring Division

Horseshoe Ring of high ground south and west of Sant' Angelo, the objective of 8 (Indian) Division

London Bridge site over the Rapido at Sant' Angelo in 8 (Indian) Division's sector

Nebelwerfer German multi-barrelled rocket launcher

Nunton Codeword for Diadem deception plan

OKW Oberkommando der Wehrmacht; the German Supreme Command

Overlord Code name for invasion of Normandy

Oxford Bridge in 8 (Indian) Division's sector south of Sant' Angelo

Panther German medium tank

Phantom Ridge Nickname of false crest of Colle Sant' Angelo

Plymouth Bridge at southern end of 8 (Indian) Division's sector launched from the back of a tank

Pytchley Second report line in 78 (Br) Division's attack towards Monte Cassino

Red Line 4 (Br) Division's third objective at Cassino

Rover David Code name for air controller directing cab rank of fighter-bombers over battlefield

Snake Explosive-filled pipe for breaching minefields

Snake's Head Nickname of Pt 593 ridge above Monte Cassino

Strangle Code name for air interdiction plan linked with Diadem

Tiger German heavy tank

Turtle VI (US) Corps plan for break-out from Anzio to Alban Hills via Campoleone

William target Concentration of guns of an Army's artillery on a single target

Notes on German and Allied Divisional Organisations

1 Most German and Allied divisions were made up of three regiments or three brigades. The title of regiment used by the Germans, Americans and French approximates to the British use of the word brigade. A regiment or brigade consisted of three infantry battalions and was normally supported by its own artillery, engineer and logistic units. The method of providing tank support varied and was one of the two principal differences between the various divisional organisations. The other difference was the degree of mechanisation. In the German Army, only the *panzer* (armoured) and *panzer grenadier* (armoured infantry) divisions were fully mechanised; the bulk of the German Army consisted of infantry divisions which still depended largely on horses for towing guns and supply vehicles. The British and American Armies rarely used horses and then only in special pack transport units to supply their divisions in mountain country.

2 The Germans had three types of mobile division and three types of the slower moving horse-drawn division:

MOBILE DIVISIONS

a *The Panzer Division* in which the tank was the principal weapon and which contained a higher proportion of tanks than any other German division. It normally contained one panzer regiment and two panzer grenadier regiments.

b *The Panzer Grenadier Division* which was essentially a motorised infantry division with three panzer grenadier regiments and one tank battalion.

c *The Parachute Division*, the élite of the German Army, which had three parachute regiments and was usually given motor transport when fighting as an infantry division. It had no tanks of its own.

NON-MECHANISED DIVISIONS

d *The Infantry Divisions* which comprised the bulk of the German Army and in which the infantry marched or were lifted by pools of transport, or, more often, by rail. The standard division had three infantry regiments and no tanks of its own.

e *The Jaeger Division* which was a light division used on the flanks or in difficult country and possessed only two lightly equipped infantry regiments and no tanks.

f *The Mountain Division* which was specially trained and equipped for mountain operations and had only two mountain regiments and no tanks.

3   The main difference between the British and American divisions was the British system of concentrating their tanks in Independent Armoured Brigades which supported infantry divisions as required. The Americans allotted individual tank battalions to their infantry divisions on an as required basis. Otherwise their three types of division were very similar. These were:

a *The Infantry Division* of three infantry regiments or brigades in which only the infantry marched and then only in the battle area; otherwise they were lifted by pools of transport.

b *The Armoured Division* which had tanks and infantry permanently grouped together and which was fully mechanised.

c *The Airborne Division* consisting of three parachute regiments or brigades, and, in the case of the British only, one glider-borne air-landing brigade instead of the third parachute brigade.

4   Comparative strengths of divisions are misleading because the different logistic system caused varying numbers of logistic personnel to be included in the totals. Even a rough cross-check of the number of battalions is difficult to make because the British, for instance, had four rifle companies to all other nations' three. It is simplest in a strategic study to equate all divisions, i.e., Major-Generals' commands.

Index